THE SEA IN SOVIET STRATEGY

Also by Bryan Ranft

THE VERNON PAPERS

TECHNICAL CHANGE AND BRITISH NAVAL POLICY, 1860–1939

Also by Geoffrey Till

AIR POWER AND THE ROYAL NAVY

MARITIME STRATEGY AND THE NUCLEAR AGE

THE SEA IN SOVIET STRATEGY

Bryan Ranft
and
Geoffrey Till

First published 1983 by
THE MACMILLAN PRESS LTD
London and Basingstoke
Companies and representatives
throughout the world

ISBN 0 333 26226 3

Typeset in Great Britain by
PREFACE LTD
Printed in Hong Kong

For
Marjorie, Simon and Philippa

Contents

List of Figures and Tables   x

List of Plates   xi

Preface   xiii

List of Abbreviations   xv

1 Problems of Interpretation   1
   Points of Contention   6

2 The Framework   13
   Introduction   13
   Politics and ideology   17
   Ideology, the Party and the Constitution in the
     Brezhnev era   19
   The Party and the armed forces   22
   Economic priority of defence   27
   Current problems of the Soviet economy   28
   The burden of defence expenditure on the economy   32
   Soviet defence industries   35

3 The Foreign Policy Background   38
   Introduction   38
   Ideology and foreign policy   40
   Priorities in Soviet foreign policy   44
   The Soviet Navy as an instrument of foreign policy 48
   The Soviet Union and the international law of the sea 53
   Maritime arms control   56
   Conclusion   58

4 The Strategic Background   59
   Geography and history   59
   Marshal Sokolovskiy's 'Soviet Military Strategy' and
     the role of the Navy   62
   Marshall Grechko's 'The Armed Forces of the Soviet
     State'   68
   Admiral Gorshkov's contribution to Soviet strategic
     thought   71
   'Navies in War and Peace'   74
   'The Sea Power of the State'   76
   The impact of technological progress   80

5 The Development of the Soviet Navy   84
   The Soviet Navy before the Second World War   85
   The Soviet Navy in the Great Patriotic War   88
   Stalin's post-war naval policy   90
   The Navy under Stalin's successors   91

6 The Soviet Navy: an Inventory   95
   The offshore defence force   95
   Destroyers   98
   Cruisers and battlecruisers   100
   Aircraft carriers   102
   Ballistic missile firing submarines   107
   Cruise missile and torpedo attack submarines   111
   The Soviet Naval Air Force   114
   The Soviet Navy's amphibious capacity   116
   Fleet distribution and ocean access   118
   Command and control   122
   Soviet naval personnel   125
   The Soviet merchant marine   129
   Soviet naval design and construction   134
   Other navies of the Warsaw Pact   140

7 The Missions of the Soviet Navy   142
   Controlling the seas   142
   Defence against maritime attack   152
   Strategic defence   160
   Strategic strike   166
   Amphibious warfare   175

Contents ix

Maritime interdiction   181
The protection of shipping   190
Naval diplomacy   193
In search of priorities   202

8 Present and Future Prospects   205

Notes and References   214

Bibliography   227

Index   235

List of Figures and Tables

FIGURES

1 The development of Soviet destroyers	98
2 Weapons systems of the *Kiev*	106
3 Soviet diesel torpedo attack submarines	113
4 Soviet naval fleet areas and ocean access points	119
5 Command structure of the Soviet Navy	123
6 Principal naval shipyards of the Soviet Union	136
7 Western ASW barriers – the Soviet view	186
8 Western convoy tactics – the Soviet view	187

TABLES

1 Patrol boat transfers by country and year	97
2 US and Soviet shipbuilding deliveries 1961–75	137
3 The Soviet Navy: proportionate numbers and tonnages over 20 years	138
4 The naval balance, 1981	212

List of Plates

1 The *Krivak*, a local water combatant
2 The *Nanuchka III* armed with SSM triple launchers
3 Modified version of *Kashin* class destroyer
4 Modernised version of *Kotlin* class destroyer
5 Guided missile destroyer *Sovremenny* on sea trials
6 *Sovremenny* after being fitted with weapons and sensors
7 The *Udaloy*. an anti-submarine surface warship
8 The *Udaloy*'s armoury
9 The *Sverdlov* class cruiser
10 The *Kynda* class guided missile cruiser
11 The *Kresta I* class cruiser
12 The *Kara* class cruiser
13 The battle cruiser *Kirov*
14 Close-up of forward part of the *Kirov*
15 The *Moskva* class helicopter carrier
16 The *Moskva* with *Hormone A* helicopters on deck
17 The *Kiev* class aircraft carrier
18 The *Minsk* class aircraft carrier
19 The *Kiev* refuelling at sea
20 A modified *Golf* submarine
21 The *Whiskey Twin Cylinder* submarine
22 The *Yankee* class SSBN
23 The *Delta III* class SSBN
24 The *Whiskey* torpedo-firing submarine
25 The *Zulu* torpedo-firing submarine
26 The *Charlie* nuclear-powered cruise missile firing submarine
27 The *Victor* nuclear-powered torpedo-firing submarine
28 The *Alpha* hunter–killer torpedo-firing submarine
29 The *Hormone A* helicopter
30 The *Forger* aircraft carried on *Kiev* cruisers

31 The *Tu-95 Bear* aircraft
32 The *Backfire Tu-26* bomber
33 The *Ivan Rogov* class amphibious warfare ship
34 The *Ropucha* class tank landing ship
35 Soviet Naval Infantry in action
36 The *PT-76* amphibious light tank
37 The *Primorye* class intelligence collectors
38 The *Reduktor*, an *Okean* class small intelligence collector
39 The *Teodolit* accompanying the frigate *HMS Juno*
40 Admiral Gorshkov and other Soviet Naval officers in Sweden,
    1981
41 Officers and men from the flagship *October Revolution*
42 Signalmen of the cruiser *Alexander Suvorov*
43 The merchant ship *Krasnokamsk*
44 The seine-net fishing boat *Aterina*

Preface

In preparing this book we have been particularly indebted to the wide range and high quality of specialised research and writing on the Soviet Navy carried out in Canada and the United States. The most original and significant contributions have emerged from the University of Dalhousie, Halifax, Nova Scotia, under the authorship and direction of Michael MccGwire, and from the Centre for Naval Analyses, Alexandria, Virginia, in the work of James McConnell and his distinguished colleagues. Our friendship with these two eminent specialists has been one of the main influences behind our work, although we are well aware that they will not agree with all of our interpretations.

In addition to the many authors and editors cited in the bibliography and notes we would also like to express our thanks to our students in the universities and service colleges, and to the participants in the seminar on the Soviet Navy held at King's College, London, from 1978 to 1981, for the continuous stimulation they have given us.

We would also particularly like to thank Donald C. Daniel of the United States Navy Postgraduate School, Monterey, Eric Grove of the Britannia Royal Naval College, Dartmouth, and Lt-Cdr D. J. Pickup of the Royal Naval College, Greenwich, for their expert help. Of course we alone are responsible for the opinions and judgements expressed, none of which can in any way be held necessarily to reflect official opinion.

We are also grateful to Judithe Blacklawe and her staff in the Library of the Royal Naval College, Greenwich, for their constant help and patience, to the photographic staff of the Ministry of Defence, and to Lt-Cdr C. E. Evans of the Royal Naval College, Greenwich, and Mrs Valentina Ward for their help in various problems of translation. Finally, our considerable thanks are due to Kathy

Mason, Sylvia Smither and Cherry Till for their devoted typing efforts on our behalf.

We believe that the increased significance of sea power in the current strategy of the Soviet Union is one of the most important developments of recent years. The growth of the Soviet Navy in strength and capabilities has raised new questions about the balance of forces between the Warsaw Pact and NATO and about possible new directions in Soviet foreign policy and the extent to which they demand new military and political responses from the West.

While there is a general awareness of the importance of the new emphasis given to the sea in Soviet strategy, we have learned, through our teaching in universities and service colleges, that the great bulk and sophistication of the writing on the subject have made it difficult for students, serving officers and readers with a general rather than a specialised interest in maritime affairs, to assimilate the vast amount of information provided, and to interpret the divergences of opinion which specialised research into so complex a subject have inevitably produced. Such divergences have been particularly apparent in the different views which are held on the motives which originally led the Soviet Union to increase its maritime capabilities, and on the strategic concepts determining the construction programmes and deployment patterns of her Navy.

We have tried in this relatively short book to show how the Soviet Union's maritime policies have emerged from the country's general political and ideological background, and to analyse the specialised research in a way which we hope will enable readers to clarify for themselves the issues already raised and to identify the most important future developments to watch for.

BRYAN RANFT
King's College, London
GEOFFREY TILL
Royal Naval College, Greenwich
1982

List of Abbreviations

ACW	Anti-Carrier Warfare
ASM	Air-to-Surface Missile
ASW	Anti-Submarine Warfare
AVMF	The Soviet Naval Air Force
BKR	Large Missile Ship
BPK	Large Anti-Submarine Ship
CPSU	Communist Party of the Soviet Union
EEZ	Exclusive Economic Zone
EM	Destroyer
GIUK	Greenland–Iceland–United Kingdom Gap
GNP	Gross National Product
JFS	*Jane's Fighting Ships*
MFR	Mutual Force Reduction (Talks)
MIRV	Multiple Independently Targeted Re-Entry Vehicle
MPA	Main Political Administration (of the Army and Navy)
NATO	North Atlantic Treaty Organisation
PVO-Strany	National Air Defence
RK	Missile Ship
RKR	Missile Cruiser
Ro-Ro	Roll-on/Roll-off ship
SALT	Strategic Arms Limitation Talks
SAM	Surface-to-Air Missile
SKR	Guard Ships/Patrol Ships/Escorts
SLBM	Submarine Launched Ballistic Missiles
SSBN	Nuclear Propelled Ballistic Missile Firing Submarine
SSG	Guided Missile Firing Submarine
SSGN	Nuclear Propelled Guided Missile Firing Submarine
SSM	Surface-to-Surface Missile
SSN	Nuclear Propelled Attack Submarine
TAKR	Heavy Aircraft Carrying Cruiser

UNCLOS   United Nations Conference on the Law of the Sea
VDS   Variable Depth Sonar
V/STOL   Vertical/Short Take-Off Aircraft

1 Problems of Interpretation

There is no disputing that the Soviet Union is now one of the world's leading sea powers. The emergence of its Navy from relative obscurity to a position where it can pose a credible challenge to the US Navy for mastery of the oceans has been one of the most remarkable features of the post-war period. But, though there has been general agreement that this phenomenon has actually taken place, there remains nonetheless considerable dispute about what it all means. Experts are divided about what the Soviet Navy is for, about its roles and priorities and about how effective it is. They do not agree about what the rise of the Soviet Navy tells us about Soviet policy in general. Since they also assess the level of threat posed by the Soviet Navy quite differently, they often make quite different recommendations as to how the West should react to it. Even though the Soviet Navy is very evidently a new element on the world scene which must be properly understood for the sake of general security, and responded to appropriately, it nevertheless so far remains something of a puzzle. To a large extent the nature of the evidence explains why it is so difficult to arrive at a consensus about the strengths and purposes of the Soviet Navy. Information about its ships and weaponry is difficult to come by since the Soviet Navy has inherited, along with much else, the traditions of furtiveness associated with its Tsarist predecessor. It has always been difficult to be sure about the Russians at sea. In the 1890s, for instance, there was much speculation and alarm in Western Europe about a new Russian ship called the *Rurik*. Believing this to be a large and powerful cruiser capable of attacking British commerce, the Royal Navy responded by building two armoured cruisers even more powerful than the Russian ship was supposed to be. The *Rurik* made her debut at the Kiel Naval Review of 1893 and the British were both relieved and chagrined to discover her to be a full-rigged three-masted sailing ship twenty years behind the times. Though trivial in itself, the *Rurik* incident is a useful example of the way in which the Russians have in the past been able to conceal information about their ships and weaponry and spring surprises of one sort or another on the West.

But, as is always the case in assessing the problems of military capability, the information-gathering agencies themselves bear a measure of responsibility for the darkness in which their subject is occasionally enveloped. Available information is not always efficiently processed, sometimes through sheer incompetence, sometimes through fear of compromising its sources and sometimes because its release would not serve the interests of the agency or service collecting it.

Nevertheless, the main problem is that the evidence is intrinsically ambiguous, whether it is derived from what the Russians have got or from what they say and do. The extent of the ambiguity is a matter of debate however. Some experts repose high confidence in the analysis of hardware:

> Analysts of Soviet naval policy are unusually fortunate in having available a range of specialised and reasonably concrete data from which to derive, and against which to test their hypotheses. By its very nature, the significant evidence comprises large, discrete items (warships) whose composition can only change gradually in number and characteristics, and such evidence is available outside the country's land frontiers.[1]

Others are more sceptical. They point out that warships and weapons may be and in fact usually are, used for purposes and in ways quite other than those for which they were originally designed. This is possible because naval weapons systems have an inherent flexibility which allows a diversity of use on the one hand, but which also makes it difficult to deduce their exact purpose with confidence, on the other. A recent study of the *Kresta II* cruiser demonstrates the extent of the problem very clearly. Forty-three experts were asked to decide on the extent to which they thought this warship was designed for use against submarines. The percentage so allocated ranged from an adjusted low of 35 per cent to a high of 95 per cent.[2] This spread of opinion indicates the potential inexactitudes of hardware analysis.

But even when analysts are reasonably confident about the basic purpose of a particular ship or weapon, there still remains the task of interpreting the Navy's hardware as a whole. How, for instance, are we to discover from the Soviet Navy's general size and shape its order of mission priorities? By how many roubles are spent on the various tasks? Or the relative number of platforms given over to each? Or proportionate tonnages? Such difficulties are by no means new: the naval past is replete with examples of maritime powers grossly misperceiving the purposes and/or effectiveness of their opposite numbers in peacetime, only finding out the hard way when the fighting starts.[3] There is little real reason to suppose that assessments of the opposition's technology and operating procedures should be any more reliable now than they were in the past.

Another rather obvious way of assessing Soviet maritime intentions and aspirations is to look at what the Russians say about the subject. Certainly we have a significant body of literature to go on. Admiral Sergei Gorshkov, the Navy's Commander-in-Chief, himself apparently wrote a series of eleven articles entitled 'Navies in War and Peace' which appeared in *Morskoi Sbornik* (the Naval Review) in 1972–3, for instance. These articles reviewed the history and importance of sea power in general, and Russian sea power in particular, concluding with a look at the role of navies in the post-war world. In 1976 these articles were expanded into a book which also incorporated a good deal of new material on the development and use of modern navies. A second and further expanded version of this was produced in Moscow in 1979, at the same time as the English-language version *The Sea Power of the State* appeared in the West.

There are, however, considerable problems in simply taking at face value this evidence of Admiral Gorshkov's thinking. How far we can use it as an indicator of what the Soviet Navy has been, is and will be partly depends on what we think it was written for in the first place. It is important at this stage to distinguish rather carefully between what the Soviet Union understands by 'military doctrine' on the one hand and 'military science' on the other. Military doctrine is 'a system of scientifically substantiated, officially approved views on preparation for and victorious conduct of war . . . compiled by the state political leadership with the assistance of the higher military bodies'.[4] Since it is defined at the highest levels of the state it is extremely authoritative: it sets the parameters within which the military are expected to conduct their operations. At the same time, however, it will tend to be highly generalised, permissive in concept and not entirely free from inherent though carefully balanced contradictions. Military science, on the other hand, is more contemplative and exploratory: it 'conducts research into the objective laws and law-abiding patterns of armed conflict (and) works out questions in the theory of military art'.[5] Since it is so much more open-ended and investigative, it is obviously much less authoritative as a statement of agreed policy.

There has been much esoteric discussion as to whether Admiral Gorshkov's work should be regarded as 'doctrine' or 'science' – whether, in fact, it is announcement or advocacy. Detailed textual investigation, some rather ambiguous evidence about possible delays in the printing of *Morskoi Sbornik* articles and the public expression of some admittedly rather oblique criticism about the book support the general conclusion that Gorshkov's writings are a uniquely authoritative type of naval science.[6] They are much more forceful, confident and successful than mere advocacy, but they have not yet become doctrine. Accordingly, to the extent that they deal with 'what ought to be' Gorshkov's articles and books (and of course all the rest of Soviet naval literature as well) will be inaccurate as a guide to 'what is and will be'.

There are some other more mundane difficulties in using Soviet naval literature as an indicator of the present and the future. The phraseology, conceptual framework and even the presentational style (which seems often to make use of Western surrogates and indirect allusion for the advocacy of points not yet fully accepted in the Soviet Union) are all uniquely Russian and frequently sufficiently ambiguous to permit quite different interpretations. But probably the main weakness of this method of analysis is that it offers unreliable guidance for the future. Intentions and priorities may change much faster than can the capabilities and the hardware. What is true now may not be so in five years time, especially as Soviet military doctrine is not in any case expected to provide for more than the present and the *immediate* future.[7]

In dealing with the naval present and future, Soviet writers frequently make extensive use of the naval past. Soviet naval history, both in the sense of what was done and what is written about it, is therefore frequently instructive. Admiral Gorshkov himself made great use of it. He wrote: 'Progress is impossible in modern naval theory without turning to historical experience.' Lessons for the future are often explicitly derived from past experience. Occasionally, this is indicated in the literature by significant shifts from the descriptive to the prescriptive: 'Thus the experience of the Second

World War gives a graphic idea of the role which the ensuring of the operations of submarines directly to the ocean *ought to play*.' Or, frequently, by telling changes in tense: 'Landing operations *are* characterised by a particularly high saturation of combat clashes of varying degree.'[8]

Quite naturally, the Russians have accumulated over the centuries a body of experience in maritime operations and developed their own outlook and ways of doing things. This will certainly have an influence on, and therefore be an indicator of, their future behaviour too. But although there are clear continuities linking past, present and future, the use of history as prophecy has its dangers. Gorshkov himself reminded his readers repeatedly that each age has a 'naval art distinctive to itself' because political, military, economic and technical circumstances change as time goes by. It is obviously dangerous to assume that this is what the Russians will do, because this is what they have always done.

Analysis of the Soviet Navy's present activities, especially its peacetime exercises and deployments, might be a more reliable guide to the future because like all navies it must practise what it means to do. But, of course, it will know that it is being watched and may deliberately try to confuse observers about its real intentions. It may indeed consciously design its activities for purposes of political display rather than for operational rehearsal. For instance, many people have interpreted the stress put on operations against NATO's maritime communications, in the Soviet Navy's *Vesna–1975* exercise, more as a political message highlighting NATO's vulnerabilities and aggravating a tendency for Europe and the United States to drift apart than as an indication of Soviet wartime intent.

Another problem with this approach is that detailed information about the Soviet Navy's war-related activities is not readily available because it is so sensitive militarily, or is more than a little ambiguous when it is. During the 1973 Arab–Israeli war, for instance, the Russians rather obviously kept some of their best ships (such as the *Kara* class cruiser *Nikolayev*) out of harm's way. But what did this imply? Was the emphasis on the presence of older, rather less powerful and more dispensable warships like the *Kynda* class cruisers intended to indicate resolve by showing that they were prepared to risk losses if need be: or was it a signal that they did not intend to get too heated over the crisis; or was it merely an operational decision to keep their vital anti-submarine forces safe and concentrate on the more immediately relevant business of countering US Navy strike carriers in the eastern Mediterranean?[9] Did they, moreover, mean anything by it at all?

This brief review shows that there are various ways of looking at the Soviet Navy and of trying to deduce its strengths and intentions. Analysts sometimes come to different conclusions because they give different emphasis to these various approaches. But each method has its own weaknesses and difficulties. Effective analysis depends on an appropriate combination of approaches; analysts must avoid being hypnotised simply by the Soviet Navy's latest ship, Admiral Gorshkov's book or the exercise reported in today's newspaper. To understand the Soviet Navy, they need to look at it as a whole. But they must also beware of the danger of 'mirror imaging', that is of assuming that the Soviet Navy thinks and functions more or less as do its Western counterparts. In fact, the structure of its doctrinal conceptions, its operational procedures and even its system of designating ship types are quite unique. It may well be that the Soviet Navy is marching to the sound of its own drum. But, as we shall see, the extent to which this is true is in itself a matter of dispute.

POINTS OF CONTENTION

One of the most basic points at issue is the extent to which the Soviet Union is reckoned to have a genuine maritime past. Is the modern Soviet Navy a totally new departure, or merely the latest manifestation of a long tradition to which the West habitually pays too little attention?

Certainly Russians have been seen on all the world's high seas for many centuries, a point which Soviet publicists are eager to bring home to ignorant Westerners. They embarked on countless voyages of discovery long before the celebrated reign of Peter the Great (1672–1725) who is often over-simply regarded as the father of the Russian Navy. From his time on, Russian ships bustled about the Northern waters, the Baltic, the Black Sea and the Pacific. Many of these activities were undertaken for a variety of scientific, exploratory and mercantile reasons. Russian conceptions of sea power, from the start, were well rounded and not restricted merely to the narrowly naval.

Naturally, like any self-respecting sea power, Russia became involved in maritime wars. One of their first successful endeavours was the Great Northern War of 1703–21 (a war, significantly, which is little studied in the West); this conflict established Russia as a great power and in order to impress on his subjects an important source of their success, Tsar Peter had a full-size man-of-war dragged through the streets of Moscow in the victory celebrations.[10] Later in the century, Russian squadrons engaged in important operations in the Mediterranean as a part of their long struggle against the Turks. In 1795 a squadron of twelve ships of the line and eight frigates operated in the North Sea with the British against the French and their allies, participating in amphibious operations, patrolling and conducting blockades. Ashore they behaved as riotously as any other navy of the time, on one occasion scandalising the citizens of Yarmouth by drinking the oil out of their street lamps.[11] Soon after, however, they were models of impeccable rectitude; in 1797, while the Royal Navy mutinied at the Nore and Spithead, it was the Russian squadron which held the line, a point given some emphasis by their successors.

The Russians also kept abreast of naval technology and thinking. In Admiral F. F. Ushakov they produced a leading naval strategist and tactician evidently of sufficient repute to irritate Nelson. Through the eighteenth, nineteenth and early twentieth centuries they were amongst the first to experiment with explosive shells, torpedoes, mines and naval aircraft. They showed considerable innovative skill in producing warships specifically tailored to their own requirements, ships like the *Vermicular* of 1788, a 200 foot galley with a draft of four inches, propelled by 100 rowers and with a hull jointed in seven places so she could get round river bends. Russia also showed herself to be amongst the leaders in more orthodox naval technology. Her naval construction programme just before the First World War, with fast battleships like the *Borodino* class, and the celebrated *Novik* class destroyers, demonstrated a foresight in naval development which was particularly impressive in view of the generally poor state of her social and industrial base.

This kind of evidence is emphasised by those who stress the continuities in Russian maritime development. Admiral Gorshkov, for instance, was at pains to establish the fact that Russia had an important and diverse maritime past and to argue therefrom that the construction of a modern fleet was so entirely natural that it hardly needed justification. Past periods of weakness were aberrations; present strength was the norm; the onus of proof was on those who sought to argue otherwise. In Gorshkov's view, only such diverse disreputables as 'influential satraps of Russian czarism', bourgeois propagandists, President Nixon and 'English politicians and leaders of the British Admiralty' could fail to accept the genuineness of Russia's maritime past or the legitimacy of her present and future aspirations. As Gorshkov himself put it: 'Hostile propaganda tirelessly affirmed that Russia was not a maritime but only a continental country and needed a fleet only for resolving the modest task of coastal defence.'[12]

Nevertheless, sceptics stress the indifferent performance of the Russian Navy in the two world wars and its disastrous conduct of the 1904–5 war with Japan. They point out that Russia's greatest periods of maritime success were distinguished by an enormous reliance on foreign personnel and expertise. Nine of the seventeen Russian ships of the line which fought the battle of Hogland in 1788, for instance, were commanded by British captains, and the whole fleet was led by Commodore S. Greig, a Scotsman. They argue that most of Russia's maritime wars were coastal and rarely decisive in strategic consequence. They stress the relative absence of a merchant fleet and a proper maritime community. Emphasis is given to the constant waxing and waning of Russian maritime development and its generally weak foundations. To take Russia's eighteenth- and nineteenth-century endeavours in the Pacific as an example, while the Russians may have reached as far as Hawaii and California, establishing themselves on shore, and while they may have had a multitude of impressive objectives, the whole enterprise in fact fizzled out with little to show for it. The government's support was intermittent. Their scientific and mercantile interest was erratic: strategically, they were apprehensive about foreign reaction to these endeavours and preferred to concentrate scarce resources on the much more important European theatre. The naval contribution was weak and unreliable, operating as it was so far forward of its base. In sum, while individual exploits were often remarkable and occasionally heroic, the whole enterprise lacked a proper foundation, and so contrasted strongly with the equivalent efforts of the West Europeans at the time.[13] Many analysts take such things as this to show that the Russians were not, in the useful phrase of Admiral Sir Herbert Richmond, 'natural' sea powers like the Athenians, the Carthaginians, the Venetians, the Dutch and the British.[14] If this is so then it surely follows that the contemporary rise of an oceanic Soviet Navy should be regarded with apprehension, as an unparalleled development hardly justified by genuine considerations of maritime need.

Irrespective of whether their present maritime endeavours are a new departure for the Russians or not, there is also considerable controversy about the nature of their intentions. Specifically, are they aiming to produce a general-purpose navy designed ultimately to contest mastery of the world's oceans, or would they be content with a limited navy fit only for narrow, more localised purposes?

One of the earliest authoritative attempts to tackle this problem was Robert W. Herrick's *Soviet Naval Strategy* which appeared in 1968. Herrick argued that 'current Soviet naval strategy is an essentially deterrent and defensive one'. Contemporary Soviet policy was aimed, as it always had been, at the defence of the Russian homeland against sea-based attack:

> the Soviet Union, with a weak Navy has been forced to adopt a strategically defensive maritime strategy, one designed primarily for deterrence, but failing that to ward off, as best it can, the sea-borne attacks of a 'NATO Navy' which can exercise command of the sea at the times and places of its own choosing.[15]

Another authoritative analyst, Michael MccGwire, maintained that Soviet Naval development should be seen as a series of reactions to Western maritime initiatives. First in the late 1940s the Soviet Navy concentrated on the threat posed by Western amphibious forces: then in the 1950s it switched to the task of dealing with US Navy strike carriers of increasing range and power: then from the early 1960s the menace of Western ballistic-missile firing submarines dominated its naval horizons. The result was 'a predominantly task-specific fleet with a narrow, defensive mission'.[16] Its primary concern was to guard the homeland against sea-based attack, partly by being able to destroy or damage the hostile forces actually so engaged, and partly by offering a countervailing capability against its enemies' homelands which would deter them from launching an attack in the first place.

More generally, such analysts have warned against regarding the Soviet Navy as a versatile blue-water force capable of going anywhere and doing anything. On the contrary the Russians did not intend to pursue 'command of the sea', being content with a second-rate fleet for a strategically defensive mission. In fact the Russians had their own perspectives on maritime power: they did not necessarily go along with Western traditions that the only legitimate maritime aspiration was one that aimed at mastery of the world's oceans. Theirs was a different tradition, more in line with the alternative philosophies of the French *Jeune École* of the nineteenth century or the German Navy of the twentieth. Their intentions were specific and limited, not general and absolute. It did not follow that the Soviet Union would necessarily develop a first-class fleet 'for general purposes of greatness', merely because it had become a superpower. This 'puberty theory of sea power'[17] was facile and inaccurate both as history and prophecy. In short the Soviet Navy had not so far demonstrated any apparent desire or intention to become a general-purpose oceanic navy, nor did there exist any iron law of nature to say that it should.

Other commentators are sceptical about all these propositions. Some profess their suspicions of deterministic and monocausal explanations. They claim that Admiral Gorshkov is constructing a balanced navy capable of an increasing variety of war and peacetime tasks. While the Soviet Navy may have been primarily defensive in orientation at the beginning, it has become much more ambitious since. It has developed a capacity for sustained operations in distant and contested waters; it may well be aiming at a capacity to achieve significant degrees of sea control; it may attack Western maritime communications if need be, or project its power ashore. In fact, the Soviet Union is increasingly realising the 'normal' strategic potentialities of the great naval power. In peacetime too the Soviet Navy has become an important vehicle for the protection of Soviet interests and the spread of Soviet power. In short, such analysts suggest that 'the ever-growing Soviet Navy has outrun the legitimate requirements of national defence', and is now capable of posing a serious all-round challenge to Western maritime supremacy.

To people of this persuasion, the incremental growth of Soviet naval capability and intent over the years seems in fact a rather familiar and normal pattern of development which other nations have followed before. Neither is there anything distinctively Russian, or distinctively novel about most of their conceptions of sea power. While the Soviet Union has occasionally strayed from the straight and narrow (as in its unorthodox notions of the late 1920s and the mid-1950s), this had best be seen more as a manifestation of operational weakness than as an alternative philosophy of maritime strategy. The argument goes that in the main we can expect the Soviet Union to think of sea power in more or less the same way as do its major Western counterparts.

The fact that the leaders of the Soviet Navy were educated as Marxist–Leninists will, of course, affect the presentation and method of their arguments; it will influence their conceptions of maritime strategy; it may even help decide their aims. But, fundamentally, the main motor of their thinking will be a response to objective military, geographic and technological circumstances. Soviet maritime strategy need not necessarily be different from anyone else's simply by virtue of the fact that its practitioners use Marxist–Leninist concepts. Gorshkov's rather obvious effort to draw lessons from the naval past, and from the naval experience of other states, itself shows that he and his audience think that the Soviet Navy has enough in common with other navies to make the exercise worth while.

However, we may be wrong in any case to assume that the Soviet Navy is developing in accordance with some kind of master plan. Perhaps, on the contrary, the Soviet Navy is just rolling along in a directionless way with a bureaucratic and technological momentum all of its own. Maybe the Russians do not know the exact purposes of their Navy any better than we do, because it is constantly subjected to a variety of technological, social, economic and political changes over which Soviet leaders have less than adequate control. Of course, a navy which is just 'happening' like this is not necessarily less (or more) of a threat to Western interests than one whose construction is proceeding to a conscious and rational design: it merely makes that navy more difficult to understand, and to respond to appropriately.

Assessing the strength of the Soviet Navy relative to Western navies and its capacity to do the West harm is in fact the third major area of contention between analysts. Connected with it is the issue of how the West should respond. It is difficult to come to clear-cut verdicts about these issues for we are frequently comparing like and unlike. For instance, the Soviet Navy is still more localised than the US Navy: in global terms and distant waters the balance still seems tilted against it, but in European waters, which are perhaps where the balance really matters, the Russians are at their strongest. The Soviet Navy has its strengths (in submarines, anti-ship missilry, inshore combatants) and its weaknesses (an adverse maritime geography, few bases, no strike carriers to date) and this also makes it difficult to arrive at a settled conclusion. Of course, the problem lies not so much in deciding the balance now (though this is difficult enough) but in assessing how it is likely to develop in the future. The maritime balance is not static; it may change, and arguably has changed, and the verdicts of individual analysts have changed along with it.

The evidence is sufficiently ambiguous to produce a variety of conclusions about the relative balance which can be artificially polarised into two views for the sake of simplicity. First, there is the view that the Soviet Navy remains basically a defensive one, inferior in global terms to the US Navy. The rate of its expansion (whether measured in terms of expenditure, operational activity, personnel or the construction of major combatants) has slowed considerably in recent years. Were it not for the strategic strike mission, concluded one analyst, 'we would be speaking now of stagnation in Soviet naval development'.[18] If this is so, then the West should obviously not overreact, despite 'the thought of the big bucks we inherit if we can really scare everybody on The Hill about Gorshkov's Sailing Circus'.[19] In fact, alarmism about the Soviet Navy may be playing the Russian game, since it might give them a capacity to influence events which their real operational strength does not warrant; in Michael MccGwire's phrase, the West should be careful not to plug an amplifier into the Soviet naval propaganda machine.[20]

Against this, however, is the view that the Russians may already rule the waves, or will soon do so unless the West does something. Likely future developments afford many commentators little comfort. Even Michael MccGwire has warned that:

> Additional resources have been allocated to naval construction and there are clear indications that the Soviet leadership has accepted that the importance of the navy's role has increased, both absolutely and relative to the other branches of service, and this process may continue in future.[21]

If true, it plainly behoves the West to take precautions. This way of looking at the problem and the solution were well summed up by Admiral Thomas B. Hayward in the spring of 1979:

> My near-term optimism about the Navy is tempered by serious concern over the longer-term trends, should the momentum of past improvement in the Navy's capabilities not be maintained. My recent predecessors testified repeatedly that the long-term trends do not favour the US Navy, and that one can project a point in the not-too-distant future when the trend lines will cross, and we will lose our margin of superiority to a Soviet Navy which remains embarked on an aggressive programme of expanding its capabilities for maritime operations worldwide.[22]

2   The Framework

INTRODUCTION

At the twentieth Congress of the Communist Party of the Soviet Union (CPSU) in 1956 Khruschev not only denounced the errors and excesses of Stalin but proclaimed a new era in Soviet history to be characterised by economic progress at home and increased influence abroad against a background of peaceful coexistence with states of different social systems. The years which followed have been marked by a striking contrast between the absence of fundamental internal changes and an increasing flexibility in foreign policy and military strategy. Khruschev's promises of substantial improvements in agriculture and industry which would enable the Soviet Union to overtake the United States by the 1980s have certainly not been fulfilled. Political dissent is still repressed. Despite theoretical constitutional and legal advances, in practice individual rights against the state remain minimal. There has been no opening up of the political system. The Politbureau of the Central Committee and its supporting Secretariat have maintained a monopoly of initiative and a totality of control over every aspect of national life. On occasions of divisions within the leadership, such as those which followed the death of Stalin in 1953, or those which led to Khruschev's fall in 1964, the larger Central Committee, with a membership approaching 300, has played some part in bringing about change, but once the new leadership has been installed, the 14/15 man Politbureau has reasserted its total control.

When age, ill health or political failure bring Brezhnev's primacy to an end, there seems no reason to expect fundamental change. The other members of the Politbureau will secretly decide on a new distribution of responsibilities and power. Those most skilled in the processes of bargaining and manipulation which characterise Soviet

13

decision-making, will come to the top, recruit like-minded followers for the most influential positions in the Politbureau and Secretariat and continue the cautious internal policies to be expected from a conservative and self-perpetuating bureaucracy.

There are clear indications that the problems to be solved will become more complex and difficult. The already observable decline in the rate of economic growth and the changes in the demographic pattern of Soviet society, resulting from the faster increase in the non-European elements of the population, will figure largely. The growing reliance on technical expertise, which the pursuit of economic improvement will inevitably produce, will increase the friction between the demands of professionalism and the continuance of the Party's bureaucratic control which has always impeded efficiency. This friction may well be intensified by the impact of Western technology and managerial methods, which the present leadership sees as necessary. Faced with such difficulties, any likely new leadership will tend to reinforce existing methods of centralised planning and control, rather than risk new methods, which, however attractive as means of increasing productivity and efficiency, will also be perceived as challenges to the preservation of the monopolisation of power whose preservation is the predominant, if unacknowledged objective of the ruling elite. This dominance and detailed Party control will also characterise the working of the state (as distinct from Party) institutions, such as the Council of Ministers and the individual ministries responsible for administration and the execution of policy.[1]

If past rigidity and future predictability are the salient features of the Soviet Union's domestic life, the same can not be said of her foreign and defence policies. It is true that her government, like any other, will remain primarily concerned with the security of its national territory and the preservation of the regime. But in the past there have been significant and sometimes sudden changes, both ideological and practical, in the methods used top achieve these aims. The future course to be followed is full of uncertainties.

Even the most conservative government's external policies are liable to be more fluid than its internal ones. The most powerful state must react to the behaviour and aspirations of other nations, especially in today's interdependent international system. But the Soviet Union, with its great resources, population and military power, need not just react: it can take initiatives. And when such a state feels that it does not enjoy the world influence which its strength and capabilities deserve, and when its leadership is ideologically conditioned to see the *status quo* as being both morally unacceptable and doomed by the inexorable laws of historical development, it is inevitable that it will have active external policies.

This is not the place for a history of Soviet foreign policy[2] or an analysis of the relative contributions of national interests and Marxist–Leninist ideology to its formation, but it is impossible to arrive at a meaningful evaluation of Russia's present and future maritime policies without some understanding of her government's interpretation of the workings of the international system and its perceptions of how the country should seek to influence them. Just as in domestic matters economic issues, for example, will be decided not primarily on technical grounds but on their overall political implications, so matters such as relations with other governments, or the nature of the armed forces and the strategic principles which govern their use, will remain under the firm control of the Politbureau. In the Soviet Union war is too important a matter to leave to generals – or admirals.

That this tight political control has not led to the rigidity and paralysis which have resulted from the Politbureau's conduct of internal affairs has been due to factors not subject to its influence or within its capacity for foresight. International relations since 1945 have been characterised by fluidity and surprise. The emergence on the world stage of so many new states, each with its particular problems and interests; the formation of new regional groupings such as the EEC; and the growth of divisions and conflict among Communist parties, and governments, with the Sino-Soviet split as its most significant feature, are only three of the more important elements in a constantly shifting scene. In such an uncertain world the first concern of Soviet foreign and defence policies, relations with the United States, has assumed a complexity and ambiguity which have demanded a high degree of flexibility in the handling of strategic and diplomatic affairs.

In defence policy the pressure for change and the causes of uncertainty have come not only from the shifting patterns of international relations but also, and more directly, from developments in military technology. Here the main influence has been the wide variety of advances in nuclear weapons; the greater accuracy and destructive power of long-range land-based systems; the apparent invulnerability of submarine-based missiles, and the uncertainties arising from the emergence of short-range, low-yield weapons. In the light of such developments no great power, especially one so apprehensive of external threats as the Soviet Union, could be expected to be resistant to innovation in its military doctrine and practice.[3]

The increasing complexity and technicality of modern war has inevitably led to a high degree of specialised professionalism in the Soviet armed forces and thus increased the significance of their contribution to national decision-making. This is not to say that the military leaders have usurped political authority, but rather that political leadership is to a large extent militarised, as is the Soviet economy. The political leaders see military strength, in its varied forms, as being the country's most powerful instrument for ensuring its security and enhancing its global influence. They are therefore ready to pay great attention to military arguments, give military equipment the highest priority in research, development and production and, in their firm determination to maintain control, to take a strong personal interest in military affairs. This last element has bulked large in Brezhnev's leadership.

Since 1945 the greatest obstacle to the increase of the Soviet Union's influence has been the United States with its stronger technological and industrial base. To counter this she has had to concentrate on those aspects of scientific and industrial development necessary to military strength, to the comparative neglect of consumers' interests. So successful has this concentration been that initial handicaps in both the nuclear and conventional fields have been overcome and a military parity achieved, which might, if there is any meaning in the term, be transformed into a superiority. In a world which contains another potential superpower, China, whose closer relationship with the United States in the last decade can be interpreted as threatening the encirclement of the Soviet Union, there is no likelihood of the belief in the primacy of armed strength being abandoned. This is not to accept the view that Russia is planning pre-emptive war against either or both of her rivals. Her leaders' realisation of the unpredictable consequences of nuclear war is too clear for that, but they firmly believe in armed strength both as the only reliable deterrent against attacks on their country and as an essential means of altering the global balance of power in its favour. They are realistic enough to know that the attractive power of the Russian version of Marxism–Leninism and of the political and economic system it has shaped, is virtually non-existent and that if the Soviet Union is to be accepted as a superpower on equal terms with the United States it can only be on the basis of her military might.

The determination to balance the military power of the United States and its allies has dominated Russian military policy and strategic thought since 1945. To do so in terms of land power was well within the capability of a country which had produced the armies and associated air forces which had defeated Hitler. Concentration on the relevant fields of science, technology and industry enabled her to catch up in nuclear weaponry at a rate which took her rivals by surprise. Maritime capability was a very different matter. In 1945 the United States and Great Britain were unchallengeable at sea. The numerical strength, combat experience and equipment of the victors in the greatest maritime war of all time were perceived as a strong threat to Russia's security, especially when they achieved a nuclear capability. In comparison the Soviet Navy was numerically small, except in submarines, technically backward and had played only a minor role in the Great Patriotic War.

Within the last thirty years this great gulf has largely been filled. The Soviet Union has overcome what seemed an insuperable handicap and now possesses a maritime strength which although not equal to that of the United States and its allies, is sufficient to present an effective challenge to that ability to use the seas in peace and war, which they see as essential to survival. To understand how this increase in maritime strength has come about and its possible future development, it is necessary to look more closely at the political and economic framework within which it has grown.

POLITICS AND IDEOLOGY

An eminent student of Soviet politics, comparing the present rulers' style in 1968 with the ebullience of Khruschev, describes them as 'a tight-lipped collective of faceless, cautious and pragmatic men, agnostic in everything but their commitment to the greatness of Russia and to the need for orderly procedures'.[4] True though this is, except for the emergence of Brezhnev as an identifiable personality during the years since it was written, it would be a mistake to deduce from it and many other similar comments in contemporary writing on the Soviet Union, that ideology plays no part in the formulation of Soviet policies and can therefore be ignored in forecasting their future course. The truth is more complex. The present Politbureau, in which effective leadership lies, and the Secretariat which directs its decisions into the Party and governmental organs, are composed of men who have worked their way to power through the Party's administrative organisations. Like all rulers they accept the necessity of establishing the legitimacy of their authority and, in their case, of its dictatorial and totalitarian nature. The history and nature of the CPSU ensure that the only possible grounds for such legitimacy is for themselves and their subjects to accept the Marxist–Leninist dogma defining the Party as the only full expression of the will of the working class and therefore entitled to a monopoly of initiative and power.[5] As Marxism–Leninism is a tightly integrated system of political philosophy and practice, acceptance of one part demands acceptance of the whole. Therefore today's and tomorrow's Soviet leaders, however unfanatical they may be, will, because of the permanent need to legitimise their authority, continue to present their internal and external policies in Leninist terminology and will refuse to accept that they are determined by purely national objectives. The dominant role of the Party in every element of Russia's life; the possibility of normal state relations with capitalist countries combined with the impossibility of ideological coexistence; the duty to assist colonial peoples struggling for freedom by wars of national liberation, and the duty to support newly liberated nations to escape from imperialist economic exploitation, are and will continue to be justified as logical twentieth-century developments of Marxism–Leninism. An additional dimension was added to the doctrine in 1968 with the Brezhnev Doctrine's proclamation of the right and duty of governments representing the international working class, led by Russia, to intervene in countries such as Czechoslovakia, where communism was being betrayed from within.

It is unconvincing to explain these claims to legitimacy based on a rationally compelling philosophy as being merely conscious hypocrisy adopted to disguise personal self-interest and chauvinistic ambition. Throughout their lives Soviet leaders and the ranks of the Party bureaucracy have been brought up to believe in them. They have come to positions of power and influence in a country which has achieved internal progress and international influence to a degree never achieved by the Tsars, through a governmental system inspired by the teachings of Marx and Lenin. Is it not natural that the presuppositions on which they base their interpretations of contemporary political and international issues should be heavily conditioned by this experience and that they should continue to observe the world through Marxist–Leninist spectacles?

If this is so, it is possible to put forward some of the ways in which their ideological presuppositions will influence Soviet policy-makers. Inside Russia, they will continue to see the Communist Party as the vanguard of the working class, and therefore the only legitimate source of leadership, and to stress the consequent necessity of repressing any forms of dissent or challenges to its authority. Abroad, they will see the capitalist countries, led by the United States, as the inevitable opponents not only of the Soviet Union but of all socialist and progressive regimes. China, as a heretical deviant from true Marxism–Leninism, will, unless it returns to orthodoxy, also be seen as an enemy. On the other hand, the peoples of the Third World, with their aspiration for economic and social progress and complete political and economic freedom from imperialism, will be seen as the natural allies of the Soviet Union in its confrontation with the forces of reaction.[6]

IDEOLOGY, THE PARTY AND THE CONSTITUTION IN THE BREZHNEV ERA

Although it is true that the leading role in the Communist Party is grounded on the historical experience of the Revolution, the Civil War and the transformation of Russia's society and economy since 1917, and although it has been rationalised and inculcated through the educational system in an ideology which can still be seen as 'the indispensable foundation of the legitimacy upon which the entire Soviet structure reposes',[7] it has only recently been given formal recognition. This can be seen as part of that concern for orderly procedures which has characterised the post-Khruschev collective leadership in which Brezhnev as the Party's General Secretary has increasingly appeared to be the dominant figure in the Politbureau. It would seem that his authority has been based not only on such bureaucratic skills as installing his protégés in key appointments, but also by identifying as his own, policies which have been accepted by all the major interest groups, including the military, as holding out hopes for the future without threatening the stability of the system – a tactic which finally made Khruschev unacceptable.[8] His internal policies have been characterised by an abandonment of utopian visions and a concentration on measures designed to further gradual and continuous economic development and improvement in the standard of living based on science and technology, and accompanied by similar advances in education and culture. In all this the Party is destined to continue its initiating and directing role and to ensure that progress is not impeded by dissidence or obstruction. From this have sprung Brezhnev's current economic problems with their attendant political difficulties. The economic progress achieved has fallen far short of the aim and the case for liberalising reforms of the economic system is compelling. But how can these be implemented without shaking the centralised and detailed control of the Party and how can the active co-operation of a massive bureaucracy stubbornly attached to existing procedures be obtained? Brezhnev's attempted solutions have been admirably described as 'As much economic reform as is absolutely necessary and as tough a course in the intellectual sphere as is possible.' This may seem the essence of pragmatism but, for the reasons already stated, it must be incorporated into a Marxist–Leninist ideological framework, and this has been done through the proclamation of the characteristically Brezhnevian concept of 'developed socialism'.[9]

This term, occasionally used by Lenin, has been increasingly employed by Brezhnev since 1967. It was given considerable emphasis in his opening address to the Twenty-fourth Party Congress in 1971, and has been frequently cited since then. It can thus be accepted as the leadership's view of their country's situation today and of where it stands in the inevitable progress to the Marxist–Leninist goal of true communism. It is defined as involving a long period in the process of development from capitalism to communism, characterised by three main elements: technical and organisational change in production; advances in the political and spiritual life of the Party and Soviet society; and changes in the international system through peaceful competition with capitalism. In other words, it is a cautious and gradual progress towards communism, accompanied by an equally cautious foreign policy.[10] The scientific and technological developments which are the basis of developed socialism, and even more necessary for the advance to true communism, will demand new skills and knowledge in the Party, which will retain its monopoly of power and control.[11] This increasing emphasis on the need for fuller understanding of science and technology and of managerial techniques is repeatedly echoed in the writings of Marshal Grechko and Admiral Gorshkov about leadership in the armed forces.

The continuing emphasis on the unique role of the Party was formally recognised in the Brezhnev Constitution which in 1977 superseded Stalin's 1936 enactment. This embodies a full description of the Soviet system as perceived by the leadership and as it wants to be perceived by the Soviet people and the rest of the world. It can be seen as yet another instance of the search for orderly procedures and has been hailed by Brezhnev as being of great practical importance and thus, by implication, not mere decoration to mask a repellent reality as was its 1936 predecessor. Brezhnev's strong personal association with the Constitution is suggested by the fact that its adoption in October 1977 was preceded in May and June by meetings of the Central Committee and the Supreme Soviet which removed Nikolai Podgorny from membership of the Politbureau and from the post of Head of State and promoted Brezhnev to the latter. Since Brezhnev remained Party General Secretary, he thus headed both the state and Party hierarchies. The Constitution's most significant novelty is that, unlike its four predecessors, it formally enshrines the leading role of the Party and legitimises its authority. Article 6 states that, 'The Communist Party of the Soviet Union operating within the framework of the Constitution as the ruling party, has determined and will determine the political line in decisions on all major questions of governmental affairs . . . The CPSU is the leading and guiding force of Soviet society and the nucleus of its political system and of all state and public organisations.' A reminder of the dictatorial nature of the Party's rule is made in the statement that government in developed socialism will continue to be based on the principle of democratic centralism, 'the mandatory fulfilment of the decisions of higher organs by lower organs'.[12]

In his report to the Twenty-sixth Party Congress in February 1981, Brezhnev claimed that the new Constitution had invigorated the country's political life, but complained that some officials had not observed the primacy of its principles and had failed to maintain proper standards of legality. He equally stressed the need to impose strong curbs on individuals guilty of dissidence and anti-state activities; again the search for orderly administrative procedures and political conduct. The whole of the concluding section of his report, successfully designed to bring the Congress to its feet in tumultuous applause, concentrated on the leading role of the Party. In the five years since the last Congress it had increased its membership by 1.8 million and now totalled 17.48 million men and women. The number of applicants was constantly growing but there was always the danger of admitting the unworthy, and 300,000 had been expelled since the Twenty-fifth Congress. He gave some insight into the working of the governmental system by his report that the Central Committee had held eleven full meetings in the past five years, which had been chiefly devoted to discussions of the economy. In the same period the Politbureau had met 236 times. In both bodies there had been keen debates but they had all ended in unanimous decisions. 'It is this unity that is the strength of collective leadership.' He describes the Polit-bureau as embodying the Party's collective wisdom and using it to shape policies in the best interests of society. Its intellectual task was to promote creative developments in Marxist theory as it applied to the concept of developed socialism. The present Party programme had been drawn up in 1961 and it was now up to the Central Commit-tee to start work on a new programme to present to the next Con-gress: a programme which would have as its keynotes the achieve-ment of communism and the upholding of world peace.[13]

Earlier in his report Brezhnev had stated that, 'In the period under review the Party and the State did not for a single day lose sight of questions of strengthening the country's defensive might and its armed forces.' This responsibility for national security also figures largely in the Constitution, which stresses the subordination of the armed forces to civil authority. The primary duty of the forces is to defend the Soviet Motherland by maintaining constant combat readi-ness, 'guaranteeing an instant rebuff to any aggressor'. In return the state must guarantee to provide them 'with everything necessary for the security and defence capability of the country'.[14]

It remains to examine the relations between Party and the armed forces in greater depth and to analyse to what extent political and economic realities have enabled it to provide 'everything necessary'.

THE PARTY AND THE ARMED FORCES

In a world in which unsuccessful political regimes have so often been replaced by military governments and in a Russia where only the military appear to have the resources and organisation to take over power, it is inevitable that there should be speculation about the present and future relations between the Party and the armed forces. There is no case for predicting a military coup but there does seem at least a possibility that, if the political leadership were divided, for instance over the succession to Brezhnev, for a time at least, the military, with their patriotism, prestige and professionalism, might gain strong influence over Party policy. Indeed, such is the opaque-ness of Soviet decision-making that there is no certainty that this has not already happened. What is indisputable is that the Party has, since the Revolution, been keenly aware of 'Bonapartism' and has aimed to prevent it by a complex system of political indoctrination and organisational control which is an important part of the framework inside which the Soviet Navy has to operate. 'The policy of the military department, as of all other departments, . . . is conducted on the precise basis of the general directives issued by the Party, in the person of its Central Committee, and under its direct rule.'[15] The Party's immediate concern after the end of the Civil War was that the new Red Army had to rely on the professional skill of thousands of ex-Tsarist officers of uncertain political loyalty, but in the event they maintained the pre-Revolutionary Russian practice of remaining loyal to the political regime and identified their interests with it as long as it was effective and gave them adequate resources and status. This is the case today and for the foreseeable future.[16]

The apparently glaring exception to this perceived harmony of interests between Party and armed forces is of course the Stalinist purge in 1937, in which it is calculated that three out of five marshals, 90 per cent of general officers and 80 per cent of colonel's rank, were either executed or imprisoned. The navy lost all of its senior admirals and several of the professors at the Leningrad Naval Academy. It is however fair to argue that this was not a Party policy in any real sense but one of the most outrageous examples of Stalin's megalomania, which, along with his similar purges of the Party, was to be denounced after his death as his greatest offence. Even if some future individual or collective leadership should wish to act in a similar fashion, all internal and external realities would stand in his way. On the other hand, the only likely circumstances in which the military might attempt a coup would be a perception that the Party was seriously weakening the country's security by reducing its military strength. Short of this most unlikely development, Party and armed forces seem permanently welded together in a complex system of shared interests.

In such a relationship there are bound to be differences of emphasis and disputed priorities in such matters as the allocation of resources between civil and military requirements; disarmament and arms control; relations within the Warsaw Pact; and detailed decisions in foreign policy. There are also bound to be inter-service disputes and rivalries which the political authorities will have to resolve, as they do in all countries which are not military dictatorships. An attempt to understand the Soviet Navy's growth in strategic significance and combat capability, based as it has been on the acquisition of a considerable share of Russia's advanced technology, must take into account this non-monolithic nature of defence decision-making.[17]

The most significant recent clash of interests came in the late 1950s with Khruschev's plans for substantial reductions in conventional forces, which would benefit the economy, and greater reliance on strategic nuclear weapons. The Navy's surface fleet would have been one of the greatest losers. The plans were seen by the military professionals both as an attack on their traditional faith in large ground forces and on their personal prestige and career prospects. That they were never implemented and that Russia continued to build up both her conventional and nuclear forces was due to the military being able to find allies in the many elements in the Party leadership hostile to Khruschev's whole style of government; an alliance which led to his downfall in 1964.

A particularly interesting element in this controversy was that the organisation upon which the Party depends for the political control of the military machine, the Main Political Administration of the Army and Navy (MPA), which is directly responsible to the Politbureau as well as to the Ministry of Defence, appears to have sided with its professional military colleagues against the Party's General Secretary.[18] The Political Administration, whose present title dates from 1958, has existed under different names since 1918, when it was given the specific role of ensuring the loyalty of the ex-Tsarist officers. Since then its main role has been to carry out 'Party work' designed to inspire loyalty, enthusiasm and morale throughout the armed forces. It is manned by specially trained officers working from ship and unit level up to the highest levels in the Ministry of Defence and is normally headed by an officer of general's or marshal's rank. Political officers, in addition to their general education, are given specialised training for their work in the particular service to which they are assigned and where they tend to remain. Those for the Navy are trained at the Kiev Higher Naval Political School and are headed by an Admiral.[19] The history of their activity in the armed forces has often been characterised by conflicts with the military operational commanders of their units. Today these conflicts have been largely resolved in ways which establish the supremacy of the military professional, but tensions still persist which must have some impact in the workings of the Soviet Navy.

The main controversy centres around the concept of 'one-man command' and, while both operational and political officers accept that this is essential for military efficiency, they differ in their interpretation of what it means in practice. The military professional sees it in simple terms and expects the unit's political officer to accept his ultimate authority and act as his subordinate in maintaining the unit's morale, efficiency and combat readiness. The political officer will tend to stress the obligations on the commander to make his decisions 'on a Party basis' and to pay attention to the Party organisations within his unit, even to the extent of listening to criticism of his own conduct.

Political officers will also insist on adequate training time being allotted to political education and on Party work not being sacrificed to the increasing demands of mastering complex military technology. This is a central item in the Party's and MPA's dogma that belief in the Soviet cause is as important for the fighting man as is professional competence. As such it is a cause of the strains between professionalism and Party zeal which occur in all Soviet institutions. Another manifestation of this has been claims by the MPA that its officers are as fully qualified to exercise command as the military professionals. This has been met by charges that political officers are so ignorant of the significance of technological developments as to be incapable of fulfilling even their specialised role of maintaining morale and discipline.[20]

Such tensions are inevitable, granted the system, but they could be creative by acting as correctives to the inertia and complacency characteristic of military hierarchies in peacetime. Moreover it is probably wrong to believe that they overshadow the general contemporary tendency for the political and operational officers to work together in the interest of their service or unit. There is good reason to believe that when, in 1969, the Politbureau was stressing the claims of détente and seeking strategic arms limitation with the United States, the MPA and the military high command united in criticism of what they saw as threats to Russia's security.[21] Perhaps the normal practice is reflected in a statement by the chief of staff of the Baltic Fleet in 1972 that he and the head of the Fleet's political administration kept close contact and 'try to solve similar problems by mutual efforts'.[22]

More significant recently than the MPA's role in ensuring political control of the military has been the development of a close relationship at the highest level between the Party and the military professionals. In earlier days it was expected that the loyalty of the armed forces would become more assured as former Tsarist officers were replaced by younger generations, educated in the new military academies where ideological and political instruction would figure largely. One indication of the success of this procedure has been the

increasing number of military officers becoming Party members and
the emergence of a significant military contingent in the Central
Committee. In the 1920s only 20 per cent were Party members, by
the 1930s this had risen to 70 per cent and, since 1945, the proportion has risen to its present size of some 90 per cent. In 1977 the
total Party membership of 16.2 million included some 940,000
military members. Even more significant is the fact that virtually all
professional military officers of the rank of major and its equivalents
are Party members.[23] This reflects a wider process which has
resulted in an increasing number of members having higher educational qualification, over 21 per cent in 1977, thus showing military
men as figuring among the other professional elites likely to identify
themselves with the political system from which they have benefited.
This close identification of the military profession with the political
system is further illustrated by the presence of a sizable contingent
in the Central Committee, the one major Party body in which there
seems to be some genuine debate on major issues and some capacity
for influencing policy decisions and appointments to high positions.
In the Central Committee elected at the Twenty-fifth Party Congress in 1976 they amounted to 7 per cent of the whole and were
'the largest contingent from any bureaucratic constituency'. There is
also a substantial military element in regional and local Party com-
mittees.[24] This is not to suggest that the armed forces aspire to any
usurption of political authority within the Party – there is no evidence that they act as a united pressure group – but to show their
general integration into the total political system with which they
identify their professional and personal interests.

This symbiosis is further demonstrated in the workings of the
Party's supreme decision-making body, the Politbureau. Here the
important factor is not that professional military men such as
Marshals Zhukov and Grechko have, as Ministers of Defence, been
full members, but that the dominant Party leaders, the General Sec-
retaries, Stalin, Khruschev and Brezhnev, have as it were militarised
themselves by assuming military ranks and, in Brezhnev's case, acting as Chairman of the Defence Council, the highest military
decision-making body. This amalgam of political and military
leadership has been further illustrated by the appointment as Minister of Defence on Grechko's death in 1976 of D. F. Ustinov, who,
although in some respects a civilian with a successful career in heavy
industry, supplemented by work in the Party Secretariat and candidate (non-voting) membership of the Politbureau, has also been for
many years a colonel-general in the Army's technical branch. On his

succession as Minister he was promoted to the military rank of marshal, as well as to full membership of the Politbureau. His appointment has been seen as a sign of Brezhnev's determination not to allow any military obstruction to his hopes for détente and arms control agreements with the United States, but it certainly does not indicate any fundamental lack of support for the armed forces.[25] Like most of the senior leadership, Brezhnev appears to have relished his military experience in the Great Patriotic War. It may well be that, in view of the armed forces' remarkable adjustment to new technology, in contrast to the backwardness in civil industry which he denounced at the Twenty-sixth Party Congress in 1981, he finds himself in considerable sympathy with the military leadership. This could provide a clue to Admiral Gorshkov's success in gaining political support for his naval ambitions. He has always stressed that it has been technological change which has produced the Navy's ability to make a larger contribution to Soviet strategy than in the pre-nuclear age.

Be that as it may, the present pattern of Soviet civil–military relations is not one of conflict but of the recognition of mutual interests. Party and government have no doubts that military strength is the basis for the Soviet Union's ability to act as a global power. The military are instinctively in favour of the strong central control which the Party's monopoly of power ensures and they as Party members share its aims and its privileges. However, events in Poland are bound to have reminded them that, should the Party fail, they are the only alternative source of power. For the time being they show no outward sign of wishing to usurp political authority, wishing only to participate in policy decision-making in accordance with the importance of military strength to their country and with their own manifest technological and managerial competence. The final proof of this recognition of mutual interests is seen in the ways in which the Party, in spite of all the difficulties of the Soviet economy, has ensured that the armed forces should have the first claim on all that is best among the products of Soviet science, technology and industry.[26]

ECONOMIC PRIORITY OF DEFENCE

Article 31 of the 1977 Constitution of the Soviet Union defining the role of the armed forces as the defence of the Soviet Motherland by maintaining combat readiness in order to produce an instant rebuff to any aggressor, is followed by the declaration in Article 32 that it is the duty of the state to provide them 'with everything necessary' to fulfil their task.[27] Although, like all military leaders, Soviet commanders must always have wanted more, compared with their Western counterparts they have been more successful in ensuring the allocation of a large part of the nation's resources to defence. This allocation has been high in quality as well as quantity, and made from an economic system far less efficient and far less capable of improving general living standards than that of the United States. This priority given to defence is a clear demonstration of the political leadership's conviction that unchallengeable military strength is essential to the country's security in a hostile world, as well as being the most effective means of global influence. It has of course been facilitated by the nature of the economic system in which the ownership and control of industry, the direction of investment and the organisation of scientific and technological research are all exercised by the state. This is not to say, as envious military men in the West have tended to assert, that their Soviet counterparts have unchallenged access to unlimited resources. The post-Stalin political leadership has always accepted the necessity of improving the geneneral quality of life if it is to maintain the willing support of an increasingly educated population and to convince sceptical foreigners of the merits of its system. The resulting competition between civil and military interests is made more serious by the system's admitted weaknesses in productivity and innovation. To this can be added the inevitable competition for resources between the individual armed services. What seems to be accepted by authoritative Western commentators and confirmed by official statements in the Soviet Union, is that in the last resort military priorities will prevail. Nevertheless competition and disputes there must be, and the fact that the Soviet Navy has been able to increase its capabilities so substantially in recent years can only have resulted from its advocates, headed by Gorshkov, having convinced the political leadership of the importance of its unique contribution to the security of Russia and the furtherance of its global interests.

CURRENT PROBLEMS OF THE SOVIET ECONOMY[28]

The distinguishing characteristic of the Soviet economy is that every element has to operate under the dual control of Party organisations and state ministries. This control varies from the construction of the

Five Year Plans which lay down the targets to be achieved by industry and agriculture and determine the distribution of investment and materials, to the detailed supervision of industrial plants and collective and state farms by the Party and state bureaucracy. In considering the allocation of resources to defence it is essential to remember that failure to satisfy the aspirations of an electorate, a major factor determining the fate of Western governments, is of comparative insignificance in Russia. The government is isolated from popular pressures and open criticism and not dependent upon consumers' votes for its continuance in office. But, inside the decision-making elite, there are always representatives of Party organs and state ministries responsible for consumer and service industries, as well as an awareness in the Politbureau of the dangers of the regime becoming discredited by economic failure. The dilemma is intensified by the ideological claims that a fully socialist economy is not only more just than the capitalist alternative but also more efficient. Here again failure to make this claim a reality could in the long run discredit the whole basis of the system abroad as well as at home.

A significant change came in Soviet economic pronouncements in the 1970s, compared with confident claims of the previous decade that by the 1980s the Soviet Union would overtake the United States in productivity and quality of life and thus prove to the Third World the superiority of its system. Today's reality is very different. It is true that the Gross National Product (GNP), based as it is on great natural resources, a huge labour force and high industrial investment makes the Soviet Union the world's second economic power, but in several ways she displays all the signs of an unbalanced and underdeveloped economy. Continuing agricultural failure has not only produced shortages of basic food supplies but also the need to buy huge quantities of grain abroad with a resulting drain on gold and foreign currency reserves. Her relative industrial backwardness is clearly shown by the character of her trade with the West, which largely consists of the export of raw materials in return for finished goods, and by her admitted need for advanced Western technology. Despite her great resources of men and materials she stands only nineteenth in Europe in the size of her GNP per head of population.[29]

One fundamental cause of this backwardness is the rigidity of the political and bureaucratic control of the economy. The realisation of this led to various methods of liberalisation initiated by Khruschev and continued in a limited and less dramatic form by the present leadership. But such reforms have never gone far enough and thus have not been effective, because of the leadership's determination not to relinquish its control of the economy which it ideologically perceives as the foundation of its whole position. An equally potent obstacle has been the inertial pressures of the vast bureaucracy, necessary to the operation of the system, determined to keep things as they are. Just as attempts at economic reform are imprisoned in this web, so it is possible that any moves to shift resources from defence to consumer industries would be similarly prevented by the leadership's ideologically based view of the primacy of military power and the deeply embedded position of the armed forces and the industries which serve them.

There are other factors suggesting that economic difficulties, demonstrated by slow-down in growth, will persist in the 1980s. One of the main reasons for Russia's great economic growth since 1917 has been the availability of manpower reserves for its new industries. All the signals point to a decline in population growth, particularly in western Russia. This will be compensated for numerically in Central Asia, but amongst people who show no desire to move into the industrial zones. This labour shortage could be compensated for by greater inputs of capital investment, but this would involve reduction of consumer goods. A further source of weakness is that the reserves of energy and other natural resources, which are the country's greatest economic advantage, are situated far from the industrial centres so that their exploitation and transport are becoming increasingly difficult and costly. All these factors foreshadow a slower rate of economic growth in the 1980s and greater difficulties in meeting consumers' expectations.[30]

It is against this background that the problems of future defence expenditure and production must be seen. Is there any likelihood that, if it becomes accepted in the Soviet Union that the quantity and quality of military expenditure seriously inhibit general economic development, this will increase the strength of those in the leadership advocating détente with the West and a consequent reduction in the rate of growth of military expenditure, an expenditure currently estimated as exceeding the rate of overall economic growth? The effect of such a change on Soviet naval development could be considerable.

A valuable illustration of the Soviet leadership's awareness of economic problems and their interrelation with foreign and defence policies is provided by Brezhnev's report to the Twenty-sixth Party Congress of the CPSU in February 1981. This speech, formally the report of the General Secretary of the Party, but given greater authority by his known prominence in the Politbureau and his position as Head of State and Commander in Chief of the armed forces, was a report of achievements in the five years since the Twenty-fifth Congress and a criticism of shortcomings, leading to an exhortation for better future performance. Given to an audience which included the most influential members of the ruling Party and laying down principles for action in the next five years, the speech, although it must be interpreted with caution, provides as clear a guide as can be expected from the Soviet system, to the leadership's future intentions.[31]

The contradictory pressures bearing on the leadership emerge in the opening passages on the world situation. Russia's overall aim is to bring about the external conditions necessary for completing the constructive task of the Soviet people by the consolidation of the world socialist system and the co-operation of all socialist countries. Because of the hostility of capitalism these advances must have the protection of the armed forces of the Warsaw Pact, a political–military defensive alliance essential for the preservation of peace. 'It has everything necessary to reliably defend the people's socialist gains and we will do everything to keep this the case.' There must also be economic competition with capitalism but at the same time trade with it must be encouraged as a factor in international stability. But this must not make the socialist states vulnerable to political pressures nor lead to any weakening in the ideological struggle against the West's continuing attempts to turn the people away from socialism. In this respect any domestic failures threatening the foundations of socialist society must be remedied.[32] Whatever its impact on its immediate audience, this part of the speech with its contradictory emphases on military strength, and on the need for domestic achievement; the need to compete economically with the West and yet to trade with it despite the fear of political and ideological infection, summarise for the outsider some of the underlying causes of the Soviet Union's economic failures.

The section of the report dealing with the 'CPSU's Economic Policy in the Period of Developed Socialism',[33] insists that the direction of the economy is the central activity of Party and state and that everything else, social progress, foreign and defence policies, are dependent upon its success. What is needed is economic growth through increases in efficiency and quality in all sections of the system. Although substantial progress in total GNP and productivity has been made since the last two Party Congresses, as well as rises in wages, and the supply of consumer goods and housing, there are still substantial shortcomings, unsolved problems and difficulties. In the 1980s there will have to be increased investment to develop the eastern and northern regions. This will make special demands on transport and communications which already are lagging behind the demands of the economy. These developments will have to be pursued despite a smaller growth in the work force. The guidelines for success in the period up to 1990 to ensure the people's well-being can be summarised as 'The changing of the economy to the intensive path of development'. This entails making full use of science and technology, rational planning of production, the most economical use of all types of resources, and improvements in the general quality of work. Ultimate success primarily depends on such improvements in heavy industry, 'where the USSR still lags behind the best world practice' in productivity and efficiency. The demand will not only be for the increased application of science and technology but also for the highest qualities of management and leadership. These demands added to the earlier reference to the husbanding of resources might well seem in opposition to the increasing demands of defence for the same scarce skills and materials.

A further contradiction emerges in Brezhnev's later assertion that improvement in the quality of life by increases in food production and the availability of manufactured consumer goods 'is moving to the forefront'. Here again the emphasis must be on efficiency and quality in production. In the past the plans for consumer goods had not been achieved in either quality or quantity and this in turn had contributed to the failure to achieve agricultural targets.[34] How can these aspirations be reconciled with the previous emphasis on the priority of heavy industry, which in turn, although this is never admitted in Brezhnev's speech, is largely necessitated by the needs of defence?

THE BURDEN OF DEFENCE EXPENDITURE ON THE ECONOMY

Despite the achievements of the Russian economy, growth has been heavily unbalanced. It has been greatest in heavy industry and in the quantity rather than the quality of finished goods. This has resulted in the bulk of the population, especially those outside the major cities, having to accept a standard of life far below that of their Western

European counterparts. There is no doubt that the concentration on heavy and other industries related to defence and the clear policy of giving military requirements higher priority, not only in quantity but also in first claims on the most advanced science and technology, scarce materials and skilled manpower, have been one of the major causes of the neglect of consumer demand.[35] The continuing determination to maintain military parity with the United States, with a GNP approximately twice as great as that of the Soviet Union, involves devoting one-eighth of it to military resources as well as one-third of machinery products and a major, but unquantifiable, share of national research and development. In addition to all this there is the strain on the economy of having to support armed forces of some 4 million.[36] Although there is probably some compensation in the education and technical training which the conscript takes back to civilian life.

The constantly changing and diverging Western estimates of Soviet defence expenditure arise from the absence of any published statistics 'on anything remotely connected with defence' in the industrial and technological fields. Interpretation of the official Soviet statistics available produces a figure of only 2.8 per cent of GNP, but this covers only the equipment and operating costs of the armed services and excludes research and development and other major elements. In addition there are great difficulties in translating rouble costs into US dollars. All that can be confidently said is that United Kingdom and American estimates indicate a growth in defence expenditure of 4–4.5 per cent in the last decade and a proportion of between 11–14 per cent of GNP currently being devoted to defence, as compared with 5.5 per cent in the United States.[37] Whatever the precise figures, these strains on an economy already marked by poor productivity and inability to meet consumer demand must be accepted as a continuing element of the framework within which the Soviet Navy has grown and must develop in future.

These strains must be accentuated by the prognosis of slower rates of economic growth in the 1980s which is at least implicitly accepted by the political leadership and must result in some degree of refusal or inability to satisfy all the demands of the military. There are however absolutely no grounds for believing that the politicians will fail to provide what they consider necessary to maintain military parity with the United States, estimates bound to be influenced by the knowledge of their rival's superior technology and industrial efficiency. Indeed, it can be argued that so great is the priority given to defence, that the Soviet economy is better designed to solve the problems of war than those of peace. Since the first Five Year Plan of 1928 heavy industry has had priority, and inside heavy industry those branches related to defence have shown the greatest sustained growth. This has only been achieved by allowing military needs to play a major part in the planning of capital investment, which is claimed to be the determining factor in Soviet economic development.[38] A further complication and indeed contradiction emerges from the leadership's apparent determination to remedy the shortfall in the production of consumer goods as well as maintain defence expenditure, an improvement which can only come about by relying on the import of technology and techniques from the very capitalist countries whose hostility is perceived as the root cause of the need for military strength.[39]

The absence of reliable statistics for research and development and total industrial investment for defence as a whole makes it virtually impossible to arrive at a meaningful quantitative assessment of the particular burden imposed by expenditure on the Soviet Navy. It would seem obvious that the growth in its capabilities in the past twenty years must have increased its cost and there is no evidence of any compensating reduction in other areas of defence. The Navy's demands on the economy, ranging from ships, submarines and aircraft with their propulsion systems, weapons and electronics to the manifold needs of its personnel in the way of accommodation and domestic equipment, must have had a significant impact on the resources available for other purposes. The demands on the engineering industry, mechanical, electrical and electronic, have been particularly heavy. These demands must have been increased by the policies of providing increasingly complex ships and equipment and the frequent introduction of new types which have been recently implemented and which appear to be a departure from the normal Soviet practice of mass procurement.[40]

All of this is not necessarily an unmitigated burden on the national economy. There must have been some spin-off and stimulation of innovation applicable to civil needs, but it does show a conscious, and so far maintained, decision by the leadership to impose a considerable additional load on an already strained economy. Such a decision implies that naval development is seen as an essential component of the armed forces needed to further Soviet interests in the future. This must also be the case in the policy decisions on forward naval deployment. These have involved not only the provision of additional ships and aircraft but also substantial increases in operational cost including transit time, maintenance, replenishment and general logistic support. Forward deployment, especially in the more distant seas such as the Indian Ocean, is much more expensive than concentration in home and adjacent waters and must have been perceived as having correspondingly significant advantages.[41] Such advantages are not confined to relations with the United States. Apart from the possible future benefits of maritime power in Russia's differences with China and a natural ambition to increase her global influence, the increasing importance of her merchant navy and fishing fleets, and the acceptance of the need to protect other economic and legal maritime interests may well have provided the Navy with support in its quest for resources from a wide range of interest groups in Party and government. Is this likely to continue in future years?

SOVIET DEFENCE INDUSTRIES

The industries supplying the armed forces appear to be a coherent and separate section of the Soviet economic organisation, with one of the Deputy Chairmen of the Council of Ministers supervising each of the eight departments involved. These also have substantial representation in the Party's Central Committee and Secretariat. They are:

1. Defence industry, responsible for conventional weapons
2. Aviation industry, responsible for aircraft and their components
3. Shipbuilding industry, responsible for ships
4. Electronics industry responsible for all electronic equipment and components
5. Radio industry
6. Medium machine-building industry, responsible for nuclear weapons
7. General machine-building industry, responsible for strategic missiles
8. Machine-building industry, responsible for armour.

The Navy is an important customer for all these, and could well have their support in its bargaining for resources. In some circumstances this group of important industries could well have substantial political influence. It appears, for instance, that in the 1960s Ustinov, later to become Minister of Defence, and other leading figures were amongst those strongly opposed to Khruschev's plans to cut conventional military forces and strongly supported his removal in 1964.[42] Under

Brezhnev's general policy of circumscribing military and other sectional influences it has not played so overtly a political role since, though it could in any future leadership crisis. But it does seem to have maintained the primacy of defence demands on the economy. This is particularly so in applied research and development in nuclear technology, electronics, rocketry, aviation and weapons systems. There are estimates varying from 40–80 per cent of what proportion this is of the whole national research and development effort, but it does seem clear that it is far more effective than its civilian counterpart, as is demonstrated by the higher growth rates in the military supply industries. Other factors influencing this are higher allocations of resources and more skilled management because of the armed forces' ability to impose their detailed requirements and supervise the whole procurement and manufacturing process. This has produced both better technology and a more rapid rate of innovation. These in turn have been facilitated by the ability to offer preferential rates of pay to skilled workers, another scarce commodity in the Soviet Union.[43]

Another proof of the defence industries' privileged position is that they were exempted from Khruschev's economic reforms which disbanded most central industrial ministries and substituted regional control. Instead they operated under long-term plans prepared by the General Staff in the Ministry of Defence and then given Politbureau approval. These plans, based as they are on the hitherto accepted strategic doctrine that a major war will be so short and destructive that there will be no time to build up supplies once it has started, insist on the necessity of having everything ready beforehand, including stockpiling of reserves, and thus postulate mass production of a high order. Not only does their implementation have the dynamic force of the Politbureau behind it but the whole research and production process is supervised by a joint Military–Industrial Commission chaired by a minister, a post held by Ustinov before he became Minister of Defence. In its detailed supervision of production the military leadership can itself be innovative. For instance, when Marshal Grechko was Minister of Defence he emphasised the need to pursue two new developments: the reduction of physical labour in military work by increased mechanisation and automation, and similar improvements in troop control. He also stressed the need for economic uses of resources and for inter-service co-operation in production.[44] Similar themes are developed by Admiral Gorshkov in his views of naval procurement. So the defence industries may well set standards challenging emulation in their civilian counterparts.

Military leaders seem to share the general Soviet apprehension that, despite all their efforts, their research, development and production are not so flexible and innovative as the West's. This is probably the case but it would seem that the determination of the political leadership to maintain military equivalence with the United States is likely to lead to a continuance of the remarkable progress in military equipment already achieved. In recent years the Soviet Navy has benefited from a substantial share of this progress and there is no reason to believe that this share will diminish as long as the leadership remains convinced of the significance of the sea in Soviet foreign policy and strategy.

3 The Foreign Policy Background

INTRODUCTION[1]

The Soviet Union's increased concern with the sea can only be understood in the light of the changes which have taken place in her foreign policy since 1953. Stalin to the day of his death saw his country as encircled and threatened by a hostile world, as she had been since the Revolution and the Civil War. His slogan of 'Socialism in one Country' symbolised this siege mentality in both internal and external policies. Hitler's invasion and the near defeat and signs of internal break-up which followed it confirmed this attitude which did not disappear at the end of the war. Based on Stalin's conviction of the inevitable hostility of capitalist to communist countries, it merely transferred historical and ideological suspicions to Russia's erstwhile allies, particularly the United States. The latter's open commitment to capitalism, her opposition to Russia's claim to suzerainty over Eastern Europe and her monopoly of atomic weapons made her the chief threat. When to these she added the commitment to support a militarily united Western Europe through the North Atlantic Treaty Organisation (NATO) in 1949 and thus deny the Soviet Union the influence in Europe to which Stalin believed her performance in the war had entitled her, the onset of the political and military confrontation of the Cold War was inevitable. Its transformation into actual hostilities involving the new weapons of mass destruction now possessed by both sides seemed more than likely as long as an increasingly megalomaniac Stalin ruled the Soviet Union.

A new era in Russia's external policies was announced by Khruschev at the Twentieth Party Conference of the CPSU in 1956, when, in addition to his denunciation of Stalin's internal mistakes and excesses, he rejected his predecessor's negative and defensive view of her place in the world. While accepting a continuance of an adversary relationship with the United States Khruschev claimed that his country's growing strength, both economic and military, now enabled her to conduct the confrontation with confidence. Moreover the United States, aware of her opponent's new strength and of the futility of nuclear war, would be less and less tempted towards aggression. This would enable the competition between the two powers to be conducted by non-military means. To this pragmatic analysis Khruschev added ideological legitimisation by proclaiming as a principle of Marxist–Leninist thought the concept of 'peaceful co-existence between states of differing social systems'. Henceforward this was to be the basis of the Soviet Union's relationships with the non-communist world. The security of the state and the expansion of socialism no longer demanded a war to the death with capitalism.

A more positive departure from Stalin's immobilism was contained in Khruschev's announcement of the Soviet Union's intention to take advantage of the emergence of a great number of newly independent states since the end of the war and the struggles for freedom from colonialism still to be decided. Stalin had been suspicious of these developments because of the nationalist and bourgeois nature of their leadership but to Khruschev they represented a great opportunity. By backing them Russia could simultaneously weaken the economic and political influence of capitalist–imperialism and establish her own leadership of a global movement of progressive states, thus substantially increasing her world influence. In addition there would be economic advantages in the opening up of new export markets and wider access to raw materials. It is noteworthy that between 1955 and 1965 Russia's foreign trade increased from 5.2 per cent of her total trade turnover to 11.9 per cent. There has also been an increase in economic assistance, first to support general development, but increasingly from the mid-1960s, concentrating on military aid. This has noticeably been given to nations with acceptable political systems or strategically important locations: Egypt, Libya, Algeria, Vietnam and Angola, to say nothing of Cuba, where Castro's regime has become completely dependent upon Soviet economic aid, and which in return has become an essential agent of Russia's African policy. Another element of this active foreign policy has been the supply of military advisers, often coupled with demands for base facilities as in Egypt, Somalia and Aden. Future substantial strategic advantage would come if the Soviet Union's aid to Angola, Mozambique and

Vietnam were to be repaid with extensive base facilities in the South Atlantic, Indian Ocean and South China Sea. There is no need to assume a carefully prepared overall plan but a skilfully conducted opportunistic foreign policy of this kind, increasing both political influence and strategic reach, has important implications for the future development and effectiveness of Soviet naval power. In addition, the provision of armaments, beginning with the Czech-fronted supply in Egypt in 1955 and which by Khruschev's fall in 1964 had built up to an estimated total of 3 billion dollars distributed between thirteen countries, amounting to about one-third of her total foreign aid programme, has continued to be one of the most effective instruments of Soviet foreign policy.[2]

Khruschev's successors have not departed from his basic policies, although they have so far avoided the 'adventurism' exemplified by his 1962 plan to install nuclear missiles in Cuba and the consequent climb down in face of America's determined opposition which had led the two countries to the brink of nuclear war. Imperialism must be constantly challenged, wars and political movements for national liberation supported, but not in ways likely to lead to open military confrontation with the United States.[3] Since the mid 1970s however, with the Soviet leadership's confidence that they have achieved nuclear parity and their perception of an apparent weakening of America's will after the disillusionment of Vietnam, there are signs of a greater willingness to take risks. These have been demonstrated by intervention in the former Portuguese colonies, in the Horn of Africa and in Afghanistan.

It has been the coincidence of this more adventurous global foreign policy with the Soviet Union's growth in maritime activity and power which has led some Western commentators to see a unique causal relationship between the two. This view has been challenged by other experts who stress a more narrowly strategic motivation. A balanced judgement demands a fuller analysis of the formative influences behind Russia's foreign and defence policies and of the relative priorities which govern the allocation of resources between her various objectives.

IDEOLOGY AND FOREIGN POLICY

As a preliminary to dealing with these questions it is necessary to deal more fully with a problem already referred to (see pp. 17–19). Are the Soviet Union's external policies motivated by national or ideological aims?[4] This is of particular importance in any attempt to assess the reasons for her growth in maritime power. Different answers have led to different interpretations of the purposes of the build-up of the Soviet Navy and other maritime activities. By and large those Western commentators who give pre-eminence to national and superpower motivation have seen an increase in war-fighting capability as the main cause of naval development and the strengthening of the national economy as being the main role of the merchant and fishing fleets. Others, more impressed by the Soviet Union's concern to spread socialism, have tended to stress the political potential of naval deployments and merchant shipping activity in support of progressive and in opposition to reactionary regimes in conditions short of war.

It is likely that the truth is more complex than an assumption that one of these two explanations must be adopted to the exclusion of the other. There is a great deal of evidence in the course of Soviet foreign policy since 1945, and indeed since 1917, to suggest that the Communist regime in its actions, if not in its words, has made the preservation and enhancement of the Russian state its main priority and has given little regard to the spread of revolution. It would however be completely wrong to deduce from this that ideology has played no part in the formulation of foreign policy or can be disregarded in attempts to forecast future developments. To do so would be to ignore the factors of legitimacy and perception which play so large a part in forming the policies and attitudes of the Soviet ruling elite.

This has led them to describe and justify every major development in foreign policy in Marxist–Leninist terminology and to assert that theirs is the correct form of the ideology as compared with the 'revisionism' of Tito and the Eurocommunists, the 'dogmatism' of Mao Tse Tung, or the even more heretical concepts of his successors. This ideological position has been used to legitimise the concept of peaceful coexistence with capitalist states while simultaneously seeking to weaken them by all means short of war. Similarly, it has provided the theoretical basis for helping countries fighting for independence in wars of national liberation and for supporting revolutionary movements in states which, although nominally independent, are stifled by 'neo-colonialism' through the dominance of their economies by capitalist ownership and investment. In the latter instance interference in their internal affairs can be justified by attributing their economic exploitation to the machinations of an indigenous capitalist class which must be liquidated and replaced by a government based

on the proletariat. These concepts and the Brezhnev doctrine claiming the right of the Soviet government to intervene in socialist countries, such as Czechoslovakia, where an established socialist regime is
threatened by internal reaction, have been strongly re-emphasised in
the Soviet Constitution of 1977. This not only proclaims the leading
role of the CPSU in internal affairs but stresses its duty to strengthen
world socialism and support all peoples struggling for national liberation and social progress. Thus an active foreign policy based on ideology is enshrined in the Constitution of the Russian state.[5] That progressive governments and revolutionary movements supported on
these ideological grounds are expected to reciprocate with political or
even military backing for their benefactor demonstrates the very
advantageous relationship for the Soviet Union between ideological
rectitude and the promotion of national interests.

This element in the formulation of Soviet foreign policy of claiming
legitimacy by acting in accordance with the teachings of a scientifically established political philosophy is complemented by an ideologically conditioned perception of the nature and working of the international system. Because of their upbringing and experience, Soviet
leaders will tend to accept the fundamental Marxist doctrine that the
economic organisation of a society dominates its political structure
and aspirations and that capitalist states, however strongly they claim
to be democratic and peace loving, will in fact be dominated by the
class interests of big business and its military lackeys. Such states are
bound to be hostile to the Soviet Union which must therefore be
strong enough to deter or defeat the attacks which they may be
tempted to launch in an attempt to stave off the collapse of their own
regimes inevitably doomed by the process of historical development.
If it is this basic Marxist teaching which colours Russia's leaders'
perception of the developed world, it is by Lenin's doctrine of
'capitalist imperialism' that they interpret the situation in the Third
World.

In his later writings, disappointed by the failure of communist
revolutions in Europe, Lenin turned to what he called 'the revolutionary and nationalist East' where the majority of the world's population lived under appalling conditions of poverty and exploitation, as
the more likely basis of world revolution. This theme has been constantly restated by Lenin's successors and, since the death of Stalin,
has played a substantial part in forming their policies towards the
whole underdeveloped world. They see an inevitable progression
towards political and economic independence as a reaction to capital-

ist exploitation. This may well be started off by nationalistic middle-class movements ideologically out of sympathy with communism but ready to accept Russian support against their exploiters. Russia in her turn should help them because, in time, these bourgeois regimes will inevitably be overthrown by revolutionary movements and in the meanwhile their assertion of independence will increase the economic difficulties of capitalism which hitherto has been saved from collapse by its exploitation of backward peoples.

It would seem that, if the dual elements of a need for legitimisation and ideologically conditioned perception play so large a part in the formulation of Soviet foreign policy, there is little significance in the question as to whether nationalism or ideology provides the dominant motive. The Soviet Union's present and likely future rulers will see no contradiction between the two and will give priority to either as circumstances change. They will remain convinced that their ideology gives them a true insight into what is happening beneath the surface of world events. They will believe that if the catastrophe of general nuclear war can be avoided, the internal contradictions of capitalism will weaken it and ultimately ensure its final collapse. In such a situation cautiously active policies, especially in the Third World, will hasten the decline of their rivals and add to their own power. Added to these ideologically based perceptions will be the practical political resentment that the Soviet Union, despite all her strength and achievements, has not yet secured her due share of global power and influence and that she should therefore be ready to take moderate risks to remedy this whenever favourable opportunities occur. If ideology thus theoretically legitimises their global aspirations the Soviet leaders are realists enough to accept that it is of diminishing influence as a direct means of attracting support to their cause and they will be increasingly tempted to play their only high card, military strength.[6]

In such circumstances the possession of maritime power will be of great value. If the Soviet Union is to succeed in increasing her global influence at the expense of both the United States, the leader of the capitalist world, and China, the rival claimant to communist leadership, the ability to deploy presence and project power in the world's oceans is a necessity. How this capability is likely to be used is again likely to be determined by a combination of ideological and pragmatic perceptions. In recent years a great deal of emphasis has been placed on the concept of 'correlation of forces', which includes both the political and economic balance between the capitalist and socialist world systems, their relative strength of will, as well as their respective military capabilities.[7] Maritime power in this context, with all its mobility and flexibility, provides an admirable means for Russia to probe and test her opponents' strength and resolution. Its mere existence, without any need to employ it in combat, may well be a most effective way of checking the United States' use of its own hitherto unchallengeable sea power to further its global interests.

PRIORITIES IN SOVIET FOREIGN POLICY[8]

In attempting to define priorities between the various objectives of Soviet foreign policy it is essential to remember that the categories used are closely interdependent, sometimes in mutual harmony and sometimes in conflict. Any meaningful analysis of present and future policy decisions must look for a complexity of causation rather than for a single aim.

For the Soviet Union, as for the United States, the first priority must be the avoidance of general nuclear war, which, once begun would be uncontrollable in its course and cataclysmic in its consequences. This was publicly stated by both of Stalin's immediate successors, Malenkov and Khruschev, and has been constantly reiterated by their successors. There is no reason to doubt their sincerity in this. It has been demonstrated in practice by their conduct of relations with the United States in the various crises which have arisen over conflicting policies in the Middle East, most recently in the 1973 October war. Complementary to this aim, and of equal importance, is a determination to ensure the safety of Russian territory and that of the Eastern European states which are considered as essential to Russia's own security. These two fundamental aims will continue to be the dominating factors in formulating both foreign policy and the defence policy needed to make it effective. No hardships to her people and no distortion of her economy will be allowed to hinder the maintenance of such an array of military power, nuclear and conventional, that her enemies will be unable to defeat her pre-emptive attack or to blackmail her into major political concessions by threats of the use of superior force. If this security from war can be assured, the Soviet Union will be in a position to pursue her third external aim of enlarging her national and ideological influence at the expense of her two main rivals, the United States and China.

In working towards these aims, relations with the United States, at present its only comparable rival in economic and military strength, must take the first place although the behaviour of China will increasingly have to be taken into account. In its dealings with the United States the Soviet Union will insist on maintaining parity in strategic nuclear weapons which it sees as the minimum acceptable basis for their relationship. It is impossible to know whether she would deliberately seek nuclear superiority if it were technologically within her grasp. It is likely that there are members of the ruling elite, including the military, who would press for this, but there are others, including Brezhnev himself, more aware of how unacceptable it would be to the United States and of the increased strain it would put on the Soviet economy. This element would prefer the continuation of the present parity and would be willing to continue with arms limitation talks provided that Russia's overall position was not weakened. In all this, acting as a world power dissatisfied with the *status quo* and determined not to accept any form of inferiority to the United States, the Soviet Union will never negotiate meaningfully as long as she perceives any weakness in her position.[9] In such a context it must seem natural for her to aim at maritime equivalence as essential to her overall aims.

As a corollary to maintaining parity with the only existing superpower is a determination to prevent any future attainment of that status by China, Western Europe or Japan, or any combination of them. The Soviet Union feels relatively secure in a bi-polar world and any substantial change in the global distribution of power would rekindle the fears of encirclement always lurking in the Russian mind. With only the United States to deal with on equal terms she can feel confident of maintaining a working relationship which will enable her to control any crisis which may arise and of being able to take advantage of any favourable opportunity to increase her prestige and influence at the expense of her rival and its allies.

Europe is the area in which the Soviet Union would most like to increase her influence and be accepted as the leading power. This ambition is blocked by America's commitment to NATO and the cohesion of the European Economic Community (EEC). At the 1975 Conference on Security and Co-operation in Europe Russia achieved *de facto* acceptance of the post-1945 frontiers and distribution of power in the continent. She would like to see further conferences producing some form of pan-European Commission in which she could play a leading part, and challenge America's influence. In the meanwhile she will aim at preventing any further increase in the unity of the EEC or the military strength of NATO. In pursuit of this last aim she will continue to maintain a holding position in the long drawn-out talks on Mutual Force Reductions (MFR) and the more recently begun negotiations on Theatre Nuclear Forces, in the expectation that political and economic pressures will weaken the Western position.

Until 1977 China played a secondary role to Western Europe in Russia's strategic thinking but recent developments, such as her treaty with Japan, much improved relations with the United States, and her seeking of help for industrial and military modernisation from Western Europe must have raised the question of whether, in the long run, the Eastern danger would become the greater. Moreover, by her courting of Romania, the maverick member of the Warsaw Pact, and her constant warning to the West of the dangers of détente, China has become a serious hindrance to two of the Soviet Union's important aims: the maintenance of the unity of the Pact and of the dialogue with the West. In the Third World China's attempts to improve her relations with India and her 1978 invasion of Vietnam were clear warnings of increased uncertainties in Asia. Prospects of rapprochement with China seem remote and, although recourse to major war is unlikely, Russia will have to maintain increasingly effective forces on its eastern frontiers, both as a deterrent to China and as a reminder to other Asian states of its ability to deploy massive strength in the area. Maritime force would be a substantial asset in both these tasks. It must be remembered that the shortest and strategically safest route between European and Asiatic Russia is via the Suez Canal and the Indian Ocean. Even with the planned improvements, the Trans-Siberian Railway will remain limited in capacity and vulnerable to Chinese attack.

Soviet foreign policy has been at its most active in the Middle East, combining confrontation with the United States and substantial support for sympathetic regimes in an area of great strategic importance to both superpowers. Significant involvement began with the 1955 arms sale to Egypt, followed by strong denunciations and diplomatic manoeuvres during the Anglo-French Suez expedition in 1956, and has continued with further provision of arms, military advisers and diplomatic support to those Arab states most hostile to Israel. It has been a story of mixed successes and rebuffs. Great influence was obtained after the Arab defeat in 1967 and during and immediately after the 1973 October war. But there have been recurring strains due to Arab dissatisfaction with the arms supplied, the insensitivity of

Soviet advisers, and an unwillingness to become completely dependent on one superpower. This has been most clearly demonstrated in Soviet–Egyptian relationships which also show the most significant interaction between foreign and naval policies. Egypt was seen as the Soviet Union's most profitable ally in the area, because of its centrality in the Arab–Israeli conflict and the geographic advantage arising from its control of the Suez Canal and the possession of port and base facilities ideal for Soviet air and naval forces detailed to watch and challenge the United States' Sixth Fleet. Great gains were made here but ultimately the facilities were denied, advisers expelled and, under President Sadat, Egypt turned to the United States and began peace negotiations with Israel, resulting in the virtually complete exclusion of the Soviet Union from Egypt's affairs.[10]

It is probable that Russia sees her future interests best served by a continuance of 'no war no peace' conditions in the region, in which her position as an arms supplier and a counter-balance to the United States' support of Israel will give her substantial influence. The overthrow of the Shah of Iran must have reinforced her hopes that the reactionary regimes in Saudi Arabia and the Gulf states which wish to reduce her role in the area, will soon meet a similar fate. In such a fluid situation the ability to deploy substantial maritime force in the Mediterranean, the Gulf and the Arabian Sea would be a significant political and strategic advantage.

In addition to this long-established activity in the Middle East, in more recent years the Soviet Union has also ventured into a more active foreign policy in Africa. This has been most evident in the former Portuguese colonies and in support of the left-wing military government in Ethiopia. The main means used have been massive arms supplies and, in a novel departure, the bringing in of large numbers of Cuban combat troops. It is worth a short digression here to mention the naval advantages which the Soviet Union has gained from her close alliance with Cuba; the extension of Soviet presence into a region so close to the American mainland and possible assistance to the deployment of SSBNs in sea areas giving extensive coverage of all parts of the United States.[11] In Africa, although a considerable part of the transport of troops and equipment was by air, Soviet merchant shipping and naval back-up were also employed, and there are reliable reports of Soviet naval bombardments in support of her most favoured client in the Horn of Africa, Ethiopia. The breach with Somalia, which lost the Soviet Navy the extensive base facilities it had established at Berbera with its commanding position at the entrance to the Arabian Sea, is particularly interesting as an example of sacrificing a strategic advantage for a political interest perceived as more important. Support of the strongly Marxist Ethiopian regime had the greater attraction, although it may well be that a later reconciliation with Somalia was hoped for, a hope which more recent American interest and presence have made remote.

If the Soviet Union's policies of playing a more active global role continue, they will offer increased scope for the deployment and use of maritime power. The sea may well figure more largely in Soviet strategy but it would be wrong to assume that peripheral activities will achieve higher priority or win for the Soviet Navy greater resources than will developing demonstrations of what it can contribute to success in dealing with the three high priorities of foreign policy, relations with the United States, Western Europe and China. In particular, the best understanding of Soviet naval policy must be based on seeing its dynamism originating in a determination to achieve parity with the United States in all aspects of power and influence.

THE SOVIET NAVY AS AN INSTRUMENT OF FOREIGN POLICY[12]

The major treatment of the subject in Russia has been in the writings of Admiral Sergei Gorshkov, commander-in-chief of the Soviet Navy since 1956. His work as the advocate and architect of the modern Soviet Navy and his strategic and tactical doctrines are dealt with in Chapters 5 and 7, here we are concerned only with his views on the unique contribution a strong navy can make to furthering his country's international interests. These are most fully developed in two publications: a series of articles under the general title of *Navies in War and Peace*, published in the journal *Morskoi Sbornik* in 1972–3, and a book, *The Sea Power of the State* which followed in 1976.[13] The appearance of these writings by so authoritative an author and their emphasis, unprecedented in Soviet military publications, on the vital importance of sea power produced not only great interest but also considerable controversy in the West.[14] Were the new capabilities already achieved by the Soviet Navy which they extolled and the further development which they advocated, signs of a forthcoming fundamental change in Russia's strategy with a far greater emphasis on the use of the seas both for the deployment of strategic nuclear missiles and for conventional naval operations? Or, as other commentators contended, did not the whole thrust of Gorshkov's writings centre on the peacetime use of naval forces as instruments of diplomacy and foreign policy? Those who stressed this role drew attention to the new world-wide deployment patterns of the Soviet Navy and interpreted them as being designed to fulfil the traditional naval mission of showing the flag in order to increase Russia's influence and its support for radical regimes, thus giving a badly needed impetus to the spread of socialism. Others,[15] more addicted to a conspiratorial view of Soviet policies saw the new navy as one instrument of a long-term plan to dominate the countries of the Middle East and Africa upon which the West depended for its energy and mineral supplies, and thus weaken it by economic strangulation.

Certainly Gorshkov's writings draw constant attention to the peacetime role of the Soviet Navy and to its potential for direct or indirect intervention in local limited wars, but it is a misjudgement to isolate these roles and to interpret them as being the primary reasons for its growth and global deployment. It is more rational to see the main linkage between Soviet naval and foreign policies in terms of the priorities set out earlier: in particular, the avoidance of nuclear war, the determination to achieve overall equivalence in power and influence with the United States, and to be in a position to deter or deal with any future threat from China. For the Soviet Navy to have obtained its already considerable resources and to be hopeful of future development, it must already have convinced the political leadership of its ability to contribute to these principal policy objectives. Of course its peacetime missions have been used by its advocates, presumably in efforts to find wider support in influential places, but activities such as the support of client states, the increase of global political influence and the protection of commercial maritime interests are best understood as contributions to a wider overall national strategy. Far from there being any contradiction between the strategic and foreign policy roles of the Soviet Navy, they are complementary and interlocking and will be given relative priority according to the priorities of overall national policy. The aims and hopes of naval leaders as exemplified by Gorshkov are that they will be able to persuade the political leadership to provide them with the very wide and expensive range of equipment needed for playing all the roles from strategic nuclear deterrence to peacetime port visits.

In considering the Soviet Navy's views on its priorities it is misleading to concentrate on particular parts of Gorshkov's writings, such as the article 'Navies as Instruments of Peacetime Imperialism' in *Navies in War and Peace* and the corresponding section in *The Sea Power of the State*.[16] The two works must be taken as a whole. What do they advocate? First is the insistence that if the Soviet Union is to fulfil her potential as a global power she must be a strong maritime power because, not only her own history, but that of the world, demonstrates that the rise and fall of great nations has been causally connected with the strength or weakness of their sea power. 'History shows that those states which do not have naval forces at their disposal have not been able to hold the status of a Great Power for very long.' This has been due just as much to the economic as to the strategic importance of the sea, and today this economic significance is greater than ever before. 'All of the modern Great Powers are maritime states.'[17] Gorshkov illustrates this theme from Russia's history by showing how her strength and prestige had suffered from rulers who had not given her adequate sea power. The chief examples are the humiliating peace forbidding her to maintain a Black Sea Fleet after her defeat in the Crimean War and the inadequacy of her fleet in the war with Japan in 1905. These disasters contrast with the greatness she achieved under Peter the Great and the successes of Admiral Ushakov in the Mediterranean during the Napoleonic Wars. Gorshkov gives this historical experience contemporary point by his claim that these recurrent naval weaknesses had partly been due to mistaken views within the country that as a land power she did not need to be strong at sea. In contrast, he praises the present political leadership for its wisdom in understanding the need for strong maritime forces and the great advantages it had already gained from supplying the necessary resources. This had been most clearly demonstrated in the Mediterranean where Russian maritime forces not only deterred nuclear attacks by the American Sixth Fleet but also checked aggressive imperialist diplomacy against the littoral states. Gorshkov obviously found the contemporary Mediterranean situation the best illustration of the Navy's varied contribution to his country's interests. The littoral states are deeply divided in their political allegiance. Some belong to the aggressive NATO block, others to the 'so-called' non-aligned countries, and another group is still struggling to gain independence from imperialism. It is thus an area of important political confrontation in addition to its prime strategic significance as providing the shortest route for oil supplies to Europe and America. The presence of strong Soviet naval forces thus fulfils both foreign policy and strategic roles as well as being ideologically legitimised as a factor in fostering the security of progressive states.[18]

The second plank in Gorshkov's advocacy was more narrowly strategic, and can be summed up in his approving citation of an extract from Peter the Great's Maritime Regulations of 1720, 'Any potentate with a land army has one hand, but he who also has a fleet has two hands.'[19] The wartime significance of this is discussed in Chapter 7 below, but its peacetime relevance to the rules of a state which owes its global influence chiefly to military strength is obvious. The maritime component of this strength has unique utility as an agent of foreign policy, an economic role in protecting merchant and fishing fleets, and an increasingly important function in ensuring that the Soviet Union and her associates get their fair share of sea-bed resources. This latter has of course important implications for Russia's attitude to negotiations on international maritime law and, together with the Navy's foreign policy role, might well gain support for Gorshkov's naval advocacy from those sections of the political elite concerned with foreign policy, ideology and the wide range of economic and industrial interests which would benefit from increased maritime activity.

The title of the tenth article in the *Morskoi Sbornik* series, 'Navies as Instruments of Peacetime Imperialism', is typical of Gorshkov's indirect approach to the advocacy of the value of the traditional naval activities of deployments in support of foreign policy and goodwill visits to foreign ports. In the past these have been the virtual monopoly of the imperialist powers but now it is possible for the Soviet Union to use them for beneficent purposes. Purposes which he treats not as ends in themselves but as organic components of Russia's major strategic objective of balancing the United States in all components of power and influence. His argument is that since 1945 the U.S. [sic] Navy has contributed most towards its country's aim of world domination. In particular its aircraft carrier and amphibious forces, sometimes in combination with allies, have been responsible for some thirty threats or actual use of force against movements of national liberation. The United States also based its hopes for gairing a predominant share of sea-bed resources on being able to enter the competition for them from 'the infamous position of strength', springing from its superior naval power. The only way for this unacceptable domination to be challenged and checked is the emergence of counter-balancing Soviet maritime power. In the diplomatic role, modern navies based on the up-to-date science and technology are powerful demonstrations of a country's achievements, while their mobility enables them to project this image in every region of the world. This can be a threatening image designed to intimidate weaker states by the ability to launch attacks by missiles and aircraft and the actual landing of troops, as the imperialists have frequently demonstrated. The time when they could do this with impunity has now passed. Russia, by building up her own maritime strength has not only dramatically altered the balance of forces at sea in such a way as to check future American aggressive uses of its navy but, more positively, has shown that the navy as an instrument of state policy can be beneficial and not malevolent. 'The instrument of a policy of peace and the friendship of peoples, a deterrent to military adventurism and a resolute opposition to the threats to the security of peace loving peoples on the part of imperialist powers.' However it is noteworthy that these high claims for the Soviet Navy's peacetime role are followed immediately by an insistence that it still sees its main mission as the defence of the homeland against attacks from the sea and the deterrence of the United States by its ability to launch nuclear attacks on her metropolitan territory.[20]

In true naval tradition Gorshkov's writing extols the value of port visits in promoting friendly relations with other peoples, not only by the impressive standards of the ships and their equipment but also by the exemplary behaviour of the sailors who demonstrate the high qualities and achievements of Soviet society, including, because of the presence of men from every part of the Soviet Union, its complete freedom from racialism. As a result of widening deployment patterns, in 1972 alone visits were paid to more than sixty countries in Europe, Asia, Africa and Latin America by over one thousand combat and support ships and their ships companies of more than two hundred thousand men:

> bearing the truth about the first Socialist country in the world, about Communist ideology and culture and about the Soviet way of life, to the masses of peoples of other states. They are clearly and convincingly spreading the ideas of the Leninist peaceloving policy of the Communist Party and the Soviet government through many countries of the world. It is impossible to overestimate the significance of this ideological influence.[21]

It is presumably passages of this type which have persuaded some Western commentators that the main threats from the Soviet Navy are political and ideological rather than strategic. It is also possible

that Gorshkov included them to impress Party ideologues and func-
tionaries and, in particular, to convince them of the legitimacy of
naval forces and deployments and thus persuade them to be more
sympathetic to their costs.

THE SOVIET UNION AND THE INTERNATIONAL LAW OF THE SEA

When he wrote Gorshkov was fully aware of the significance of
attempts by the international community to come to an agreement on
the major issues of maritime law which have occupied the three
sessions of the United Nations Conference on the Law of the Sea
(UNCLOS) in 1958, 1960 and 1974 (the last still in progress at the
time of writing). Naturally it was not their legal significance which
most concerned him but the implications of any agreement reached
for his vision of the Soviet Union as a global naval power. It is this
element which features most emphatically in the advocacy of his
writings, especially in *The Sea Power of the State*. The interrelated
items on the conference's agenda which most directly affect naval
policy-makers are: the extent of the territorial sea; the nature of the
regime in large areas of what has hitherto been the high seas, but is
now claimed by coastal states as Exclusive Economic Zones (EEZ);
the regime for international straits; and the control of activity on the
deep sea bed. It is generally agreed that the Soviet Union's negotiating position has gradually changed since the beginning of the conference.[22] Originally, with her relatively small merchant marine and
what was essentially a coastal navy, she figured as the leader of those
coastal, and largely Third World, states hoping to regulate the
activities of the traditional maritime and capitalist powers in their
adjacent seas. For instance, at the 1958 Geneva conference she led
the opposition to the United States' attempt to get the widest possible
freedom of transit for warships through other nations' territorial seas.
Her specific stance was that prior notification was not enough and
formal permission would have to be obtained. At the time of writing
she has not openly abandoned this position but has been content to
let the United States and Britain make the running in favour of
notification only.[23] This is one example of the gradual shifting of her
position which now more and more approximates to that of the
United States, sharing with her the attitudes of a major maritime
power wishing to keep to a minimum the restrictions placed by inter-

national law on the free movement of naval and other vessels. Naval strategic mobility and the influence of naval presence off other countries' coasts were seen to be of more significance than the sensibilities of minor coastal states. An additional and very important economic interest which has moved the Soviet Union in the same direction has been the increasing importance of fish in its diet, and the growing importance of distant water fishing to meet its needs.

Russia's delegations at the UNCLOS sessions have been led by Foreign Ministry officials and have normally included two naval representatives as well as single delegates from each of the other maritime interests, such as the merchant marine, fishing, and marine technology and science. It seems clear, however, that the Navy's interests have figured most powerfully in establishing the Soviet Union's negotiating position. In 1960 she formally enacted a twelve-mile limit for her own territorial sea and has pressed for this to be internationally accepted, strongly resisting those other nations, notably the Philippines and several Latin American states, who have sought much wider limits. This resistance to national encroachment on the freedom of navigation by extending their territorial sea has been matched by a similar approach to the consequences of what she has reluctantly accepted as an irresistible demand by virtually all countries for a 200-mile EEZ. She has insisted that coastal states' control over the huge areas of sea so designated should be restricted to the preservation of their economic interests and should not be allowed by a creeping growth of regulation to develop into an extension of the territorial sea, with the consequent right to control the passage of other countries' naval and merchant vessels.[24]

Because of its geographical position Russia has been particularly concerned with establishing and, if possible, increasing rights of freedom of passage through international straits. Her specific aim has been to gain acceptance for a special straits regime which would give a greater degree of freedom of transit than that through territorial seas. This would result in shipping, naval and mercantile, using the straits (and aircraft overflying them) being entitled to pass without any interference. It would appear to legitimise submerged passage by submarines, which under the 1958 Territorial Sea Convention are required to navigate on the surface and fly their national flags. This convention also gave coastal states the right to expel from their territorial waters any ship which broke their national regulations.[25]

The Soviet Union's position on the military use of the sea bed, though not entirely clear, seems to have changed substantially from its original aim of complete demilitarisation. This policy both reflected its technological backwardness in sea-bottom anti-submarine devices and could also be seen as a propaganda move on arms control against the United States. But in the 1971 conference reviewing the Sea Bed Treaty, perhaps because the technical problems of the installation of sensors had been overcome, she agreed with the United States in insisting only on the banning of weapons of mass destruction.[26]

In contrast to her demands for the maximum freedom of navigation and unimpeded passage of warships in the world's oceans, the Soviet Union has not abandoned older claims and practices aimed at closing sea areas adjacent to her own coasts which other nations might well consider high seas or international straits. The significantly named statute, 'The Protection of the State Boundary of the USSR', promulgated in 1960, partly as a riposte to the 1958 Geneva Convention on the territorial sea, brought out the defensive strategic attitude behind this. It denied that there is any internationally accepted right allowing the innocent passage of warships through the territorial sea without the express permission of the coastal state and laid down detailed procedures and limitations under which this permission would be granted in Soviet waters. In its Naval International Law Manual of 1966 the Soviet Union strongly re-emphasised the obligation of submarines to transit territorial waters on the surface by stating that any boat ignoring this will be liable to destruction. The same manual made large claims for what it avers have been historically recognised as Russia's internal waters and therefore completely under her control. These included the Sea of Azov and the White Sea. These claims have since been softened, perhaps as inappropriate to a maritime power which would be hampered by similar claims made by other nations. Similarly wide assertions have been made about the Northern sea route, but in practice the tolerance of voyages by American icebreakers indicates a less rigorous attitude. Historically Russia has never accepted that only completely land-locked waters can be treated as closed seas and has made repeated claims that the Baltic and Black Seas should be accepted as such. Since 1945 she has unsuccessfully tried to pressurise Turkey and the Baltic states to support the view that only the littoral states should regulate access to these waters. But here too she has more recently diminished these efforts, again probably because as a strong maritime power she sees no reason to adhere to doctrines originating in the days of her weakness, and also because of the disadvantages she would suffer if other littoral states, say in the Indian Ocean, made similar claims.[27]

Against this background it is not surprising to find that Gorshkov stresses as the two most important aspects of international law, freedom of navigation and the immunity of warships from interference. This leads him to strong denunciations of states wishing to bring increased sea areas under their control by regulating passage through their 200-mile EEZs and to reassert that the Soviet Union will never accept anything more than a twelve-mile territorial sea. He is equally insistent on the impossibility of accepting any restriction of navigation through international straits, any claim to restrict scientific research beyond the territorial sea or to impede the free passage of shipping under the pretext of pollution control. On the other hand, he claims that as a great maritime power the Soviet Union wishes to see generally accepted international agreement on these and all other disputed international legal issues which affect the safety of sea-borne trade, and fair access to the sea's resources by all nations great and small.

Behind all this is the conviction that the central point of the Soviet Union's maritime concerns is the possession of strong and effective naval forces which alone can safeguard her maritime interest.[28] Although other elements in the maritime bureaucracy may differ and attempt to influence policy, there is no reason to doubt that Gorshkov and his supporters have always asserted that no developments in international law can be allowed to obstruct the Navy's freedom of action. Rather they must be exploited to increase it.[29]

MARITIME ARMS CONTROL[30]

The same applies to the Soviet Union's attitude to proposals for arms control at sea, although this has produced some presentational difficulties since the main ideologically based claim for her foreign policy is that it is one of peace and disarmament. Her general arms control policy has been marked by two characteristics, sweeping declarations, such as the one for total renunciation of nuclear weapons, and hardheaded and protracted negotiations on specific matters such as the Strategic Arms Limitation Talks (SALT) and those on Mutual Force Reductions in Europe (MFR). In her proposals for maritime arms control there have been no calls for general reductions such as those implemented by the Washington and London Conferences between the wars. This is not surprising considering that it has never been Soviet practice to negotiate from a position of weakness and, whatever the propaganda claims she makes for her naval strength, she must know that she has not yet achieved an overall balance with the West. Furthermore, her realistic foreign policy-makers are bound to realise that the United States and her allies with their complete dependence on the use of the sea for strategic and economic purposes, would never concede any demand for parity.

Instead the Soviet Union has concentrated on either proposing or supporting plans for the demilitarisation of certain sea areas, particularly the Indian Ocean and the Mediterranean, and having them internationally recognised as 'zones of peace', a policy which, of course, has strong propaganda value among smaller nations. In the late 1950s she urged that the Mediterranean should become a nuclear-free zone. This campaign intensified in the 1960s after the addition of SSBNs to the United States' existing nuclear strike capability from carrier-borne aircraft. With Russia's general arms control policy of not treating any element in isolation, these Mediterranean proposals have been linked with SALT as involving forward-based systems which must be included in the overall strategic balance. She also sees them as impinging on MFR because of the theatre role of the Sixth Fleet's nuclear weapons. As part of her peace propaganda the Soviet Union has also proclaimed her support for the reduction or complete prohibition of external powers' naval operations in the Mediterranean. She is unlikely to press for negotiations on this as long as she wishes to be able to intervene in the Arab–Israeli struggle. In any event she claims to be a Mediterranean power herself because of her access from the Black Sea, as compared with the aggressive interloper, the United States.[31]

Some of the non-aligned littoral states of the Indian Ocean have made pleas for their sea to be made a zone of peace, and the Soviet Union, seeing the propaganda advantages involved, has supported these proposals in the United Nations and elsewhere. The exclusion of outside naval intervention has also some strategic attractions as the Indian Ocean is one of the most difficult areas for her to sustain major naval deployments. She has been particularly strong in denunciations of any intention by the United States to deploy SSBNs there. More recently she has strongly protested against the increase of carrier groups' presence and the development of the base facilities at Diego Garcia, which have been part of the United States' response to the invasion of Afghanistan.[32] This invasion has given the Soviet Union potential strategic advantages in the area which the United States can only challenge from the sea, and if she were to mobilise regional opinion effectively against the American presence, it would be a striking example of the strategic gains to be made from a skilful use of arms control proposals.[33]

CONCLUSION

Since the death of Stalin the Soviet Union has developed from a superpower to a global power. Despite this extension of her political and strategic reach, she remains apprehensive of the superior economy and technology of the United States, the future threat from China and the prospect of encirclement which co-operation between the two could make a reality. The first priority of her foreign policy is the avoidance of war with the United States, while not being willing to accept a position of inferiority in any element of national power. This includes the ability to influence world events and it is here that she does not consider that she has achieved equivalence with her rival. This is a situation she will try to remedy whenever international developments offer favourable opportunities.

The significance of her naval strength is not to be assessed by any one criterion, be it nuclear strategy, limited war or diplomatic influence. Its development to date and its future course depend on the political leadership's perceptions of what it can contribute to the total equivalence with the United States which they believe necessary both to the avoidance of general war and the furtherance of the global interests to which they are ideologically and patriotically committed. It is the task of advocates of Soviet sea power to convince them that strong balanced, but necessarily expensive, naval forces have a unique contribution to make across the whole spectrum of these interests.

4 The Strategic Background

GEOGRAPHY AND HISTORY

If a credible analysis of the significance of the sea and of maritime forces in Soviet strategy must begin in the realms of her internal political structure and foreign policy, it must continue with an examination of Russia's overall strategy and an acceptance that hitherto it has been predominantly land-based. Geography, history, as well as perceptions of contemporary threats, all point to this conclusion. It is true that current Soviet strategic writing admits that the advent of nuclear weapons has transformed the nature of war and that the Strategic Rocket Forces have now displaced the Ground Forces as the chief determinants of victory, but the basic concepts are still land-orientated. The main stress is on general nuclear war, beginning with heavy nuclear strikes against the enemy's armed forces and economic centres, and immediately followed up and exploited by highly mobile mass armies and their associated air power. On the defensive side, the Soviet homeland must be protected by the Air Defence Forces and damage further limited by extensive civil defence measures covering the population and essential industries.[1] In the light of this emphasis, if maritime forces are to have a significant role in Soviet strategy and gain an adequate share of resources, their advocates must convince the political leadership that they have a unique contribution, which cannot be made by land forces, to the central aims of strategic planning; the prevention of nuclear or conventional attack on Soviet territory, or, if deterrence fails, the country's ability to fight and win a nuclear war.

The primacy of the Army in Soviet defence thinking has been founded on the geography and history of the Russian state. The empire of the Tsars originated in the ability of their predecessors, the Grand Dukes of Muscovy in the late fifteenth century, to defend their territory against Mongol invasions. Its survival, expansion and control of its increasingly diverse peoples, depended entirely on the strength and loyalty of its armies. As its land mass, with its wide range of natural resources, increased, the empire became largely self supporting, with little need of maritime trade. This source of strength was counter-balanced by a lack of natural frontiers which the Tsars sought to remedy by centuries of war and internal colonisation, in which success depended on the Army's ability to conquer and control resentful subject peoples. New frontiers made Russia contiguous to strong and suspicious rivals in both Europe and Asia, and thus called for the permanent deployment of a massive conscript army. Even when, in the nineteenth century, Russia established herself as a major European power in the West and fought her way to the Pacific in the East, she remained primarily a land-locked state. With the exception of Murmansk, her oceanic ports were ice-bound for a greater part of the year and her outlets from the Baltic and Black Seas commanded by potentially hostile powers. It was thus inevitable that she should have seen her internal stability and external security as primarily dependent on the Army, with the Navy relegated to ancillary roles in coastal defence and support of land operations.

Extensive territory, poor communications, diverse and often rebellious populations, added to the autocratic traditions of the Tsars, all combined to produce a government based on military resources and organisation. It is arguable that in the centuries before the 1917 Revolution the Russian empire was a more militarised state than Prussia and Imperial Germany. The survival of the regime depended entirely on the active loyalty of the Army to the Tsar, and that loyalty in turn depended upon the Army's confidence in the Tsar's ability to govern. In 1917 military defeats and the breakdown of internal government undermined this confidence and the Army raised no effective opposition to the Tsar's removal and replacement by Kerensky's Provisional Government. Similarly, when it in turn was overthrown by the Bolsheviks, the Army as a whole produced no effective resistance and mutineers and deserters played a prominent part in what fighting there was. If all this demonstrated that Russian governments could be overthrown merely by the Army's negative attitude, the four years of civil war and foreign intervention which followed the October Revolution were to show that the Communist regime depended for its survival on the loyalty of the newly organised Red

Army, which eventually defeated its internal enemies and forced the withdrawal of their foreign supporters. This dependence continued and was reinforced during the troubled years which followed, when the Red Army loyally supported the regime in carrying out its unpopular policies of agricultural collectivisation and enforced industrialisation with a consistency which even Stalin's excesses and purges did not shake.

In the 1930s, when what was perceived as the continuous hostility of the capitalist powers was reinforced by the rise of Hitler, the Red Army provided the only hope of survival. When war actually came and the Red Army, after initial defeats which threatened the very existence of the regime, halted the invaders and then destroyed the major part of the German armies and thus brought the country to a hitherto unequalled eminence in world affairs, the identification of the regime with its army was complete. This was further accentuated by the overlapping of civil and military leadership during the war. Just as many of the early Party leaders had served in a quasi-military capacity during the Civil War, so, under Stalin's overall command, his principal colleagues, including those destined to be his successors, were closely involved in military affairs and worked intimately with the military commanders.[2]

This organic relationship between the army and the political leadership is reflected today in the predominance of ground force officers in the highest levels of the defence decision-making apparatus. Since 1953 the Soviet armed forces have been controlled by a unified Ministry of Defence. With the exception of the present incumbent, D. F. Ustinov, a civilian previously in charge of the defence industries and who has held army rank, the Minister of Defence has always been a professional soldier. The highest organ of military decision-making, the Defence Council, which is presided over by Brezhnev as Commander-in-Chief of the armed forces, has as its chief professional adviser the Chief of the General Staff, a soldier. Although it would seem likely that the Commanders-in-Chief of each of the armed services, Admiral Gorshkov, who ranks as a deputy minister of defence, among them, would be consulted on matters within their spheres of responsibility, it is equally likely that professional advice on fundamental matters, such as general strategy and the allocation of resources, would come from the Chief of the General Staff. It is also noteworthy that the Commander-in-Chief of the Warsaw Pact forces, also a soldier, has precedence over Gorshkov in the hierarchy of deputy defence ministers. At the political level it is significant that of the nineteen places in the Party's Central Committee occupied by leaders of the armed services in 1978, Gorshkov was the only naval member.[3]

In the light of the Army's historical predominance in the history of the Soviet Union and of its established strength in the decision-making apparatus, it is not surprising that the major authoritative book on Soviet strategy has been written by a team of soldiers, headed by Marshal V. D. Sokolovskiy, and that its main emphasis is on land warfare.

MARSHAL SOKOLOVSKIY'S 'SOVIET MILITARY STRATEGY'[4] AND THE ROLE OF THE NAVY

When the first edition of the book appeared in 1962, shortly before the Cuban missile crisis, it was described in the Soviet Union as the first complete work on strategy based on a correct Marxist interpretation of the nature of war. It ignored the strategic writings of the Stalinist era and was obviously designed to expound the changes in military thought necessitated by the appearance of nuclear weapons. By the time it appeared, the concept of 'minimum deterrence' favoured by Khruschev, with its rejection of the need for large conventional forces, had been substantially modified. Although the Strategic Rocket Forces were accorded pre-eminence, nuclear weapons had also been allocated to the other services and the official doctrine underlying the whole of the book was that victory depended on the co-ordinated use of all arms, nuclear and conventional, and that massive ground forces were still a necessity.

Marshal V. D. Sokolovskiy, its principal author, had been Chief of the General Staff from 1952 to 1959, a first deputy defence minister and a candidate (non-voting) member of the Party's Central Committee; obviously a politically acceptable figure of the Army establishment, admirably qualified to expound the accepted principles of Soviet strategy. A second edition of the book appeared in 1963 containing little substantial change. The third version of 1968, by which time the Soviet Union could reasonably think of the achievement of nuclear parity with the United States, contained considerable deletions and additions but not any fundamental shift in doctrine or strategy. The team of contributors was substantially unchanged and the political upheaval culminating in the replacement of Khruschev by Brezhnev and Kosygin in 1964 seemingly made no direct impact.

Throughout the book heavy emphasis is placed on the revolutionary effect of strategic nuclear weapons on warfare. In this new era military strategy must be based on rocket strikes deep into enemy territory to destroy both his economic and military strength and thus secure the achievement of war aims in the shortest possible time. The new technology of long-range missiles and aircraft will extend operations over far wider land and sea areas than in earlier wars. In contrast to the pre-nuclear age, when wars were decided by ground troops with the co-operation of aviation and, in coastal areas, the Navy, now:

Under conditions of nuclear rocket war the resolution of the main aims and problems of war will be accomplished by strategic rocket troops by delivery of massed nuclear rocket strikes. Ground troops, with the aid of aviation will perform important strategic functions in modern war: by rapid offensive movement they will completely annihilate the remaining enemy formations, occupy enemy territory and prevent the enemy from invading one's own territory. The strategic operations of the other armed forces will consist of the following: the national PVO [Air Defence] troops will protect the country and groupings of the armed forces from nuclear strikes of the enemy; the Navy will perform military operations in naval theatres aimed at the destruction of enemy naval formations, the disruption of enemy naval communications and defence of one's own communications as well as coastal areas, from strikes from the sea.[5]

This ancillary role for the Navy features in all three editions but in the long analysis of imperialist strategy and threats featured in the 1963 version, a possible shift emerges. This comes from the recognition of the new threat to the homeland presented by the *Polaris* submarine launched ballistic missile (SLBM), soon to be increased by the expected appearance of the *Poseidon* missile with an estimated range of over 4,000 kilometres. These weapons would not be accurate enough for counter-force strike and would therefore be aimed at cities and industrial complexes. SSBNs, operating from a variety of bases in the United States and Europe, would surround the Soviet Union with a network of mobile strategic nuclear forces, soon to be strengthened by the deployment of a British *Polaris* force. This outline of a new and serious threat from the sea is followed by an extensive description of the great limited-war capability possessed by the

United States and Britain with their carrier strike forces, marines, world-wide naval bases and large shipbuilding capacity.[6]

Sokolovskiy does not offer a direct answer to this dual maritime threat but instead develops a strongly critical examination of the Soviet Union's past naval policies, implying that whatever response is needed to this new danger it is not a traditional navy based on the large surface ship. He is particularly critical of the interwar policy of accepting that surface ships were the best means of fulfilling the Navy's roles and of the consequent underestimation of submarines and aircraft. Moreover this emphasis on surface ships ignored the Soviet Union's geographical disadvantages in naval warfare with two of her fleets based on inland seas and the difficulties of even the Northern and Pacific fleets in gaining access to the open seas. Submarines and naval aviation would have been much less hampered by these factors. A hint that this criticism, amounting to a complete condemnation of the large surface ship, met with opposition from the Soviet Navy, is given by the omission, in the later 1968 edition, of the trenchant judgement, 'thus our theory with regard to strategic utilisation of the Navy was influenced by antique concepts of naval warfare and the predominance of the surface fleet'.[7]

In Sokolovskiy's evaluation of the lessons of the Great Patriotic War only three out of thirty pages are allotted to naval operations. They reiterate the same two themes; the Navy's subordinate role and the mistaken stress on the importance of surface ships. The essence of success in the war is seen as having been the co-ordination of large ground forces on several fronts: 'A strategic operation is accomplished as a rule by the efforts of several Army Groups with the participation of long range aviation and with the participation of naval forces in coastal regions.' Pre-war theory had been that the Navy's role would be independent operations by large formations of surface vessels, but, in the event, the main tasks had proved to be combined operations with the ground and air forces. These had taken the forms of: covering the ground troops' coastal flanks; coastal defence; amphibious landings from seas and rivers; blockade of surrounded enemy groups and support of the regrouping of Soviet troops. There had also been some independent naval operations against enemy sea lines of communication and the defence of Russia's own, including convoy operations in the Baltic and Northern Seas. The most important naval lesson to emerge from the war was a regrading of the importance of the various arms. Naval aviation, formerly a supporting arm, emerged as a primary one, as did submarines. These two together 'were the main means of armed conflict in naval theatres . . . Large surface ships, considered before the war to be the mainstay of our fleet, lost their leading role in solving tasks placed before the Navy.'[8] In common with all Soviet writing on the Second World War, the book downgrades the importance of maritime as compared with land operations and provides no grounds whatsoever for the post-war Soviet Navy to claim a primary role in national strategy or for the construction of a balanced fleet. Such claims could only be based on a clear demonstration that the nature of warfare and also, perhaps, the foreign policy objectives of the Soviet Union, had changed so radically as to diminish the predominance of land forces and to give new scope to maritime power.

No such argument is directly propounded in 'Soviet Military Strategy' but indirect and implicit moves towards it can be detected in the repeatedly stated dogma that in a nuclear age the Strategic Rocket Forces had replaced conventional ground forces as the decisive military arm and the admission that the Navy had a distinctive contribution to make both in the defence of the homeland against nuclear attack from the sea and by itself providing a valuable addition to the Soviet Union's own nuclear strategic strike. As in all Soviet military writing, the danger of war is seen as springing from the inherently aggressive nature of capitalism which can produce predatory wars in any part of the globe. On the other hand, the Soviet Union has the duty to assist peoples struggling in wars of national liberation by political and economic support. In addition, it will 'render when necessary military support as well to peoples subject to imperialistic aggression'. So here are two possible planks for the naval platform.

But general nuclear war is the greatest danger and the book frequently states that Soviet strategy must put as its main priority the decision of the Twenty-third Communist Party Congress in 1966 that the prime necessity was to prevent such a catastrophe occurring. This can only be accomplished by the potential aggressors realising that if they do unleash such a war it can only end in their own destruction. For this the Soviet Union needs large invincible forces, constantly on the alert, to deter the enemy from launching a surprise nuclear attack. Here the role of the strategic rocket troops is pre-eminent but the Navy has gained a share of this primary strategic task: 'Simultaneously with the Strategic Rocket Forces, the main force for keeping him in check and decisively defeating him in war, is the nuclear rocket-carrying submarine fleet.' The third edition adds that the advent of nuclear weapons has led to a reconsideration of the importance and role of the Navy. In future wars this importance will arise from its achievements 'in destroying targets both on the high seas and on the dry land'. In such roles the submarine force, supported by missile firing maritime aircraft, will be far more effective than surface ships. These new instruments of naval combat have greatly increased the Navy's capabilities: 'it has now become capable of solving the active missions entrusted to it far beyond the confines of Soviet waters'.[9]

If the recognition of these new missions and of the need to break away from the coastal waters doctrine which governed the Soviet Navy in the Great Patriotic War shows an increasing awareness of the importance of the sea in Soviet strategy, the authors of *Soviet Military Strategy*, like generals the world over, persist in emphasising the obsolescence of the large surface ship:

> The waging of military operations based on large formations of surface ships will disappear from the scene, together with the surface ships themselves. In a future war the task of destroying shore targets or defeating groupings of the naval forces of an aggressor, or his assault carrier formations and rocket-carrying submarines at bases or on the high seas and disruption of ocean communications, will be accomplished by strikes of rocket troops and mobile operations of rocket-carrying submarines co-operating with rocket-carrying aircraft.[10]

This assertion of the irrelevance of surface ships to the new maritime tasks and of the possible role of land-based rocket forces in maritime operations show the determination of Soviet strategists to see naval power as only one constituent part of an overall strategy and not in any way distinct. On the other hand, the third edition, which tends to upgrade the importance of conventional land and sea operations following the nuclear strikes, states that the Navy, in addition to its primary mission of dealing with enemy carriers and SSBNs, now recognised as being capable of nuclear strikes deep into Soviet territory, will simultaneously have to engage enemy naval forces and disrupt his sea communications. Although these missions will be best fulfilled by submarines and aircraft, 'a certain number of surface ships are also necessary to safeguard the activities of submarines and to perform secondary missions such as protection of naval communication lanes and coordination with ground forces in operations carried out in coastal regions'.[11]

Chapter VI, 'Methods of Conducting Warfare' poses the basic problem of the nature of future war as: 'Will it be a land war with the use of nuclear weapons as a means of supporting the operations of the ground troops, or a war that is essentially new, where the main means of solving strategic tasks will be the nuclear rocket weapon?' The latter is seen as the more likely and this would entail the ground troops having to co-ordinate their operations with the rocket troops and not *vice versa*. As this would displace the ground forces from the primary role neither the Navy nor the Air Defence Troops will be subordinated to them as in the past, but to the rocket troops. The Air Defence Forces' main tasks will be to protect strategic targets within the Soviet Union, not ground troop formations, and 'The Navy's operations will also not be tied to ground theatres, since in modern conditions it is called on basically to conduct the struggle on the oceans often far from the ground theatres of military operations.' 'In particular naval operations' directed towards protecting Russia's coasts 'from nuclear attack from the sea, must be considered an independent type of strategic operation'. The Navy with its nuclear weapons, nuclear submarines and long-range aviation, will play a much more important part than in the Great Patriotic War with 'vast possibilities for successful conduct of armed combat over vast sea and ocean expanses against an enemy with a powerful navy'. These, like all other operations, will be co-ordinated into a single strategic plan under a unified central command; there can be no place for independent actions by units or services.[12] The Navy is thus shown as having escaped from its historical subordination to the Army, not because of any upgrading of conventional naval operations but because of its offensive and defensive contributions to strategic nuclear warfare.

The later treatment of conventional naval operations such as the destruction of enemy naval forces and the disruption of sea lines of communication still contains the old reservation. It is admitted that compared with those in the Great Patriotic War, they will be of vast scope and have to be conducted on the world's oceans but even so, 'they can hardly have a decisive effect on the outcome of the war'. Most important will be the destruction of enemy aircraft carriers which, however well protected by escorts, will be vulnerable to missile attacks.[13] Thus traditional naval warfare is included, though somewhat marginally, in this official exposition of Soviet strategy although, at the time it was written, the Soviet Navy was far from having acquired the resources needed to carry out the global operations envisaged. This was an aspiration not a reality.

This was equally so in other naval operations. The first to be treated are operations in support of ground troops which, although they will not be a major task, will demand a considerable effort. Offensively, such operations would consist of bombardment of enemy territory and forces and the transport of Soviet troops. Defensively, they would be against enemy naval forces, including carriers, threatening Soviet troops and even possibly against large-scale invasions. 'The enemy may attempt large sea-borne assaults, in which connection readiness to break up assault operations remains an important requirement of our Navy, ground troops and other services.' Mine warfare, as in the past, is seen as either offensive or defensive and may be widely used.

In conclusion the chapter sees future naval operations differing greatly from those of the Great Patriotic War, chiefly because they will have to be conducted in all the world's oceans and against a strong enemy especially well equipped and prepared for anti-submarine warfare. In this situation the Soviet Navy must in peace-time be instantly ready for war so that it can take the strategic initiative. Effective mobilisation procedures must be prepared for bringing reserves into readiness, improving base facilities, including the use of civilian ports and dockyards, and 'converting certain ships of the civilian fleet into warships and auxiliary ships'.[14]

Although in what is still the most thorough and authoritative exposition of Soviet strategy, the amount of space given to naval matters is relatively small, and no great enthusiasm is shown for conventional naval operations, and although there is no mention at all of the classical concepts of maritime strategy, such as command of the sea, there is at least a clear recognition that, in the nuclear age, the sea and maritime forces have a distinctive contribution to make to national strategy. That this admission is made in so land-orientated a book is itself of considerable significance.

MARSHAL GRECHKO'S 'THE ARMED FORCES OF THE SOVIET STATE'[15]

If Sokolovskiy's *Military Strategy*, with its emphasis on the revolutionary impact of nuclear weapons on the nature of war, offers some evidence of a growing recognition of the contribution which sea power could make to Soviet strategy, Marshal Grechko's book, published six years after the third edition of Sokolovskiy, follows much the same pattern. As it was written and published when Grechko was Minister of Defence and a member of the Politbureau, readers of the 200,000 issued copies of the expanded second edition of 1975 must have given it high authority. Its stated aim was to show the people of the Soviet Union and the whole world the unique virtues of the Soviet armed forces, the reasons for their unrivalled victories in the Great Patriotic War and the inevitability of their success in repelling any future imperialist aggression.

Marshal A. A. Grechko joined the Red Army in 1919 at the age of 16, fought in the Civil War and, in the interwar years, graduated from both the Frunze Military Academy and the General Staff Academy. He commanded various armies during the war and, after 1945, held important appointments, including that of Commander-in-Chief in Germany. He became a Marshal of the Soviet Union in 1955 and two years later was made Commander-in-Chief Ground Forces and a first deputy minister of defence under Malinovskiy, whom he succeeded in 1967. He died in office in 1976. He had joined the Communist Party in 1928 and in 1973 became a member of its supreme decision-making body, the Politbureau.[16] As far as it can be assessed his career was one of high military competence combined with political caution expressed by loyalty to the Party leadership, which was unaffected by the excesses of Stalin and the uncertain manoeuvres of the immediate post-Stalin years.

His book clearly reflects this type of career. It has a substantial ideological content, with frequent references to the military genius of Lenin who is credited with implanting in the Red Army the basic military principles of: centralisation of command; unity of command; the highest degree of military discipline; and constant readiness to repel aggression; all of course under the direction of the Communist Party. Lenin had also insisted on the need for scientific objectivity in military affairs. It has been these precepts, combined with their organic relationship with the working class and their own recognition of their historic role in defending and furthering world socialism, which have made the Soviet armed forces invincible.[17]

Despite its title the book is essentially the work of a soldier. It is mainly about the Red Army and pays only the necessary minimum of attention to what are always referred to as 'the other services'. This is particularly marked in the treatment of the Great Patriotic War, in which all the emphasis is put on the Army's achievements, which include the final defeat of Japan as well as of Germany. There is no mention of the Allied maritime campaigns in the Far East and the surrender of Japan is attributed neither to them nor to the atomic bomb, but to the Red Army's defeat of Japan's army in Manchuria. Similarly, there is no recognition of the essentiality of the Soviet Union's allies' maritime power to the final outcome of the war.[18]

If there is thus no evidence of Grechko's acceptance of the past importance of maritime power, there is a limited acknowledgement of its enhanced significance for Russia in a nuclear age. In his listing of the seven branches of the armed forces the Navy is given fifth place, following the Strategic Rocket Forces, the Ground Forces, the Air Defence Forces and the Strategic Air Force. What strategic significance the Navy has comes not from the potential of its conventional forces but from the striking power of its SSBNs. This assessment is followed by the rhetorical claim that, 'The Navy emerged from coastal waters and closed seas and mastered the expanses of the World Ocean. It has everything it needs for the simultaneous and prolonged conduct of combat operations on the oceans and seas.'[19] This must have produced a wry smile from Admiral Gorshkov, knowing that the ability to execute widespread and prolonged naval operations was precisely what the Navy had failed to gain during Grechko's tenure of the Ministry of Defence.

In the discussion of the impact of technology on the nature of war, and therefore of the Soviet armed forces, it is again the SSBNs which are emphasised. They are, 'The genuine masters of the ocean depths and expanses' and recognised as having advantages over other missile launching platforms. 'While nuclear missile submarines are not less effective in their operations than ground or air nuclear systems, they possess a number of advantages, among which the primary one would be greater survivability.'[20] At a time when the ability of land-based systems to survive an enemy counter force attack was coming under question in the Soviet Union, this could have been an admission of significant advantage to the Navy.

Grechko devotes considerable space to expounding the lessons to be learned from recent wars in the Middle and Far East which would have to be taken into account if the Soviet Union should become involved in similar local encounters. The admission of such a possibility is itself significant, especially when it is followed by the statement that scientific progress has opened up a variety of new prospects for the Navy. 'Ships of various classes are being developed, commissioned and designed for carrying out a number of missions: strike, landing, transport, anti-submarine support, etc.'[21]

This shows at least an awareness of the possibilities being opened up by the possession of conventional naval forces, especially when it is backed up by a statement of naval tactical doctrine which could well have been written by Admiral Gorshkov himself as part of his arguments for a balanced fleet. Naval force groupings will not in future be the homogeneous ones which in the past were adequate for the simple requirements of gun and torpedo attack. With today's complex new weapons, 'Successful accomplishment of the missions facing the Navy is unthinkable without the skilled organisation and conduct of naval battles with the participation of heterogeneous naval forces and various types of weapons in close tactical co-ordination. The precise and co-ordinated actions of heterogeneous forces presume exemplary mastery by personnel of surface and underwater warships and naval aviation and their weapons and combat equipment, an ability to manoeuvre, avoid enemy attacks and attack him suddenly.' [22]

What is remarkable about Grechko's book is not that it concentrates so much on the Red Army but that, in the space which it does give to naval matters, it admits the unique contribution Soviet SSBNs can make to overall nuclear strategy and, at least by implication, the importance of operations against the enemy's counterparts. When to this is added an acceptance of the possibility of the Soviet Union's becoming involved in local wars, accompanied by a description of the varied roles which could be filled by balanced naval forces (although the term is not used), it seems an arguable conclusion that a shift had occurred in general Soviet strategic thinking which gave a significantly greater part to sea power.

ADMIRAL GORSHKOV'S CONTRIBUTION TO SOVIET STRATEGIC THOUGHT

The problems of interpreting Admiral Gorshkov's writings have been discussed earlier (see pp. 3–5). Here he will be considered as the man who has been Commander-in-Chief of the Soviet Navy since 1956, has presided over a radical transformation of its role and equipment, and, in his publication, has made a significant contribution to the debates on strategy which have been in evidence in the Soviet Union since 1956.

Sergei Gorshkov was born in 1910 and commissioned in the Navy from the Frunze Higher Naval School in 1931. His earlier service included tours as a navigating officer in the Black Sea and Pacific Fleets. By 1938 he was in command of a squadron of destroyers, probably as a captain, second rank. As such he was too junior, or too politically quiescent, to become a victim of Stalin's purges of the armed forces and could well have benefited in future appointments and promotions from the disappearance of many of his seniors. In 1939 he returned to the Black Sea Fleet and graduated from a senior officers' course at the Voroshilov Naval Academy. On the outbreak of the war with Germany in June 1941 he was in command of a cruiser squadron in the Black Sea and in September distinguished himself in the combined operations unsuccessfully aimed at the holding of Odessa. By October, after only ten years of commissioned service, he was a Rear-Admiral and in command of the Azov Flotilla. As such he was probably largely responsible for the biggest Soviet combined operation of the whole war, the landings at Kerch in late December of some 40,000 troops in an attempt to relieve the pressure on Sevastopol. In 1942, with Germany still advancing on the southern front, he was appointed deputy naval commander and a member of the military council responsible for the defence of Novorossisk. This was an integrated command which included the 47th Army under General Grechko. The city fell but, in February 1943, Gorshkov was able to organise amphibious counter attacks which, against the wider background of the battle of Kursk and the subsequent German retreat, were to lead to the recapture of the city in September. The remainder of Gorshkov's war service was spent in support of land operations in the Crimea and finally in command of the Danube Flotilla in support of Marshal Malinovskiy's armies as they loosened Germany's grip on the Ukraine and the Balkans. His wartime career was thus a complete demonstration of the Soviet Navy's ancillary role of support for the Army which he was later to transcend.

After the war his advancement was rapid. In 1948 he became chief of staff of the Black Sea Fleet and, three years later, its Commander-in-Chief as a Vice-Admiral. The really significant step came in 1955 when he went to Moscow as first deputy Commander-in-Chief of the Soviet Navy under Admiral N. G. Kuznetsov. At this time Khruschev was building up his pre-eminence in the Politbureau and was known to be opposed to the concept of a big ship navy, including aircraft carriers, which Kuznetsov had persuaded Stalin to accept. It was presumably on Khruschev's urging that Gorshkov replaced Kuznetsov in June 1956, in the belief that the new Commander-in-Chief's ideas on the Navy were compatible with his own, especially with his known interest in new technology, including missiles. Probably equally important in enabling Gorshkov to further his plans for the Navy were his wartime connections with men now rising to pre-eminence in the military and political establishment; Malinovskiy about to be appointed first deputy minister of defence, Grechko soon to be Commander-in-Chief of the ground forces and Brezhnev who was increasing in importance in the Party leadership. By his access to these men he could hope to have influential listeners to his arguments for what a modernised navy could contribute to the security and world influence of their country.

Until the early 1960s Gorshkov's published speeches and statements echoed the traditional Soviet doctrine that the Navy's primary task was to support the ground forces and defend the maritime boundaries of the homeland. He apparently retained Khruschev's confidence for, not only did he receive the Order of Lenin in 1960 and secure promotion to Fleet Admiral two years later, but, more important, persuaded Khruschev to abandon his intention of abolishing the bulk of the Navy's cruiser force. On the positive side came the building programme for large missile armed destroyers which ensured the survival of major surface ships in the future naval build-up. These successes were presumably assisted by the Cuba incident's revelation in 1962 of the Soviet Union's general weakness at sea. The fall of Khruschev in 1964 did not weaken Gorshkov's position and three years later his achievement of the newly created rank of Admiral of the Fleet of the Soviet Union, which gave him formal equality with the Commanders-in-Chief of the Ground and Strategic Rocket Forces, was a public recognition of the increased importance of the Navy, as were the appearance of the *Moskva* helicopter carrier and the Yankee class SSBN a demonstration of its greater capability. From this time onwards Gorshkov's published statements and articles placed increased stress on the Navy's oceanic missions and their essential and unique contribution to the country's overall strategy.[23] In this context it is noteworthy that his wartime colleague Grechko became Minister of Defence in 1967. If Gorshkov was to have any success in increasing the Navy's role he must have realised that his arguments must not appear too heretical to a man convinced of the primary importance of land warfare.

There is no evidence that Gorshkov has ever been politically active. He did not join the Communist Party until 1942 and, although he has been a member of every Party Congress since 1952, it was only in 1961 that he became a full member of the Central Committee.

Gorshkov's contribution to the strategic debate can be most fully evaluated by an examination of his two major works, *Navies in War and Peace* and *The Sea Power of the State*, in which by a combination of critical surveys of the place given to sea power in Russia's history, and in analyses of the contemporary scene, he has presented a powerful case for the build-up of the Soviet Navy.

'NAVIES IN WAR AND PEACE'

Of the eleven articles which make up the series only the last two deal with contemporary affairs at any length, the others are primarily historical surveys of the development of navies up to 1945, with four specifically devoted to the Russian Navy. From the beginning Gorshkov insists on the political and strategic orthodoxy of his views. Marx, Engels and Lenin are quoted in support of the importance of sea power in war but he emphasises that he is not claiming a separate or superior role for naval forces. History and the facts of the contemporary world prove that each armed service has a particular contribution to make, but also that they must operate harmoniously according to a common doctrine and with identity of operational views between their commanders. Furthermore, in any major war final victory demands the occupation of enemy territory by land forces. Nevertheless, the facts of geography make it essential for any country wishing to be recognised as a great power to be strong at sea. The sea covers seven-tenths of the earth's surface and the continents are islands between which it is the strategic and economic link. To this has been added the increasing importance of the sea as a source of food, energy and other vital resources. Because of this wide range of significance the sea has always played a large part in determining the rise and fall of nations.[24]

It is from this basis that Gorshkov builds up his message to his political leaders and fellow service chiefs. If it is to fulfil its aspirations, the Soviet Union must strengthen the maritime component of her strategy. Too many of their predecessors, both before and after 1917, had failed to recognise this and had neglected the Navy, and Russia had been humiliated in consequence. Some had even actively resisted the development of sea power by arguing that the country's geography made it unnecessary for her to have more than coastal

forces. Such arguments are still heard today but, of course, Gorshkov adds, only among Russia's enemies. One of his consistent
refrains, directed presumably at the Party chiefs, is of praise for the
wisdom of the present leadership shown by the practical steps it has
taken to increase the Soviet Union's strength at sea. This has
already produced great strategic benefits, such as the ability to
maintain naval forces in the Mediterranean strong enough to challenge the United States' nuclear threat to the homeland and to
check its expansionist policies in the region.[25]

The clear recognition of the importance of sea power after the
Revolution had begun with decisions made in 1928 and culminating
ten years later in the policy to build a large ocean-going fleet of
capital ships to add to the already considerable force of submarines, cruisers and escort vessels. At the same time, because the
main threat came from Germany, the basic strategic conviction was
that the next war would be decided on land, and that the Navy's
missions must be based on co-operation with the Army, supplemented by coastal defence and attacks on enemy sea communications. There was considerable discussion and wide differences of
opinion in the service academies as to whether the Navy's specific
strategic role was offensive or defensive. The final decision was that
it should be strategically defensive with tactical offensives against
enemy forces threatening the fulfilment of Soviet missions. It is here
that Gorshkov introduces a critical note with obvious implications
for his contemporary political leaders and military colleagues. Between the wars the Soviet Navy more than any other had realised the
importance of air power in maritime operations, but the roles and
aircraft allotted restricted it to reconnaissance and other secondary
tasks. Similarly, although the Soviet Union had led the way in formulating a correct doctrine for amphibious operations, no landing
craft nor specially designed gunnery support ships were provided.
This was partly due to economic restraints but even more to the
failure of some army commanders to appreciate the importance of
the naval contribution. No unity of doctrine was achieved and the
Army's amphibious training was given low priority. This criticism is
followed by a direct attack on the naval doctrine of the time.
Although the Soviet Union has the largest submarine force in the
world no consideration had been given to its long-range offensive
use. All its missions were assumed to be in local waters and its
oceanic offensive potential neglected.[26] Gorshkov's account of the
Soviet Navy's overall contribution to the Great Patriotic War is very

reserved and most significant for its repeated assertions that the war's particular nature made it inevitable that ground forces played the primary role and that the Navy's strategic and operational contributions had to conform to the Army's requirements.[27] The implication is clearly that in any future war the circumstances could be so substantially different as to give the Navy a primary role.

That circumstances have so changed is of course the underlying theme of the whole series of articles. In today's international situation and alignment of forces, combined with the new technological capabilities of naval forces, the relative contribution of sea power to national strategy has substantially increased. This has been realised by the Party which has equipped the Soviet Union with a Navy capable of fulfilling strategic missions in the world's oceans. Thanks to this she will in future not only be the strongest land power but 'also a mighty sea power, a faithful guardian of the peace of the world'.[28] Gorshkov must have known in 1973 that the Navy's actual capabilities fell far short of these claims and that sustained advocacy would be needed if the Navy was to maintain, let alone increase, its strength. This advocacy was to culminate in 1976 with the publication of a much extended and more forceful justification of sea power.

'THE SEA POWER OF THE STATE'[29]

Michael MccGwire, who has always been the most cautious as well as one of the best-informed Western commentators on the significance of the growth of the Soviet Navy, has gone so far as to suggest that the appearance of this book and the authority of the favourable reviews it received in the Soviet Union, marked a fundamental shift in the theoretical basis of Soviet naval policy. Such verdicts as that of Marshal Bagramyan in *Izvestia*, 'For the first time in Soviet literature the author formulates the concept of sea power as a scientific category', and other official reviewers' praise of the book as a major contribution to military science providing a source for developing a correct view on the sea power of the state, are cited in support of its significance. This does not mean that all Gorshkov's arguments and conclusions have been accepted and translated into material additions to the Navy's strength, but that they now form an essential ingredient of the continuing Soviet debate on defence and strategy. The first edition of the book had an exceptionally large printing of 600,000 and was rapidly followed by a second edition strengthening the Navy's claims, and formally recommended to 'The admirals, generals and officers of the Soviet Army and Navy'. Further evidence of official approval came with the promotion of two of its contributors to vice-admiral and one to rear-admiral.[30] The Navy's subsequent success in obtaining new classes of major surface ships as well as submarines points in the same direction, as does the appearance of an officially approved English language version of the book with a special 'Foreword' by Gorshkov himself.

MccGwire's evaluation is certainly sustained by an examination of the book's treatment of strategy. From the beginning it emphasises that technological changes since the Second World War have moved sea power up from a secondary to a primary strategic role because of its new capability to destroy an enemy's centres of military and economic strength. This demands the creation of a new strategic doctrine enabling land and sea power each to make its full contribution to the whole. This is in effect a demand for the Navy to be accepted on equal terms with the land forces in war as well as claiming recognition for the peacetime contribution which it alone can make in furthering foreign policy and protecting the country's commercial maritime interests.[31]

These general claims are followed by an evaluation of the relative strategic importance of the world's oceans in terms strongly reminiscent of late nineteenth-century Western naval thought, based on the centrality of sea communications in maritime strategy. The Atlantic is of prime importance in international trade largely because of the use made of it by the leading capitalist countries whose economies depend upon sea-borne trade. To this is added its strategic significance for NATO lines of communication and as a deployment area for SSBNs. The Mediterranean is important both as an oil supply route from the Middle East to Europe and America and as an area of political confrontation between states of differing social systems and interests. Geographically and strategically the Mediterranean can be considered as an extension of the Atlantic and therefore part of the sea area having the heaviest concentration of naval forces and thus the most likely theatre for future naval warfare. The Pacific's outstanding characteristics are seen as the great length of its sea routes providing the means of trade between America, Asia and Australasia, as well as for Japan's oil supplies from the Persian Gulf. Furthermore, the United States' Pacific coast is the site of many of its most important defence industries and the base for its power in

Asia and consequent domination of South Korea, Japan, Thailand and Taiwan. These countries in turn provide her with military and naval bases as the Pacific itself provides deployment areas for SSBNs and the strike forces of the Seventh Fleet. It is only when he comes to the Indian Ocean that Gorshkov declares a specific Soviet interest, in that it provides communications from the Black and Baltic Seas to countries such as India, Bangladesh, Indonesia and Burma. It is moreover an area significant for the continuing struggle of its peoples against political and economic imperialism and the imposition of foreign bases. The smallest ocean of all, the Arctic, with its great resources and its extensive territories bordering the Soviet Union, is of particular interest to her despite its being open for navigation only between June and September.[32] Strangely, nothing is said of the Soviet Union's continuing efforts to extend this period.[33]

Far more forcefully than in *Navies in War and Peace*, Gorshkov makes it clear that the strategic and economic importance of the oceans, and the Soviet Union's need for sea power to protect and further her maritime interests, are not always accepted even today. In the two concluding chapters of *The Sea Power of the State*, 'The Development of Navies after the Second World War' and 'Problems of Naval Art', he shows his determination to further his arguments, especially against those in the country who argue that the advent of nuclear weapons has made navies obsolete. What he terms 'military research circles', which are presumably clearly identifiable by his Soviet readers, have put forward views denying any significant role for conventional naval forces in any future war, which will see no maritime operations and thus demand no naval forces. Everything would be decided by nuclear missiles. Recent research, claims Gorshkov, has refuted these views in the light of new assessments of the world distribution of power and of the nature of future wars. They would be waged not only by nuclear missile forces but by all arms, each equipped with appropriate nuclear and conventional weapons which would revolutionise their mode of operations.[34] Furthermore, Russia's most likely enemies with these capabilities were maritime powers capable of major aggression from the sea. Geography would help the Western Alliance to block Soviet exits from the Baltic and Black Seas and its fleets and overseas bases were the main instruments of its bid to control the seas and hence dominate the world. Faced with these maritime challenges, the Soviet Union had no alternative but to respond in kind and to make her enemies, especially the United States, realise that the seas were no longer a barrier between themselves and punishment for aggression.[35]

Because its whole social structure and political regime are seen as legitimised by the scientific doctrines of Marxist–Leninism, every major element of Soviet life, especially vitally important ones such as its military policies, must not only be subject to the overall political doctrine but must have their own principles embodied in objective scientific thought. Alongside the practical arguments for naval development so successfully pursued by Gorshkov has been his equally important claim for the existence of a specific 'naval art', thus providing his service with the scientific theoretical basis so much praised in the reviews of *The Sea Power of the State*.[36] He defines it as a scientific theory based on a combination of rational analysis of historical and contemporary phenomena and practical experience, designed to produce correct doctrines for the conduct of maritime war. He insists that although it has the same objectives it is substantially different from 'military art' because of the differences between the elements in which land and sea forces operate.[37]

This claim for the scientific independence of naval thought, developed in the last chapter of his book, far more than anything else published in the Soviet Union, sets out to establish the uniqueness and importance of sea power and of the naval forces which exercise it. The detailed applications of it are set out in Chapter 7 below; here it is sufficient to record that they stem from a definition of the two primary missions of naval forces, 'fleet against shore' and 'fleet against fleet'.[38] The former, with its emphasis on the potential strategic decisiveness of sea-based nuclear missiles, has always been in the forefront of Gorshkov's advocacy of sea power, but here the latter, more traditional, naval activity is given more importance than in his earlier writings. There is far greater emphasis on conventional naval operations designed to gain what he terms 'sea dominance'. This in turn is defined as ensuring the preliminary conditions necessary for the Navy to fulfil its prescribed strategic tasks, be they nuclear strike, anti-submarine operations, participation in land operations or the attack on or defence of sea lines of communication.[39] All this leads to Gorshkov's planned conclusion that the execution of these tasks, essential to the Soviet Union's national strategy, can only be carried out by a 'balanced fleet' of surface, submarine and air elements all equipped with the most modern sensors, communications and weapons.[40]

The unique value of naval forces in limited war is expounded in Gorshkov's usual oblique way by stressing the contribution they have made to United States expansionism. The essential requirements have been high mobility and sea endurance. When these have been achieved through the provision of air strike capability from carriers, combined operations vessels and specially trained manpower, they have added a most potent ingredient to overall strategy, Moreover, granted the creation of balanced forces, as in the United States Sixth Fleet in the Mediterranean, they can work in conjunction with a strategic nuclear capability. Gorshkov makes no direct plea for the Soviet Union to deploy such forces and does not conceal how costly they would be, but concludes by saying that, so far, the United States had been successful in their use only because there had been no effective local opposition, supported by the socialist community.[41] The implication is clear.

In his conclusion Gorshkov returns to his central message that only a balanced fleet will enable the Soviet Union to maintain an effective maritime element in her strategy. The steps which have been taken so far in giving the Soviet Navy both a nuclear and conventional capability have removed the threat of nuclear blackmail from the sea and enabled her to offer help against imperialist aggression to friendly states. This has been instrumental in helping to bring about the present balance of world forces with its shift towards socialism, and hence the advancement of détente and peace. But, as long as capitalism and imperialism exist, so does the danger of war and therefore the necessity for the Soviet Union to be strong at sea. It is because the CPSU has fully realised this that 'the general building of the fleet is now orientated towards the creation of a comprehensively developed, that is, balanced fleet'.[42]

If this claim, and confidence in the political leadership, followed up since Gorshkov wrote by significant additions to the Soviet fleet does not fully confirm MccGwire's suggestion that Gorshkov's writings and achievements mark a fundamental change in Soviet strategy by 'challenging the primacy of the continental theatres of war',[43] it certainly points towards a conclusion that Soviet strategic thought and policy options have become more complex and varied in ways which offer greater scope for maritime strategy and power.

THE IMPACT OF TECHNOLOGICAL PROGRESS

Earlier chapters of this book have strongly stressed the primacy of political rather than military factors in the formation of the Soviet Union's strategic posture, with the implication that it will always be the intentions of the political leadership which will determine the capabilities of the armed forces and the ways in which they will be employed. True though this is, there is a danger of oversimplification. In times when technological change, particularly in the nuclear and electronic fields, has transformed the nature of war and created new combat capabilities which the Soviet Union has eagerly grasped, the military and naval leadership, which alone fully understand what can now be done, must be in a strong position to make positive contributions to strategic thought and intentions. When to this are added reasonable grounds for the Soviet Union to believe that the balance of forces between herself and the United States has swung in her favour, there is every reason to expect corresponding changes in strategic doctrine and planning for war. It is strongly arguable that factors such as these provide a more reliable basis for establishing the current and future importance of sea power in Soviet strategy than a postulation of a conscious shift to more maritime modes of thought. If indeed such technological changes and balance of power perceptions have been strongly influential in enhancing the value of sea power in Soviet eyes, then the likelihood of continuance along that path is all the greater.

It is difficult to deny that after the achievement of strategic capability and the formation of the Strategic Rocket Forces in 1959, Soviet strategic thought until the late 1960s saw only one option in the event of war with the United States, all-out nuclear war beginning with strikes against America's centres of power and population.[44] Even those Soviet writers who admitted the need for conventional military operations to effect the final decision, saw the nuclear strikes as being so devastating as to make the war very short, a matter of weeks or even days. At this stage SLBMs were seen only as one component of all the strategic nuclear forces, operating under a unified command in a targeting plan shared with the Strategic Rocket Forces and Long Range Aviation.[45]

As long as the Soviet Union saw herself as either quantitatively or qualitatively inferior in nuclear strategic systems to the United States this immediate all-out strike must have seemed the only realistic option. But, in the early 1970s, the availability of an increased number of missiles of greater payload and accuracy, coincided with a discussion in the Soviet literature of another option. This considered the practicability of a first strike, heavy and accurate enough to eliminate the United States' land-based systems, which might force her to yield before a complete nuclear holocaust ensued. Such a surrender would be more likely if the American government knew that the enemy had withheld its SLBMs from the initial strike so that they could be available for use against its cities. Such a withholding strategy would certainly have gained the Soviet Navy an important and distinctive function in overall grand strategy.[46] It also seems likely that a nuclear war limited in this way would last longer than one beginning, and ending, with an all-out nuclear exchange, and would thus give opportunities for conventional naval operations to both sides.

A further possibility detectable in the literature is that of war, both nuclear and conventional but excluding the metropolitan territories of the United States and the Soviet Union. Again, such a war, limited in geographical extent and possibly in use of nuclear weapons, could well be of longer duration.[47]

If these two strategic options offer greater scope for the use of sea power, a third possibility, actual Soviet armed intervention in support of its global policies outside the NATO area, would offer even more opportunities. Even after its intervention in Afghanistan it is difficult to establish how prominently such actions are likely to figure in Soviet strategic thinking, especially as discussions in the military literature usually take the form of condemnatory references to what the imperialists have achieved by them. McConnell's analytical approach is different, being based on his perception in Soviet writing since 1966 of departures from the hitherto accepted doctrine that such wars would inevitably escalate into superpower confrontations and nuclear war. As an example he cites:

> The armed forces of the USSR and the Socialist countries are confronted with an important task – to be in readiness for repelling the aggression of imperialist states, not only in a nuclear missile war but also in local wars with the use of conventional means of combat.[48]

More important than the details of the above arguments which are necessarily speculative, it does seem apparent that Soviet strategic thought has proved capable of substantial shifts in response to changing political perceptions of the balance of world forces and the acquisition of additional combat capabilities arising from technological development. Coincident with this has been the Navy's own acquisition of a wider range of equipment and capabilities which could give it a stronger voice in future strategic debates. The likelihood of this is increased by the fact that all the newer strategic options which have apparently been considered, controlled or limited nuclear war and armed intervention in local wars, increase the possibility of protracted hostilities, with consequent greater occasions for the use of maritime forces. Taking all this into account, and matching it with the proven ability of the Soviet industry to produce impressive ships, submarines, aircraft and weapons systems, it seems likely that the Russian Navy will overcome many of the shortcomings and frustrations which have marked its past history.

5   The Development of the Soviet Navy

It would be more accurate to see the recent growth of the Soviet Navy as the end product of a complex interaction between political aims, economic and industrial developments affecting maritime technology, and changing perceptions of strategic threats and opportunities, than as the work of any one man. This is not to minimise Gorshkov's achievements in advocacy of the naval cause and in the actual creation of a strong ocean-going navy, but to see him not so much as an original thinker but as a perceptive and able practical man who identified several currents of strategic thought and technological development which, if skilfully exploited, would result in the political leadership accepting the advantages to be gained from a greater stress on maritime power in national strategy and a consequent growth in the strength and reach of the Navy.

Granted the triple determination of the post-war leadership to transform the country's technological and industrial base, to achieve equivalence with the United States in all elements of national power and to take whatever opportunities emerged to increase the Soviet Union's global influence at the expense of America and China, growth in maritime power was virtually inevitable. Such growth could have taken various paths: that it has resulted in the creation of Gorshkov's 'balanced fleet' can be more directly attributed to his persuasive powers, particularly to his argument that the lack of such a fleet was responsible for the interwar failure to produce compatible naval doctrine and forces, which in turn resulted in the Navy's inadequate performance when war came, compared with the Army's immense and continually celebrated achievements. As has been perceptively observed, there is no naval hero enshrined in the national

84

memories of the Great Patriotic War alongside the many marshals and generals.[1]

THE SOVIET NAVY BEFORE THE SECOND WORLD WAR

The contradictions which have marked the development of the Soviet Navy go back to the very beginning of the communist regime. In the October Revolution of 1917 which brought the Party to power, it was the guns of the cruiser *Aurora* of the Baltic Fleet, already known for its revolutionary fervour, which signalled the fall of the provisional government. Thus established in the annals of the Revolution the Red Navy was formally created by Lenin in 1918 under a separate Commissariat which had considerable independence within the Defence Commissariat. But towards the end of the Civil War, in March 1921, this early prestige was overshadowed by a sailors' mutiny at Kronstadt, protesting against the increasingly tyrannical Party government. The mutiny was ruthlessly crushed by the Army and the Cheka, the new secret police. Some 5,000 sailors and workers were executed. The resulting mistrust of the Navy was exacerbated by the necessity of its being commanded by ex-Tsarist officers until a new generation could be trained,[2] a factor which must have increased its difficulties in getting adequate resources from a shattered economy.

Another contradiction, and one more important in the long delay in producing an effective Soviet Navy, was the incompatibility between the strategic concepts taught in its academies and the deplorable condition of its *matériel* and the inability of the Soviet economy and industry to remedy it. There was no reality in a strategy based on gaining command of the sea approaches to the country and the tattered and often immobile relics of the Tsarist fleet. The inevitable clamour of the professional naval leaders to have this disparity remedied was to be dismissed by their political head, the Commissar for the Navy, in an address to the Naval War College as late as 1925: 'You speak of aircraft carriers and the construction of new types of ships ... at the same time completely ignoring the economic situation of our country and corresponding conditions of our technical means'.[3]

In face of the *matériel* realities some new strategic doctrine had to be found before the Navy could present rational demands for resources. This emerged in the ideas of the so-called 'New School', which rejected the need for a high seas fleet and concentrated on advocating an inshore defensive role based on light surface craft, submarines, mines and shore-based aircraft. Despite the name of 'Young School' sometimes given to it, it is important not to identify this approach with the French *Jeune École* of the late nineteenth century. Their strategy was offensive, based on unrestricted attacks on British merchant ships wherever they could be found as a means of economic warfare which would compel Britain to surrender because of her dependence on sea-borne supplies. The Russian concept postulated enemy naval attacks in home waters which would be countered by a totally defensive strategy.

Inevitably in the new communist state, the new naval strategy had to be given ideological backing and this was done by incorporating it in the search for a proletarian theory of war which became increasingly significant after the replacement of Trotsky by Frunze as Defence Commissar in January 1925. His ideas stressed the Leninist doctrine of the unity of the armed forces, which in practice meant the domination of strategic planning and resources allocation by the Army. The doctrine of command of the sea, as advocated by Mahan, was denounced as inherently capitalist and entirely unacceptable to the new communist state. This was a denunciation to be echoed after the Second World War in discussions of the Navy's possible procurement of aircraft carriers, which were often condemned as tools of aggressive imperialism, unworthy of a peace-seeking society. But in the 1920s, as in the 1950s, it was much more likely that the real reason for not giving the Navy an ocean-going capability lay more in the inability of the economy and industry to produce the necessary ships and their equipment. During the period in which the early Five Year Plans were concentrating on building up Russia's general industrial base to the level which it had achieved before the Revolution, the relative cheapness of the New School's requirements must have been a more important factor in its success than any ideological legitimacy. Even so, by the time of the second Five Year Plan in 1933, the economy had so far advanced that it was found possible to initiate the large-scale production of submarines which, by 1939, was to result in the Soviet Union having the largest submarine force in the world.[4]

But even as the New School gained ascendancy it was challenged and finally displaced by a change in the political leadership's perceptions of the implications of other countries' naval policies. The 1920s and early 1930s had been characterised by successful attempts among the leading naval powers to bring about substantial reductions in naval armaments at conferences at Washington and London. Parallel to this had been a growing scepticism among naval men, as well as politicians, about the future utility of large battleships in the face of increasingly effective submarine and air threats. But after 1933 a reverse trend set in. First came Hitler's accession to power and his expressed determination to cast off the restraints on German armaments imposed at the end of the First World War. This was followed by the failure of the 1935 London Naval Conference, the concluding of the Anglo-German Naval Agreement in the same year, and the consequent inevitability of large-scale naval building programmes by all the major powers. For the Soviet Union perhaps the most immediate threat was seen as that from Japan, especially when, in 1936, she entered the Anti-Comintern Pact with Germany and Italy. Stalin's perceptions of the importance of sea power were reinforced by realisation of his inability to intervene navally in the Spanish Civil War because of the Soviet Navy's weakness. That these factors turned his mind to a big ship navy is confirmed by the fact that the only Fleet Commander to survive the 1937–8 purges was the Commander-in-Chief of the Pacific Fleet, Viktorov, who was known to be in favour of an ocean-going fleet.[5] The practical result of all this was the initiation of a construction programme which contained the modernisation of three existing battleships and the beginning of a new class of heavy cruisers of which six were ultimately to be completed.

The exclusion of new battleship and aircraft carrier construction was due more to the inadequacy of Soviet shipbuilding and armament industries than to any ideological or strategic theories. In the third Five Year Plan, announced in 1937, battleships were included and at least three begun. Although the building of carriers was discussed it was apparently decided to postpone it until the closing years of the Plan to allow time for the solving of problems of their construction and of aircraft design. It is noteworthy that from 1936 the Soviet Union made strong efforts to obtain advice and practical help in capital ship construction from the United States on the basis of their common interest in balancing Japan's increasing naval capabilities. In the many criticisms of Stalin which have been made in the Soviet Union since 1956 it is significant that both Admiral Kuznetsov and his successor as Commander-in-Chief of the Soviet Navy, Admiral Gorshkov, have stressed the contradictions in naval policies which aimed at producing an ocean-going navy but failed to provide it with the integral air power which would have freed it from the necessity of having to operate within the range of shore-based aircraft, with a consequent inability to carry out effective offensive operations.[6]

Stalin may have wanted a big ship Navy for deterrence and prestige and he and his military advisers may have had no plans for giving it a major offensive role in war, but it seems difficult to deny that they would have given the Navy a powerful fleet had economic and industrial realities and time made it practicable.

THE SOVIET NAVY IN THE GREAT PATRIOTIC WAR

When war came in 1941 the initial German penetration of Russian territory halted all capital ship construction and forced on the Navy an entirely defensive role: supporting the Army's coastal flanks; defending supply convoys; and using its heavy units as fortresses for besieged cities and its lighter craft for protecting sea or inland water supplies for their garrisons and civilian inhabitants. Without this latter support it seems highly doubtful if Leningrad could have held out.[7] Important though this was, it served in Gorshkov's words to 'consolidate the Navy's role as merely an assistant of the ground forces', a role which was organisationally recognised by the subordination of ships and maritime aircraft to local front commanders.[8]

The Soviet Navy fought in five naval theatres during the war: the Baltic and Black Seas; the Arctic and Pacific Oceans; and Inland Waters. In none of them, except perhaps the last, can it be said that naval forces fulfilling their normal roles made a major strategic contribution. This was often due to inferiority in *matériel* but, even when Soviet naval commanders had local superiority, they showed little initiative or offensive spirit. This was particularly true in the Baltic, where Germany had very weak naval forces, relying on mines and aircraft to give what maritime support was needed for their land operations. The Soviet Union had two battleships, at least three cruisers and substantial numbers of destroyers and submarines. Yet the surface forces were given no significant offensive tasks and even the submarines had little success. As already mentioned, there was an important contribution to the defence of Leningrad but, even after the siege was lifted and Germany's position began to crumble in January 1944, there was no surface fleet offensive, despite the fact that Russia now had air superiority.[9]

Much the same occurred in the Black Sea where there was an even greater numerical superiority. Opportunities to attack German supply routes were not taken by the surface forces and the submarine campaign was badly organised. If there had been more effort to integrate naval forces into the land operations the war could well have been shortened. Even the Navy's major contributions, the operations in defence of Odessa and Sevastopol in which Gorshkov took a prominent part, were unable to prevent defeat.[10] In the light of the apparent irrelevance of surface forces in the Baltic and Black Seas, it is as easy to understand the post-war Army's scepticism about the value of surface ships as it is to understand Gorshkov's ambition to gain a greater voice for the Navy in strategic thought and planning.

In Northern waters the most important wartime task was the protection of the Anglo-American convoys bringing war supplies to the Soviet Union. However much these supplies may have been discounted by post-war Soviet writing, it is difficult to believe that the delivery of so many weapons, tanks, aircraft and transport vehicles at a time when the Red Army barely succeeded in stemming the German invasion, was not of great significance.[11] Another indication of its importance is provided by the considerable German effort directed against the convoys by submarines, aircraft and capital ships with consequent heavy losses in both merchant and warships. Yet the whole of the oceanic protection had to come from Britain and the United States, and the Soviet Navy's contribution in its home waters was never significant in either quantity or quality.[12]

Where the Navy did make its most direct contribution to the defeat of Germany was in operations on inland waters in tactical support of the land fighting. This was particularly so in the Caspian Sea, the Volga and Don rivers and on Lake Ladoga in ensuring supplies to besieged Leningrad. Soviet *matériel* and operational expertise were much more suited to this type of warfare than they were to the open seas.

Russia's participation in the war against Japan in 1945 involved only fourteen days of fighting. In these the operations against the Japanese army in Manchuria were the most important. But there were sizable amphibious operations in Korea and the Kurile islands which, though not strongly opposed, were effectively executed, helped by an adequate supply of United States landing craft which, as Gorshkov has frequently bewailed in his post-war writings, were not available from Soviet sources.[13]

In the post-war discussion on the future nature of the Soviet Union's strategy and armed forces the Navy, unlike the Red Army, could not start off from a firm basis of vast experience and over-whelming victory against great odds. Some of the Navy's failures could be blamed on defective equipment and more on the failure to foresee the significant role it could have played in national strategy, but it was hard to deny that it had not made the best use of what opportunities it had. The surface forces in particular had made a poor showing. They had not sunk a single major German warship and yet had lost one battleship, two cruisers and some fifty destroyers. Even the elite submarine force and the mine-laying effort had not produced the results expected of them. Only the Navy's aviation, entirely shore-based, had, after initial losses had been made good by the Allies, carried out effective offensive operations, mainly against enemy supply convoys. By the end of the war the sinking rate was highly impressive.[14] This must have been a factor in influencing the high place given to naval aviation in post-war discussions, but it is not difficult to believe that the Navy's leaders, after they had digested the achievements of their British and American counterparts, must have felt strongly how much more they could have contributed to victory if the significance of maritime power had been more appreciated by their country, and if they had been provided with adequate means of exercising it.

STALIN'S POST-WAR NAVAL POLICY

Whatever views Stalin may have had about the war, he showed little hesitation in projecting a new, big ship Navy to repair the destruction which the German invasion had brought to his pre-war naval plans. His motives were presumably derived from his determination to deter the United States and Britain from taking any advantage from their enormous maritime superiority and to give every possible demonstration of his country's new place in the world. As far as they existed at all, his concepts of maritime strategy were defensive, concentrating on securing the four main fleet areas, the Northern, Baltic and Black Seas and the Pacific Ocean, from penetration by enemy fleets. He seems to have accepted the general view that the Second World War had marked the end of the battleship, and his planned naval forces were to be made up of heavy cruisers, destroyers and lighter surface craft, submarines and shore-based aviation. It is difficult to be certain whether he had any serious intention to add aircraft carriers, although Herrick claims that, by 1950, four were planned, one for each fleet. The evidence is tenuous but it was clearly decided once again that carriers would not be included in the initial building programme because of the inability of Soviet industry at the time to produce them and their planes. This meant the emergence of yet another contradiction in Soviet naval policy. Although the declared operational aim for the new fleet was the execution of tactically offensive operations against enemy lines of communication, without carriers these could only be carried out within the fighting range of shore-based aircraft. Had Stalin lived long enough to see the first part of his planned fleet completed it does not seem unreasonable to suppose that he would have furnished it with the one element it lacked, a sea-based air component. Another factor which might well have moved him in the same direction was his recognition of the obstacles to the increase of Soviet influence presented by the United States Pacific and Mediterranean Fleets. In an interesting repetition of his frustrations during the Spanish Civil War, in 1948 he had to admit his inability to give direct naval support to the Greek communist uprising because of Western superiority in the Mediterranean.[15]

THE NAVY UNDER STALIN'S SUCCESSORS

That the Navy was to suffer a severe check to such hopes under Stalin's successors was demonstrated by the abolition, shortly after his death, of the separate Naval Ministry and its closer control by the Army-dominated Ministry of Defence, especially under Marshal Zhukov in 1955–7. The full consequences became apparent with the emergence of Khruschev as the dominant personality in the new collective leadership.[16] Khruschev, like some of his Western contemporaries, including Duncan Sandys in Britain, was carried away by the advent of nuclear weapons which, he claimed, would so transform the nature of warfare that the importance of non-nuclear land, sea and air forces would become greatly diminished. They should be substantially reduced and the consequent savings in manpower and resources diverted to civil production and thus facilitate Khruschev's driving ambition of seeing the Soviet economy overtake that of the United States within the next twenty years. The Navy seemed to him to be particularly obsolescent and to offer great opportunities for economies. Large surface ships, including cruisers, could no longer serve any useful purpose. Small surface craft, submarines and land-based aircraft, especially if fitted with nuclear missiles, would be all that was required. Another indication of the severely limited expectation of future naval operations was the surrender in 1956 of the wartime gains of naval bases at Port Arthur in Manchuria and Porkalla in Finland.

It was of course to implement these ideas that Gorshkov, with his reputation of enthusiasm for missiles, was brought in to be naval Commander-in-Chief in place of Kuznetsov, who was associated with Stalin's big ship Navy. It is true that after his appointment all open discussion of acquiring aircraft carriers vanished and instead there were frequent examples of writings attacking them as symbols of imperialist aggression which in any case were now highly vulnerable to missile and torpedo attack. On the other hand, and more important, was the fact that Gorshkov and his supporters conducted a cautious campaign both publicly and in closed official discussion which succeeded in changing Khruschev's mind on the utility of large surface ships. Part of the cruiser force was saved[17] and new classes of surface ships were soon to appear. By 1962 Gorshkov was able to publish an article in *Pravda* which included the assertion: 'On the level with submarines in the armament of our Navy are surface ships carrying missile weapons and the latest equipment.'[18] In the following year he went further and stated:

> Modern submarines and missile-carrying aircraft comprise the principal strike forces of the Navy and are the essence of its power. Yet, there must be other forces besides the long-range strike forces, both for active defence against any enemy within the limits of the defence zone of a maritime theatre, and for the comprehensive support of the combat and operational activities of the main striking forces of the Navy. To such forces belong surface missile ships and small craft, warships and aircraft for anti-submarine warfare, minesweepers . . . etc.[19]

This surely marked a high point in Gorshkov's moves towards achieving a balanced fleet (although he did not use the term at this stage). He had skilfully based his advocacy of the necessity of a wide range of surface ships not on what they could do by themselves but on the essential support only they could contribute to the successful fulfilment of the strike missions of submarines and aircraft which already had political approval.

Offensive strikes, when they have figured at all in Soviet naval thinking, have always been seen as tactical moves in a strategy which has been essentially defensive. This has remained the case during the recent expansion. Of all the Western interpretations of what was the original motivation leading to the Soviet Navy's present strength and deployment patterns, the one which postulates that they stem from a determination to protect the homeland against nuclear attacks, first from carrier-borne aircraft and then from *Polaris* missile submarines and their longer-range successors, seems to be supported by the most convincing evidence. This motive alone has had behind it the ideological and strategic strength needed to move the political and military leadership towards the highly expensive procurement and deployment programmes which have been implemented since the 1960s. The basic decision having been taken on these grounds, Gorshkov's further achievement has been to convince the leadership that success in this aim demands an ocean-going fleet of great diversity, and that the possession of such a force will bring substantial advantages in conditions short of general nuclear war. The primary importance of this response to nuclear threats from the sea as being the dynamic behind Soviet naval expansion, has been most continuously analysed over a long period of years by Michael MccGwire and needs only a brief restatement here.[20]

The process began at the end of the Second World War when the Soviet Union realised that, with the defeat of Germany and Japan and the move of China towards communism, the only foreseeable military threat could come from the United States and her allies, particularly Britain. Not only were they ideologically hostile but they also presented the only serious obstacle to Russia's attaining predominance in a war-weakened Europe. They were also essentially maritime powers which, during the war, had demonstrated naval capabilities of the highest order, both in sea battles and in amphibious operations large enough to be of strategic significance. If this were not enough, they also possessed atomic weapons, some of which could be launched from the sea against Soviet centres of industry and population. With the formation of NATO in 1949 and the later rearmament of West Germany, it was natural for Russia's traditional fear of invasion from the West to revive, but now seemingly more strongly because of her enemies' overwhelming maritime power. It was inevitable that the Soviet government would react to this new threat from the sea.

The original danger in the immediate post-war years, and apparently particularly by Stalin himself, was perceived as being large-scale amphibious invasion. After 1954 this was downgraded and gradually disappeared from prominence in Soviet strategic writing, to be replaced by fear of surprise nuclear attack by NATO's carrier-borne aircraft: aircraft which rapidly increased in range and destructive power. This danger was overtaken in the early 1960s by what was perceived as the most dangerous maritime threat of all, attacks from *Polaris* submarines and their longer-range successors. Each of these developments was met by the acquisition of newly equipped forces designed to counter it in support of the basic strategic principle of the absolute necessity to defend the homeland. This was of course accompanied by the acquisition of the vital offensive and deterrent capabilities arising from the Soviet Union's production of its own SSBNs.

The Soviet Navy we know today had its origins in this powerful dynamic produced by the advent of sea-borne strategic nuclear weapons but, in the process of growth, it has extended its capabilities much more widely and acquired a range of *matériel* which must now be examined in more detail.

6 The Soviet Navy: an Inventory

THE OFFSHORE DEFENCE FORCE

The offshore defence force is a large, distinctive and important part of the Soviet Navy which is intended primarily for operations in local waters. It comprises about 1,200 frigates and minor combatants of various kinds with a collective displacement tonnage something in excess of 450,000 tons. Since this represents about one-sixth of the Navy's overall tonnage, the offshore defence force plainly deserves more attention than it usually gets from the West.

Its leading ships are the 130 or so frigate-like vessels of the *Mirka*, *Petya*, *Kola*, *Koni*, *Riga* and, more recently, the powerful *Krivak* classes. The Russians themselves describe these ships as *Storozhevoy Korabl'* (SKR) which roughly means 'guard-ship', a term which is often rather loosely translated as 'escort'. But in fact these ships have few real equivalents in the West. Certainly, they should not be thought of as modern descendants of the kind of escort that fought the Battle of the Atlantic, for this is not their function. They are usually middling sorts of ships, moderately fast (normally less than 30 knots) with a medium armament and modest endurance.[1] They are typical of the kind of naval hardware which led one early commentator to argue: 'The more the Russian surface warships are scrutinised the more evident it becomes that they have been created to comply with the Russian idea of "offensively conducted defence of the sea frontiers of the Soviet Union".'[2]

The fast and powerful *Krivak* is an interesting new addition to the Soviet Navy's SKR force. Displacing around 3,300 tons, it is equipped with the SS-N-14 anti-submarine missile and also has anti-air weapons, mines, torpedoes and 76 or 100 mm guns. Reinforced by the mistaken belief that its primary weapon was intended for use against surface ships, initial Western assessments certainly over-rated the *Krivak*'s performance.[3] Only recently has it been accepted as a frigate rather than a destroyer. Originally the Russians rated it more highly as well, calling it a *Bolshoy Protivolodochny Korabl'* (BPK) or large anti-submarine ship, only recently demoting it to the SKR category. All in all, the *Krivak* is a significant example of the way in which perceptions of a particular piece of naval hardware can change over the years.

The Soviet Navy's frigate force is backed up by a vast host of minor combatants. The Russians operate more of these than does the rest of the world combined. They maintain a particularly large mine-sweeping force which is variously specialised for deep-water, offshore or riverine operations. Huge stocks of mines argue a con-tinuing interest in offensive mine warfare too. Most of their ships have a mine-laying capacity or can be easily so converted and they are one of the few navies in recent times to have built in the tiny *Alyosha* class of 1965 a warship specifically designed for mine-laying.

But, generally speaking, the West has been much more interested in the Soviet Navy's small missile ships than it has in their mine warfare vessels. In the 1950s, the Soviet Navy tried to outflank Western naval superiorities by investing in surface-to-surface mis-siles (SSM) like the SS-N-2 *Styx*, putting them on small fast ships like the *Osa* and the *Komar* and developing a new tactical doctrine for their operation. The potentiality of this kind of warfare was brought home to the West by the sinking in 1967 of the Israeli des-troyer *Eilat* by the Egyptian Navy, then under Soviet tutelage. Since then, many other countries, perhaps most notably Israel, have fol-lowed the Soviet lead in this. In 1969 the Russians themselves pro-duced the 800 ton *Nanuchka*, armed with SS-N-9 SSM with an estimated range of 150 miles, and once described as 'a kind of capital ship of the marginal seas' with follow-ons in the *Tarantul* and *Sarancha* classes.

In addition to these two classes of minor combatants, the Russians have produced countless small patrol craft, anti-submarine ships, hovercraft and the like. The size and diversity of its offshore defence effort shows the importance the Soviet Navy attaches to this task. This emphasis goes back to the earliest days of the Soviet Navy. The SKR designation itself started in 1926, but the recent allocation of the *Krivak*s to this task shows that Soviet interest in it is by no means diminishing.

The main focus of this capability for offshore defence is naturally on waters local to the Soviet Union. But the general strategic significance of ships like these is much more than appears at first sight. Many of them do in fact operate regularly on the high seas: *Krivaks*, *Grishas* and *Nanuchkas*, for instance, frequently participate in Soviet naval activities in the Mediterranean. In wartime their presence in large numbers would be of considerable benefit to the Soviet Navy if it wished to seek control of nearby seas like the Sea of Japan or the Norwegian Sea. More immediately, this type of ship has a particular appeal to the world's many small navies for it meets their modest requirements much better than do larger more sophisticated sea-going vessels. Table 1 shows the extent to which the Soviet Union supplied Third World countries over the period 1956–78 with missile boats and other small combatants originally designed for use in Soviet waters.[4] Their arrival in more distant places often

TABLE 1   *Patrol boat transfers by country and year*

Country	P6	Komar	OSA I	OSA II
Algeria	10 (1963–66)	6 (1967)	3 (1967)	–
Bulgaria	–	–	4 (1970–71)	–
China	10 (1956–60)	4 (1965–67)	9 (1965–67)	–
Cuba	12 (1962)	18 (1962–66)	5 (1972–73)	3 (1976)
Egypt	20 (1956–60)	7 (1962–67)	10 (1966)	–
Eq. Guinea	1 (1969)	–	–	–
Germany DPR	27 (1957–60)	–	12 (1970)	3 (1976)
Guinea	4 (1968–70)	–	–	–
India	–	–	8 (1970)	8 (1976)
Indonesia	14 (1961–63)	9 (1961–65)	–	–
Iraq	12 (1969–61)	–	6 (1973)	6 (1973 & 1976)
Korea DPR	8 (1961)	12 (Mid-60s)	8 (N/A)	–
Libya	–	–	–	24 (1976–78)
Nigeria	3 (1967)	–	–	–
Poland	6 (1957–58)	–	12 (1968)	–
Romania	–	–	5 (1964)	–
Somalia	4 (1968)	–	–	3 (1975)
Syria	–	5 (1963–66)	8 (1972–76)	–
Tanzania	3 (1974–75)	–	–	–
Vietnam	–	2 (1968)	–	–
Yemen PDR	2 (1972)	–	–	–
Yugoslavia	–	–	10 (1966–69)	–

Source: Defense Electronics, September 1978, p. 74.

alters local naval balances, increases Soviet naval and political influence and gives even Western navies some pause for thought. For all these reasons, their strategic consequence is not restricted simply to the waters for which they were originally intended. There is evidence indeed that some of the newer classes have been designed with export in mind.

DESTROYERS

Over the last twenty years, the number of destroyers in the Soviet Navy has dropped by over half. Currently, the Russians have about 68 in active service compared to 157 in 1961.[5] Over the same period, total tonnage has dropped too – by nearly one-third. These reductions have taken place against a bewildering background of construction, cancellation and conversion. Broadly, the following represents the modern Soviet destroyer's family tree (see Figure 1).

Many observers have seen four admittedly indistinct phases in destroyer development. First, there were the *Skory*, *Kotlin* and the single *Tallinn* class gun destroyers. These were derived essentially from the experience of the Second World War. The *Skory* programme, initiated in 1945, was intended to produce a standard 5″ gun destroyer of conventional 1943–5 design, and in fact all three

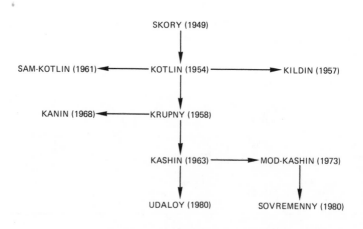

FIGURE 1   *The development of Soviet destroyers*[6]

classes suggest that naval thinking at the time of their conception was perfectly orthodox. However the Soviet Navy then moved into a second and more innovative phase. The last four *Kotlins* were completed as *Kildin* 'missile ships' (RKs) and were soon complemented by the *Krupny* class. Guns were abandoned as the primary weapon and the SS-N-1 *Scrubber* surface-to-surface missile (SSM) took their place. This dramatic new departure caused considerable perturbation in the West, which felt itself outflanked by this technological surprise. Other *Kotlins* were also taken in hand, fitted with surface-to-air missiles (SAM) and still classified as 'destroyers' (EM), became the *SAM-Kotlins*. These three ship types seemed to be designed for operations against Western carrier-based task groups. *Kildins* and *Krupnys* would shoot at Western ships (doubtless in company with submarines and land-based aircraft) and *SAM-Kotlins* would provide them with air defence.

The third and fourth phases are somewhat less distinct. Many observers argue that Soviet preoccupations moved away from the threat of Western surface ships and onto that of Western submarines. Accordingly, in the third phase, there was a shift in destroyer policy towards the deployment of anti-submarine weapons in place of anti-ship ones. The *Krupnys* were stripped of their *Scrubbers*, given more anti-submarine and anti-air capacity and were designated by the Russians BPK (large anti-submarine ships) and as *Kanins* by the West. This BPK designation was also applied to the world's first major warship to rely exclusively on gas turbine propulsion, the *Kashin* class of 1963. These ships were mainly intended for operations against submarines but had a heavy anti-air armament as well. In a sense this phase is still continuing, for in 1980 there emerged the lead ship of the *Udaloy* class, a large destroyer of about 8,500 tons whose ASW missiles and helicopters are considered to be its main armament.

However some analysts have also discerned a fourth phase in Soviet destroyer policy which is also still unfolding and which is distinguished by a shift back to anti-surface weaponry. Starting in 1971, the Russians began to turn their *Kashins* into *Modified Kashins*. On the one hand the *Kashin*'s ASW weaponry was updated with the addition of variable depth sonar (VDS) and greater air defence was added, but, on the other, and very significantly, the ships were fitted with SS-N-2C SSM, an improved *Styx* sometimes called SS-N-11. About the same time three of the *Kildins* received similar installation of new SSM. Both these modified types were re-designated BKR (large missile ship) in 1977–8. This trend towards more versatile general-purpose warships has recently produced the *Sovremenny*, another large destroyer of some 7,500 tons which, according to the US Navy's Director of Naval Intelligence, is primarily designed for anti-surface warfare with two twin 130 mm guns, surface-to-surface anti-ship cruise missiles and a new medium range surface-to-air system'. While *Sovremenny* has a secondary ASW role, and carries helicopters, it 'is their first major combatant since 1970 to deploy without significant ASW capability'.[7]

Some qualifications need to be set against this presentation of Soviet destroyer policy however, partly because experts differ in their definitions. Some for instance maintain that *Udaloy* and *Sovremenny* are not destroyers at all, but cruisers.[8] Others see in this the first indications that the Soviet Navy is about to shift all its class sizes up one stage so that its cruisers of the future will displace some 12,000 tons or more, and its destroyers some 8,000.[9] The Russians also make life difficult for their analysts by their tendency to hedge their bets in fitting weapons to warships by providing at least a little of everything. The armament of the *Kanin* and *Kashin* classes for instance is such that many observers contest the notion that they are in fact simply BPK and stress instead their anti-air capacity. Disputed evidence like this leads, as we shall see, to fundamental disagreement about what were the primary preoccupations of the Soviet Navy during the period such ships were conceived and built.

CRUISERS AND BATTLECRUISERS

Soviet cruisers have more or less followed the same lines of development as have their destroyers, although their strength has risen both in terms of ship and tonnage totals. First, the Soviet Navy built gun-cruisers of the traditional style in the *Chapaev* and *Sverdlov* classes which originated in 1939 and 1948 respectively. In the 1950s, however, the construction of these was abruptly terminated and plans for other large cruiser classes were scrapped. Instead attention switched to new style cruisers like the *Kynda* and *Kresta I*. Completed *Sverdlovs* were mainly retained, however, several being converted later to command or training ships. In this way, the Russians demonstrated their marked reluctance to throw anything away.

The *Kynda* appeared in 1962 as what the Russians call *Raketnyy Kreyser* (RKR) or missile cruiser. Though at 4,500 tons they were on the small side, they carried SS-N-3 *Shaddock* SSM and were evidently designed for operations against Western carrier forces. Their problem was that, although the *Shaddock*'s range was upwards of 150 nautical miles, the ship itself had no way of supplying it with targeting information beyond visual range and so had to rely on aircraft, submarines or other warships nearer the target. Because of this, the *Kyndas* are not usually considered to have been a success and the series was terminated quite quickly. *Kresta I* cruisers (1967) were another small class of cruiser with the same anti-ship function but which carried a heavier SAM armament and a helicopter for missile-targeting, both of which enhanced their capacity for independent operations. Rather confusingly the *Kresta Is* were classified BPK for several years. This may have reflected a shortage of more suitable ships and/or the carrying of the ASW version of the *Hormone* helicopter. Recently however they have returned to their designed role and been reclassified as RKR.

Neither of these classes had a long-range ASW missile weapon but later cruisers – like destroyers – showed 'the very marked shift away from the surface attack role towards that of ASW'. Initially, the extent to which this was true of the *Kresta II* (1970) was not fully realised in the West because it was widely believed that her main ASW weapon – the SS-N-14, a kind of flying torpedo – was in fact a SSM which NATO designated the SS-N-10. The *Kara* cruisers of 1973 were larger still at 9,700 tons and better equipped to prosecute their main ASW mission and defend themselves from attack.

This recent trend towards more versatile ships has become particularly marked with the Soviet Navy's latest cruiser, a large warship of some 12,000 tons, being built on the Black Sea, with an impressive array of ASW weapons, SSM and a good air defence system. This multi-purpose ship is probably intended to act as some kind of command cruiser.

This is also one of the suggested roles for the *Kirov*, a nuclear battlecruiser whose arrival in 1980 attracted considerable Western interest. At some 23,000 tons, *Kirov* is the largest warship (apart from carriers) to be built by any nation for the past thirty years. With a powerful array of SAM, ASW weapons and the new SS-NX-19 (a SSM capable of delivering a nuclear warhead 250 nautical miles) the *Kirovs* promise to be formidable and sophisticated components of the Soviet fleet. Currently at least two more ships of this class are reported to be under construction. *Kirov*'s precise function, however, is still a matter of conjecture. Some experts consider her to be a large command cruiser and others the centrepiece of an ASW group. Still others argue that such ships are eventually intended to operate with carrier task groups rather as did fast battle-ships in the last part of the Pacific war. Probably *Kirov* could do all these things, and more, if the requirement arose; it is difficult and perhaps profitless to seek to gauge the primary purpose of such a notably versatile ship.

The construction of *Kirov* is significant for another reason too. Present at the commissioning ceremony of the first *Kynda* cruiser, Khruschev is supposed to have remarked, with something less than perfect tact, that the ship was really just a floating coffin. This was part of a general feeling in the Soviet Union (and one that raised certain echoes in the West as well) that the day of the surface war-ship was drawing to a close. According to Khruschev, it 'has become outmoded for conducting wars in modern conditions because all sur-face means are now vulnerable from the air as well as from shore, and they can be destroyed by an enemy from a far distance'.[10] The construction of *Kirov* and in fact most of their recent cruiser and destroyer construction shows that the Soviet Navy, if ever it had this idea, has now quite definitely abandoned it. Admiral Gorshkov tells us that advances in air defence now mean that large surface ships can 'counter enemy aircraft and repel combined attacks from other naval forces of the enemy while carrying out their main mission'.[11] Accordingly, the Soviet Navy has proceeded with the construction of a versatile and balanced surface fleet of the traditional kind which need no longer be restricted to narrowly defensive tasks in local waters.

AIRCRAFT CARRIERS

In the period when Soviet writers were expressing their doubts about the future of large surface warships, the aircraft carrier came in for particularly heavy criticism. This ranged from their alleged vulnerability in the nuclear missile age to the view that they were really the irrational product of a bourgeois military–industrial com-plex whose only use was for increasingly desperate attempts to sup-press revolution around the world. Apparently for such reasons, the Russians abandoned any idea they might have had of adding carriers to their own line of battle. Instead they relied on their early and considerable expertise in SAM technology for the air defence of ships and on land-based air power for strike and reconnaissance. This was widely taken as evidence that the Soviet Navy did not intend to aim at maritime supremacy; neither did it want to develop the capacity to control the seas or to launch amphibious enterprises.[12] The absence of carriers reinforced the notion that the Soviet Navy was developing its own noticeably modest concepts of maritime strategy rather than aping those of the West. Indeed, in some quarters, Soviet views were taken as evidence that the West should not have carriers, and the ambitious maritime aspirations that seemed to go with them, either.[13]

In fact, however, Soviet attitudes to carriers were nothing like as clear-cut as this argument suggests. The link between cause and effect, for instance, is unclear to say the least. Did the Russians not have them because they didn't believe in them, or was it the other way around? Were Soviet doubts about carriers nothing more than a simple case of sour grapes, distinctly reminiscent of the public scepticism about the value of nuclear weapons expressed in the late 1940s? Certainly, criticism ran neither deep nor long. Many of their arguments about the vulnerability of carriers, for instance, were inherently implausible; the modern carrier's firepower, resilience and mobility in fact make it one of the least vulnerable of weapon systems, certainly as compared to airfields, military formations and so forth. A navy can argue that they are too expensive, that it does not need them, that there are other cheaper ways of achieving the same ends; but it cannot really argue that they are too vulnerable, *tout court*. Many Soviet criticisms were also frivolous from the operational point of view, since they focused not on the carriers' capacity but on the disreputable things the US Navy used them for. But the main reason for scepticism about the whole-heartedness of Soviet claims must be how very seriously they took the menace of US carriers to the Russian homeland. It seems unlikely that the Soviet Navy would have concentrated the bulk of their attention and maritime resources on the task of dealing with Western strike carriers if they really thought that 'aircraft carriers have become so vulnerable that their use appears to be inexpedient'.[14]

What probably happened was that there was a spectrum of opinion about carriers and scepticism became dominant, largely for reasons of expediency, for a short period in the 1950s and early 1960s when it seemed unlikely that the Soviet Navy would have them in the foreseeable future. Certainly, there had been little doubt about the ultimate need for carriers in the immediate post-war period. In 1946, Admiral Alafuzov, deputy chief of the main naval staff argued:

> The conditions of modern war at sea demand the mandatory participation in the combat operations of navies of powerful carrier forces, using them for striking devastating blows against the naval forces of the enemy as well as for the contest with his aviation. Both at sea and near one's own bases these tasks can only be carried out by carrier aviation.[15]

Carriers were dismissed along with other large surface ships in the early days of Khruschev's regime but there were signs that opinion was already beginning to swing back by the early 1960s. The Russians evidently followed with considerable interest both the debate held in Britain between about 1959 and 1966 about whether to build large or small carriers, and the later discussion which led to the *Invincible* class.[16] Soviet criticism increasingly focused not on carriers in general but on certain kinds of carrier. Thus in 1967, Gorshkov plainly only had the strike carrier in mind when he claimed that some people,

> yielding to the hypnosis of the modern use of aircraft carriers *in land wars*, continue to fight for the construction of aircraft carriers, but they lose sight of the fact that aircraft carriers, even nuclear-powered ones, cannot stand comparison with *the strike capabilities* of submarines and air forces.[17]

Very evidently, this was not intended to apply to those other kinds of ASW aircraft carriers which the Soviet Navy were already operating or planning by this date. Even more significantly, it became clear that the rehabilitation of strike carriers themselves was already under way. In 1964, although an important work called *Avianostsy* (Aircraft Carriers) detailed the weaknesses of US strike carriers, they were still regarded as 'a rather serious adversary at sea'. In the following year an article in *Morskoi Sbornik* rehearsed Western arguments in their favour but left the readers to draw their own conclusions.[18] Their value in limited war situations when 'aircraft carriers repeatedly stepped forth as the main forces of the navy' was recognised by 1969. The process was completed in 1978 by one of the Soviet Navy's most important theoreticians, Vice-Admiral K. A. Stalbo, in an article entitled 'Aircraft Carriers in the Postwar World'.

Using US Navy carriers as an example, Stalbo emphasised their mobility and flexibility as parts of 'the first echelon of its attack groupings both on oceans and in littoral regions . . . There is no basis to speak of a future reduction in the importance of carriers in armed warfare at sea'. As if to rub the point in, Stalbo also specifically pointed out the advantages of large carriers in aircraft-per-ton ratios, construction costs and so forth.[19]

This pattern of acceptance, sudden rejection and gradual rehabilitation in theoretical exposition closely mirrors that to be found in Soviet programmes of construction and procurement. Immediately after the war, there were many signs that the Soviet Navy intended to build on the foundations in maritime air laid long ago by the Tsarist navy.[20] Indeed had the uncompleted German carrier hull *Graf Zeppelin* not sunk in the Baltic when under tow to the Soviet Union and full of liberated railway engines, the Russians may have started to construct their first carrier in 1945. Such plans as they may have had to do so later seem to have been abandoned in the early 1950s. However, about 1957, they apparently recognised the need to take helicopters to sea. This led to the *Kresta I* and the appearance in mid-1967 of the 'anti-submarine cruiser' *Moskva*. Its radical design, a missile cruiser in front and a carrier behind, has many similarities to the old *Furious* produced by the British fifty years earlier when they were at an equivalent stage in the carrier development process. Of some 18,000 tons, *Moskva* carries about 16 *Hormone* ASW helicopters, other ASW weapon systems and has a certain capacity to defend itself against air attack. Originally it was intended to build up to eight of these warships but they were found to be too small for effective deployment at the distances now required, so the Soviet Navy settled for two, the *Moskva* itself and the *Leningrad*.

The apparently four-strong *Kiev* carrier class was the next stage in the process. Conceived about 1963/4, and finally decided on about 1967/8, after experience with the *Moskva* class had been absorbed, the first *Kiev* appeared with much bally-hoo in 1976 (see Figure 2). The Russians originally described these ships as anti-submarine cruisers too, and like the *Moskva* they are hybrids, ships which combine the characteristics of cruisers and carriers. Indeed very recently they have been reclassified *Tyazhyoly Avianesushchy Kreyser* (TAKR – heavy aircraft carrying cruiser). Their air group (about 20 *Hormone* helicopters and 13 Yak 36 *Forgers*) and their extensive missile armament (which includes 300 nautical mile range SS-N-12 *Sandbox* SSMs) gives them an impressive variety of ways of dealing

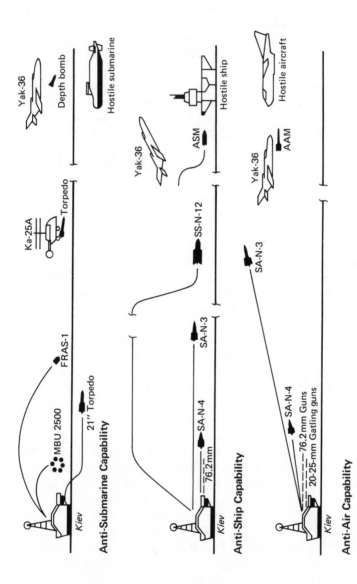

FIGURE 2 *Weapons systems of the Kiev*

Source: Proceedings of the USNI, July 1977, p. 101. Courtesy of US Naval Institute.

with submarines, ships and aircraft. Everything about them, from their versatility in performance to their gold-painted names and crests shows them to be the leading ships of a confident and ocean-going surface navy.

But, for all this, they are not strike carriers. Their air group is no match for the F-4 and F-14 fighters and A6 and A7 strike aircraft of their principal US Navy counterparts. Their chief orientation seems to be ASW and their ability to strike at land targets from the sea is limited. Early indications are such, however, that these qualifications may not have to be made about the new breed of carriers reportedly being built in the Soviet Union. The first of these ships perhaps under construction near Murmansk is said to be a large-deck nuclear-powered carrier of about 60,000 tons, similar in size to the US Navy's *Forrestal* class fast attack carriers. If this indeed proves to be the case, the Soviet carriers – as ships – would be at least equal to all but the US Navy's four *Nimitz* and *Enterprise* ships. They would appear to be the culmination of a long, steady and incremental process of carrier development begun over twenty years before.

Once, the absence of carriers was felt to limit the Soviet Navy to defensive and localised operations near Russia's own coasts. By the same logic, the anticipated arrival of 'real' carriers strengthens an impression already created by their cruiser and destroyer programmes that the Russians are determined to build a surface navy capable of sustained, impressive and multi-dimensional operations on the high seas; a navy, in other words, which need no longer be regarded automatically as second best.

BALLISTIC MISSILE FIRING SUBMARINES

The Russians have long been interested in submarines. In 1856, they built one dubbed *Le Diable Marin* which lay submerged off Kronstadt with a number of musicians aboard to play loyal music for the coronation of Tsar Alexander II. At least thirty submarines were in commission with the Imperial Russian Navy by 1914, including the world's first mine-laying submarine. This interest was kept up with such effect during the Revolution and the interwar period that the Soviet submarine force of 1939 was the largest in the world.

If anything, this emphasis has since increased. In 1960 Gorshkov remarked: 'Leading military thought correctly considers that the fleet which most fully answers the demands of modern warfare must be based on submarines. It is precisely in this direction that the Navy of the Soviet Union is now developing.'[21] Soviet naval construction since the war reflects this stress on submarines. Even by 1961, the Soviet Union already had a huge fleet of over 400 submarines. Over the following twenty years, while the total number of submarines in the Soviet Navy declined a little, their collective tonnage trebled to a gigantic one-and-a-half million tons. As a proportion of overall naval tonnage, the submarine effort rose as well, from about one-fifth in 1961 to nearly one-half in 1981. While the US Navy has built about 150 submarines since 1945, the Soviet Navy has produced some 600. Currently, the Russians have about 343 submarines in active service: 84 of them fire ballistic missiles, about 69 cruise missiles and the remaining 190 are mainly torpedo attack craft of various kinds. The equivalent US Navy figures are 36, 27 and 52 respectively.

Nuclear propelled ballistic missile firing submarines (SSBNs) form the most important part of the Soviet submarine fleet. The idea of deploying ballistic missiles at sea in SSBNs was attractive to the Russians for the same reasons which Gorshkov rather ingenuously attributed to the Americans. The submarine launched ballistic missile (SLBM) was a weapon system which allowed the enemy to be attacked from almost any direction; it avoided placing installations on home territory which might themselves attract nuclear strikes; it had 'greater viability, ease of concealment and mobility than corresponding systems positioned on land'; and, finally, although SSBNs would be difficult to find, the enemy would still feel bound to try to destroy them and this would dissipate his nuclear missile power.[22]

For all these reasons, the Soviet Navy embarked on a SLBM programme possibly as early as 1949.[23] The first stage of this programme was very experimental and all sorts of expedients were tried. According to one analyst, *Zulu* torpedo attack diesel submarines were very probably given the task throughout the 1950s of delivering nuclear mines or torpedoes into enemy ports. As a counter to the US atomic monopoly, a shallow nuclear burst in New York or San Francisco harbours was a threat worth posing.[24] More in the mainstream of development, the Russians were interested in German wartime plans to fire V2 rockets from containers towed by submarines. They eventually fired their first ballistic missile from a modified *Zulu* in September 1955, probably a version of the 75-mile range *Scud*-A launched from the surface. These experiments produced the *Zulu-V* class of 1956–7, the world's first SLBM firing submarine. The *Golf* and *Hotel* classes of 1958 were a distinct improvement on this but still had great weaknesses. The diesel *Golf* had originally to surface to fire its three missiles, though later versions could do so submerged, as could the nuclear propelled *Hotels*. But their missiles were few, primitive and very short range (350–600 miles). Because of these deficiencies the US Navy was easily able to sweep into the lead with its *Polaris* submarines (which began appearing in 1959) even though it only started its SSBN programme in 1955, some five or six years after the Russians.

About 1962, however, the Soviet Navy appears to have made a determined effort to catch up. Possibly the decision to do this was inspired by the evident superiorities of the US Navy's *Polaris* submarines or maybe it was part of a general Soviet reaction to Washington's new confidence in strategic doctrine about this time. Since Defence Secretary McNamara appeared to be outlining a strategy in which the United States could limit the damage the Soviet Union could do American society by attacking Soviet land-based missiles,[25] it made sense for the Soviet Union to invest in ballistic missile defence, to increase their missile strength on land and to put more missiles at sea where they would be safer from attack. The *Yankee* submarine of 1967 might well have been the product of such a policy. It was the Soviet Navy's first 'real' SSBN; it carried sixteen 1,300 nautical mile SS-N-6 missiles in launch tubes built into the main hull rather than two or three short-range missiles awkwardly contrived into the conning tower. As a submarine it had many similarities to the *Ethan Allen* class of *Polaris* type which entered service between 1961–3 although it was much noiser, and its missiles were shorter ranged and still liquid-fuelled. An element of doubt has to be entered against such a straightforward presentation of the development of the *Yankee* submarine however. There is some evidence to support the notion that the *Yankee* was originally intended to carry a missile dubbed the SS-NX-13 which would be used against naval rather than land targets, but which did not in the end materialise.[26] Certainly, as will become apparent later, Soviet concepts of how to employ SSBNs cannot be assumed to be necessarily the same as those of the West.

The *Yankee* submarine, however it was originally intended, eventually turned out to be a somewhat inferior version of the *Polaris*. But with their next two classes of SSBN, the Russians have clearly emerged as pace-setters once more. Towards the end of 1972 the first *Delta* submarine appeared. Displacing some 9,700 tons when surfaced it was much larger than the US Navy's largest SSBN – the *Lafayette* class of *Poseidon* submarine – and its twelve SS-N-8 SLBMs completely outdistanced American equivalents. Now, the Soviet Navy could threaten much of the North American continent without leaving Russian home waters. In this kind of submarine technology, the Soviet Navy has shown itself to be seven or eight years ahead of its American adversary. Since then the even larger *Delta II* and *Delta III* classes have emerged, the latter carrying the slightly bigger SS-N-18 SLBM. The gigantic *Typhoon* submarine of 1980, of some 25,000 tons with 20 still larger SS-NX-20 SLBMs, took this process one extraordinary step forward, confirming thereby the Soviet Navy's penchant for bold innovation.

But although the Russians were ahead in this particular field, they were behind in other quite related ones. Their SLBMs are generally said to be less sophisticated and less accurate: the SS-N-18 SLBM, for instance, was the Soviet Navy's first SLBM with independently targetable re-entry vehicles (MIRVs) and was deployed some seven years later than American equivalents. Soviet SSBNs are also thought to be much noisier than their Western counterparts. In terms of simple totals, the United States had 36 modern SSBNs (deploying 576 SLBMs, 496 of them MIRVed) in mid-1981 compared to the 62 of the Soviet Navy (backed up by a further 22 or so older types of ballistic missile firing submarines) which together carried some 989 mainly unMIRVed SLBMs. But such straightforward comparisons are almost meaningless. It is in fact extremely difficult to decide on the relative effectiveness of each side's SSBN force because there are so many variables in the maritime equation and, in any case, because such forces have to be seen not as self-contained units but as components of a national nuclear deterrent system which includes aircraft, land-based missiles and various kinds of defences as well. It is certainly true however that developments at sea have helped produce an overall strategic balance between the superpowers which is now completely different from that which obtained twenty years before. In the early 1960s, the United States was able to inflict four or five times the amount of death and destruction on the Soviet Union than it need expect in return. Over the past two decades, however, the Russians have devoted enormous effort to the task of redressing this balance. As a result, while the United States' capacity to inflict pain has remained relatively constant, it has been matched, or possibly even surpassed, by the equivalent capacity of the Soviet Union.[27] Because of the tremendous growth in its firepower and in its relative invulnerability to attack, the Soviet Navy's SSBN force has played a particularly important role in this process.

One final point needs to be made about the development of this kind of submarine in the Soviet Union and that is that it should not be seen as simply reactive to American initiatives, the similarity of *Yankee* to *Polaris* notwithstanding. The Soviet Union has not merely copied Western technology; on the contrary it has often been remarkably innovative. And nor should the Soviet Navy's concept of operations for their SSBN force be seen as necessarily the same as the West's. In the development and use of the SSBN, the Soviet Union has been marching essentially to the sound of its own drum.

CRUISE MISSILE AND TORPEDO ATTACK SUBMARINES

The Soviet Navy was at its most innovative when it developed various classes of submarine capable of firing cruise missiles. Currently the Soviet Navy has about 69 such submarines. It is generally agreed that these were intended to play a leading part in the attack of Western carrier task groups. The Russians began their programme with three not very successful conversions of the *Whiskey* diesel-powered torpedo attack submarine (known as *Whiskey Single* and *Twin-Cylinder* and *Whiskey Long-Bin* submarines) followed up by the *Juliett* class of 1961.

All these were diesel-powered submarines but the Soviet Navy was quick to realise the advantages of nuclear propulsion. Nuclear submarines can submerge for weeks at a time and are less vulnerable to ASW as they do not need to approach the surface to recharge batteries. They can travel farther and faster, carry more weapons and sensors and are better suited for attacking high-speed surface targets like carrier task groups. Accordingly, the Soviet Navy developed the *Echo I* (1960) and *Echo II* (1962) classes of nuclear propelled cruise missile submarine in parallel with their diesel *Whiskeys* and *Julietts*.

These submarines were all armed with SS-N-3 *Shaddock* cruise missiles, a missile of considerable range (above 150 nautical miles) but which needed terminal guidance when approaching the target.

The SS-N-7 *Siren* became operational about 1969; it can be launched from a submerged position and is very fast. Although its range is only 35 nautical miles, it is in fact a more potent threat to surface ships than the *Shaddock*.

The SS-N-7 was first deployed on the new *Charlie* class of nuclear-powered submarine of 1968. The steady increase in sophistication of Soviet cruise missile submarines has recently been exemplified by the appearance of a modified *Charlie II* and the new *Papa* and *Oscar* submarine classes. The *Papa* is a development of the *Charlie*, a nuclear-powered submarine which seems now to be an isolated prototype. The *Oscar* of 1980 is another extraordinary Soviet innovation; at 15,000 tons (surfaced) it is extremely large and is thought capable of launching 24 long-range anti-ship cruise missiles of the SS-NX-19 type carried by the *Kirov* battlecruiser. It is fast, and has a double-hull construction that would withstand conventional torpedoes.

The evolution of Soviet torpedo attack submarines is even more complex and more ambiguous than that of their cruise missile submarines. The shape of their diesel-powered torpedo submarine programme is represented in Figure 3. The function of these diesel submarines is enigmatic. In the early days, it was generally assumed that this large force of torpedo attack submarines was designed to attack Western shipping rather as German U-boats had done in the Second World War. Indeed the *Whiskey* class of 1950 and even more of the *Zulu* of 1952 were heavily influenced by the design of the German type XXI, a large sophisticated submarine intended for the battle of the Atlantic. But if this was really the Soviet intention, sceptics have asked, would they not have built more *Zulus* and fewer *Whiskeys*, bearing in mind the particular value of the former for such a campaign? Soviet diesel torpedo submarine policy can be interpreted on the contrary, as a means of protecting the Soviet Union from sea-borne assault. In this conception, *Zulus* would be farthest out, opening the attack on Western task forces as they steamed towards Russia's coastal approaches; *Whiskeys* would then take over as the enemy got nearer; finally, *Quebecs* would mop up any forces that had struggled through that far. For evidence, this school points to the relatively low endurance of the *Whiskeys* and argues that the 100 mm gun they originally carried would have been used against soft-skinned amphibious ships, rather than merchantmen.[28] On the other hand, the German type IXC had a 105 mm gun too and found it very useful in its attack on commerce. In

1. The *Krivak* is now designated SKR by the Soviet Navy, a combatant for local waters. But as this photograph of one in the Indian Ocean shows, it is a modern and powerful warship perfectly capable of deep-water operation. (USN photo)

2. The *Nanuchka III* is another well-armed local water warship. It is armed with two triple launchers for the SS–N–9 SSM, one of which is clearly visible in this photograph. Just forward of this can be seen the circular cover of the ship's SA–N–4 SAM. Reportedly, the *Nanuchka* is a poor sea boat with unreliable engines. (RAF photo)

3. The *Kashin* class of destroyer was the Soviet Navy's first gas turbine driven warship. The modified version shown here carries extra ASW weaponry and a helicopter pad at the stern. (RAF photo)

4. With the sheer uninterrupted line of the hull, stubby raked funnels and cutaway prow, the old *Kotlin* class of destroyer is very reminiscent of German destroyers of the Second World War. This modernised version has been converted to carry SAMs aft. (RAF photo)

5. The new large (7–8,000 tons) guided missile destroyer *Sovremenny* is primarily designed for anti-surface warfare. It has two twin 130 mm guns and anti-ship cruise missiles. This is an early photograph taken in the Baltic while the ship was on sea trials before its major weapons were fitted. (RN photo)

6. A later photograph of the ship, complete with weapons and sensors. This class is now in series production. The Soviet Navy changes the numbers painted on its ships much more readily than do its Western counterparts. (RN photo)

7. Another new class of major surface warship is the *Udaloy*, which first appeared in November 1980. This class is mainly oriented towards anti-submarine warfare. (RN photo)

8. The *Udaloy* carries two 100 mm guns (for general-purpose surface work) and eight ASW missiles in two quadruple launchers. (RN photo)

9. The *Sverdlov* class of cruiser appeared in the 1950s. It was a gun-cruiser of the traditional type. Subsequently some ships of this class have been modified to serve as command cruisers or training ships. (RAF photo)

10. The *Kynda* class of guided missile cruiser carries four Shaddock SSMs forward and four aft. Introduced to the fleet in the early 1960s, the *Kyndas* were a bold attempt to counter US superiority in strike carriers by technological outflanking. (USN photo)

11. Based on the *Kynda* class but with a better mix of weapons, the four strong *Kresta I* class appeared in the late 1960s. The huge pyramidical enclosed mast contains the ship's funnel and carries a profusion of radar and electronic warfare sensors. A *Hormone A* helicopter is carried in the hangar aft. (RAF photo)

12. A versatile ship whose appearance is dominated by the large funnel needed for its gas turbine engines, the *Kara* class of cruiser is extremely well equipped in weapons and sensors. Starting at the prow, the ship carries BMU 2500 A ASW rocket launchers, SA-N-3 SAMs, two quadruple launchers for the SS-N-14 SSM, two 76 mm guns, SA-N-4 SAMs, Gatling-type guns for air defence, quintuple banks of torpedo tubes, another set of SA-N-3 SAMs, more rocket launchers and a *Hormone A* helicopter. The Soviet Navy invariably manages to pack more weapons into its ships than do its Western counterparts. (RAF photo)

13. The battle cruiser *Kirov* is an impressive recent addition to the Soviet battlefleet. Exceptionally well equipped for all types of naval warfare, *Kirov* carries twenty SS-N-19 missiles in silos forward of the superstructure and three to five helicopters in a hangar below the flight deck aft. Its nuclear propulsion system much enhances range and endurance. Excluding aircraft carriers, *Kirov* is the world's most powerful surface warship. (RN photo)

14. This close-up of the forward part of the *Kirov*'s superstructure shows some of the hatches of the twenty silos for the ship's long-range cruise missile and, at bottom, one of its eight Gatling-type cannon (looking something like a Dalek). The two circular bins with blast deflector shields behind them hold some of *Kirov*'s SA-N-4 SAMs. The superstructure is covered with a wide variety of sensors and fire control systems. (RN photo)

15. Entering service in 1967–8, the two helicopter carriers of the *Moskva* class were the Soviet Navy's first real attempt at providing itself with organic air support. The ship carries about sixteen *Hormone A* helicopters. In the background is the assault ship *HMS Intrepid*. (RN photo)

16. Four of the *Moskva's Hormone A* helicopters are shown in this photograph. These aircraft are for use against submarines. For defence against air attack, *Moskva* relies on her SA-N-3 SAMs, two banks of which can be seen forward of the superstructure, together with their blast-deflectors. (RAF photo)

17. The Soviet Navy's next step forward was the *Kiev* class of aircraft carrier. Here the new *Kiev* is seen off the coast of Scotland in August 1976, closely shadowed by the frigate *HMS Danae*. (RN photo)

18. This photograph of the second-in-class *Minsk* clearly shows the ship's layout. The flight deck is about 180 m long and is inclined 4.5° to port of the centreline axis of the ship. (RAF photo)

19. Until recently, Soviet replenishment at sea was relatively primitive. But the advent of sophisticated ships like the *Boris Chilikin* (on the right) and a general improvement in efficiency increasingly allows ships like the carrier *Kiev* (on the left) to be refuelled from the side, Western style, rather than by the slower astern method. (RN photo)

20. A modified *Golf* submarine of the sort now deployed in the Baltic. Its SS-N-8 missiles threaten military and civilian targets throughout Western Europe. The way in which *Golf* submarines have been adapted to this new role illustrates the Soviet reluctance to scrap aging equipment (RN photo)

21. The *Whiskey Twin Cylinder* submarine of the 1950s, apparently photographed here for propaganda purposes in unlikely conjunction with the test firing of a ballistic missile, was an early Soviet attempt to take rockets to sea. (UPI photo)

22. The *Yankee* class of SSBN, which became operational in 1968, was the Soviet Navy's first ballistic missile firing submarine of modern design. The *Yankee* carries 16 missile tubes immediately to the rear of the conning tower; its SS-N-6 missiles have ranges of up to 1,600 nautical miles. The *Yankees* are now being converted into attack submarines. (RAF photo)

23. The *Delta III* submarine is the latest variant of an advanced form of SSBN which was deployed years before its American equivalent. Fired from Soviet coastal waters, its SS-N-18 SLBMS can easily reach the United States. (RAF photo)

24. The *Whiskey* torpedo-firing submarine was produced in huge numbers during the 1950s, probably mainly for defensive operations in waters local to the Soviet Union. (RAF photo)

25. The much smaller class of long-range *Zulu* torpedo-firing submarines was probably intended for oceanic operations against Western shipping. (RAF photo)

26. The *Charlie* class of submarine is an effective nuclear-powered cruise missile firing submarine which first appeared in 1968. (RN photo)

27. The *Victor* class is a nuclear propelled torpedo-firing submarine which became operational in 1967. A follow-on to the *November* class, it is one of the fastest submarines in the world. It is also very noisy. (RN photo)

28. The *Alpha* hunter–killer torpedo-firing submarine. With a revolutionary hull made from titanium alloys, this submarine can operate at enormous depth and must be considered a serious threat to Western ships and submarines. The first prototype has been scrapped but the class is now in slow series production. (RN photo)

29. The Soviet *Kamov Ka-25* helicopter known in the West as the *Hormone A*. It has a second contra-rotating rotor instead of the more normal tail rotor. The *Hormone A* is used against submarines; the *Hormone B*'s role is to help SSMs find their targets. (USN photo)

30. The *Forger* aircraft, ten or so of which are normally carried by the *Kiev* class carriers, is the Soviet Navy's only other form of organic air support. These are clumsy aircraft, decidedly inferior to the British *Sea Harrier*. They can only take off vertically, a procedure which wastes fuel and limits endurance. An improved version of this aircraft is apparently under development. (RAF photo)

31. The *Tu-95 Bear* has four turbo-prop engines with contra-rotating propellers. *Bear Ds* are used for maritime surveillance, reconnaissance and target information purposes. Fitted with a refuelling probe, this aircraft can fly 8,000 miles without using it. The Soviet Navy also has a small number of *Bear F* aircraft for ASW purposes. (RAF photo)

32. The Soviet Navy's celebrated *Backfire Tu-26* bomber, a long-range swing-wing aircraft which can cover much of the Atlantic from its bases in the Soviet Union. (RN photo)

33. With the arrival of the *Ivan Rogov* class of amphibious warfare ship, the Soviet Navy's amphibious reach was considerably extended in the late 1970s. The *Ivan Rogov* has helicopter flight decks fore and aft and a dock in the stern which can accommodate three air cushion vehicles. It can carry about 500 troops with all their equipment – including over 20 tanks. An astern refuelling operation can be seen in the background. (RN photo)

34. One of the *Ropucha* class of 3400 ton tank landing ships built for the Soviet Navy in Polish shipyards. Doors at bow and stern allow roll-on roll-off operation. (RN photo)

35. Soviet Naval Infantry in action. Company Commander First Lt Evgeni Samoilov leading his Red Banner Baltic Fleet Unit in an attack. They are equipped with AK 47 assault rifles and RPG-7 anti-tank rocket launchers. In the background are three amphibious armoured personnel carriers. (Tass photo)

36. The Soviet Naval Infantry has been equipped for many years with the *PT-76* amphibious light tank shown here. (Tass photo)

37. The *Primorye* class of intelligence collectors are extensively modified factory trawlers. The large box-like structures above and to the rear of the bridge are crammed with electronic monitoring equipment of various kinds. (RAF photo)

38. The *Reduktor* is one of the *Ocean* class of small intelligence collectors. This battered looking vessel was photographed in 1978 anchored off the Portland naval exercise area. In the background, the fishery protection vessel *HMS Wakeful* is seen watching the watchers. (RN photo)

39. The Soviet Navy puts a considerable stress on intelligence collection. Here the *Teodolit* (another *Ocean* class intelligence collector) accompanies the frigate *HMS Juno* passing through the Northern approaches in early 1979. (RN photo)

40. Admiral Gorshkov and other senior Soviet Naval officers on a vis
Sweden in 1981. (RN photo)

41. Petty Officer First Class Vasil Alekseev and some of his men f
the Soviet Baltic Fleet. Though intensely loyal, Soviet sailors ar

Signalmen of the *Sverdlov* Cruiser *Alexander Suvorov* then in the Pacific
et. (Tass photo)

ov class cruiser the *October · Revolution*, then flagship of
t to be over specialised and too narrowly trained. (Tass photo)

43. The Soviet Union's conception of sea power includes a thorough appreciation of the value of an extensive merchant and fishing fleet. Being modest in size and for general purpose rather than specialised trading, the merchant ship *Krasnokamsk* is typical of the Soviet merchant fleet. This ship was built in Finland. (RAF photo)

44. The seine-net fishing boat *Aterina*, part of one of the largest fishing fleets in the world. (Skyfotos)

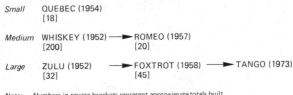

Note: Numbers in square brackets represent approximate totals built.

FIGURE 3   *Soviet diesel torpedo attack submarines*

short, the design characteristics of these early submarines do not lend themselves to easy verdicts as to their ultimate purpose.

The more recent *Tango* class, first seen at the Sebastopol Naval Review in 1973 is particularly interesting. These sophisticated submarines, like their nuclear-powered counterparts, have in the SS-N-15 a long-range tactical nuclear ASW capability and their main targets are thought to be Western submarines. Significantly they are of a highly advanced diesel-propulsion design, far superior to most of their Western counterparts. Despite the early drive for nuclear propulsion, the Soviet Navy has by no means neglected the diesel submarine, nor been blind to its advantages of cheapness, quietness and ability to operate in shallow waters. It shows the Russian tendency to back as many horses in the race as they can.

The *November* class of 1959 was their first nuclear propelled attack submarine (SSN). It was followed by the *Victor* (in three versions of 1968, 1973 and 1978) and the mysterious *Alpha* class of 1972, and *Yankees* released from their strategic task by the appearance of *Deltas* and *Typhoons*. In their SSN programme, the Russians have demonstrated once more their capacity for innovative design. The hull shape of the *November* was quite revolutionary, in no way echoing Western expertise. The *Alpha*'s titanium hull is equally novel: it defeats Western magnetic sensors and allows the submarine to operate at great depths, beyond the range for the moment at least of many Western ASW weapons. Soviet SSNs are all very fast, but noisy too. The *Alpha*, for instance, is reported to be almost capable of an amazing 50 knots underwater; on the other hand, it is so noisy that monitoring stations in Bermuda heard it thrashing about in the Norwegian sea on its operational debut.[29]

The noisiness of Soviet SSNs would be a great liability in the stealthy business of ASW but could possibly be minimised by operational practices of various kinds. Certainly their weaponry seems to be aimed principally at Western submarines, but they could doubtless be fitted for operations against Western maritime communications or for high-value surface targets like US Navy carrier task forces.

THE SOVIET NAVAL AIR FORCE

The Soviet Naval Air Force (Aviatsiya Voenno Morskaya Flot – AVMF) originated in the surprisingly impressive naval air service of the Tsarist Navy of the First World War. Naval aviators suffered badly during the Revolution and the interwar period however and entered the Second World War with obsolete equipment and poor tactical notions. Nevertheless, by 1945, the AVMF had become a large and reasonably effective force with some proficiency in the support of amphibious operations and in the attack and protection of shipping. It also had an important defensive role in the central land–air war and in fact continued to do so until 1956 when its large fighter and fighter-bomber forces were turned over to *PVO-Strany*, the Soviet National Air Defence Force. Only from that time on were the AVMF's responsibilities exclusively maritime. Since then, it has become one of the largest air forces in the world, with an increasingly global reach. It comprises some 55,000 men and 1,440 aircraft directly subordinate to the Soviet Navy and divided between the four fleet areas.

The land-based AVMF is supplemented to a certain extent by aircraft from some of the Soviet Union's several other air forces, especially the bombers of Long Range Aviation. When these aircraft are used for maritime purposes, they evidently come under the operational control of the Navy. At sea, the land-based component of the AVMF is supported by organic naval air power in the shape of the Soviet Navy's burgeoning force of ship-based VSTOL aircraft and helicopters.

Since 1967, the AVMF has also benefited from the Soviet Union's very considerable satellite programme. In 1973 alone the Soviet Union put up 75 satellites, four of them within a crucial twelve-day period during the Yom Kippur War – an impressive performance when compared to the 26 military satellites put up by the United States in that year.[30] The Russians use electronic intelligence, radar and photographic satellites and the data they produce s carefully integrated with that of the reconnaissance aircraft of the AVMF. Over the past decade they have also shown some profi-ciency in intercepting satellites and it is widely believed that they are developing an anti-satellite capacity. It is impossible to say how all his will affect the future conduct of maritime operations but an ob-scure struggle for satellite superiority will certainly be an important eature of war at sea, and this point has not escaped the attention of he Soviet Navy.

In addition to a variety of ancillary duties, the AVMF has three main operational functions. It has about 180 aircraft for reconnais-sance and maritime surveillance – mainly Tu-16 *Badgers*, Tu-95 *Bear Ds* and Tu-22 *Blinders*, supplemented by other shorter-range aircraft for coastal patrol and for the coverage of the Mediterranean and the closer European waters. The extent of this oceanic coverage has increased considerably over the past two decades and is now impressive. Information about Western naval activity gained by air-craft is carefully integrated with that derived by the Soviet Navy's 58 strong fleet of intelligence-gathering ships or AGIs. These are usually based on hulls originally designed for the fishing industry and range from the six ships of the 3,400 ton *Primorye* class to smaller vessels of more trawler-like appearance. They watch NATO exercises and monitor activity at Western SSBN bases and sea firing ranges. The Russians doubtless also have underwater surveillance systems analogous to the US Navy's SOSUS for the detection of submarines. Finally, as already noted, this extensive surveillance effort is reinforced by the use of satellites. During the exercise *Vesna–75*, for instance, radar satellites were used to monitor the progress of a simulated convoy in the Bay of Biscay.

In the same exercise, the anti-shipping function of the AVMF was given a particular stress. The main aircraft used for this purpose are the 350 or so Tu-16 *Badgers* of the C and G marks and the now celebrated long-range Tu-26 *Backfire B* bomber, which really does seem to be the tactical system the Russians claimed it to be all the way along. Their chief air-to-surface missiles are:

AS-2	*Kipper*	200 km	1961
AS-3	*Kangaroo*	600 km	1961
AS-4	*Kitchen*	300 km	1961
AS-5	*Kelt*	200 km	1968
AS-6	*Kingfish*	250 km	1977

For a long while, the AVMF's maritime bombers were arguably the

Soviet Navy's principal strike force against surface targets and Gorshkov's faith in them as a principal maritime weapon has survived advances in SSM and SAM technology. AVMF bombers could be deployed either against surface warships or against Atlantic merchant and reinforcement shipping. Either way, the US Navy recognises them to be a profound threat. According to Admiral Holloway,

> Our deployed fleets must have the defensive strength to defend themselves against attacks of land-based air, because we are seeing more and more the development of long-range aircraft with anti-ship missiles as a threat which can develop rapidly and can extend to almost any spot on the globe.[31]

The AVMF's last major role is in the war against the submarine for which its main aircraft are the Il-38 *May*, the Tu-95 *Bear F*, the *Hormone A* and *Helix* helicopters and VSTOL aircraft embarked on ships, the BE-12 *Mail* flying-boats and *Haze* large shore-based helicopters. Although Gorshkov claimed that the importance of this task is 'sharply rising', he was forced to admit that the detection of submarines 'presents no small difficulties',[32] despite constant improvement in equipment.

This is neither the only nor the main weakness of the AVMF however. That must surely be the lack of naval fighters apart from the limited *Forger* capability of the *Kiev* class and the forty *Fitter* aircraft deployed primarily for surface attack duties in the Baltic. This gap in the armoury means that AVMF aircraft must carry out their missions without escort and Soviet Navy ships theirs without aircover. This is only partially compensated for by the long range of Soviet ASMs and the generous provision of SAMs in most warships. Future carrier construction policy may well be expected to remedy this fault. Nor, with the possible exception of the *Backfire*, is there any reason to suppose that Soviet naval aircraft are any better than those of the West. But even with these qualifications, it is hard to disagree with Gorshkov's claim that '[Soviet] naval aviation has in fact become oceanic; it has been converted into a most important means of armed struggle at sea'.[33]

THE SOVIET NAVY'S AMPHIBIOUS CAPACITY

The Russians' ability to project military ashore really began in 1705 when Peter the Great transferred two regiments of foot soldiers to his newly created Baltic Fleet. Since then their capacity for amphibious assault has waxed and waned considerably. Relatively neglected in the First World War, it was much developed in the Second. Initially, Soviet amphibious operations against the Germans were largely improvised as far as ships, equipment and operating techniques were concerned and were short-range tactical enterprises, frequently undertaken, but modest in scope. By the end of the war, however, the scale and sophistication of such assaults had much improved; a total of 330,000 men had been put ashore in hundreds of landings and the naval infantry had increased to a total of about half a million men. After the war the Soviet Navy's amphibious capacity gradually declined and the Soviet Naval Infantry force itself seems to have been effectively de-activated in the 1950s, at a time when conventional forces in general, and the Soviet Navy in particular, fell temporarily from governmental favour. It was set up again in the summer of 1964, possibly in recognition of the value the US Navy derived from its much larger Marine force. For the rest of the decade ship and manpower totals were vigorously expanded; since then the effort seems to have levelled out.

In the early part of the Second World War, the Soviet Navy had very little in the way of shipping especially designed for amphibious assault; troops had frequently to be carried across the water lying cold and miserable on the open decks of motor torpedo boats. 'The lack of specialised landing ships,' wrote Admiral Stalbo, 'often led to considerable losses of landing forces and made weather conditions of special significance.'[34] The Soviet Navy slowly developed a force of suitable ships during the war but their subsequent renewal and development were much delayed, according to Admiral Gorshkov, by the view that other kinds of surface warships were more important.[35] However, the Polish-built 780–1,000 ton *Polnochny* class of landing ship began to arrive in 1965, supplemented by the much larger *Alligator* in 1966. The latter displaces some 4,000 tons and can carry several hundred naval infantry, with up to 25 tanks or armoured personnel on its deck. The similar *Ropucha* class arrived in 1975 and four years later the much larger *Ivan Rogov*, a sophisticated ship which can carry about 550 troops with all their vehicles and equipment, amphibious hovercraft and helicopters. The sea-lift capacity of this ship, and its long range, make it a considerable step forward for the Soviet Navy. Currently there are about 78 of these four classes of landing ship whose total lift capacity would be considerably enhanced by merchant ships used as transports for perhaps up to ten regular army divisions. These amphibious warfare ships

and transports are supported by the world's largest force of military
hovercraft (particularly *Gus*, *Lebed* and *Aist* classes) and, in exer
cises, by the minor combatants of the offshore defence force.

The 12,000 men of the Soviet Naval Infantry are regarded a
something of an elite. They wear a distinctive blue-black uniform
with the blue striped undershirt of the Soviet sailor. Their officers
have army ranks but the men are called 'Seamen'. As a force, they
are quite heavily mechanised, being equipped with armoured per
sonnel carriers, amphibious tanks and rocket launchers. Although
they have expertise in river crossings and in the defence of naval
bases, their main task is to act as an initial assault force. They are
plainly intended to 'hit the beaches' first, opening the way for a
second wave of Army divisions arriving later. To a certain extent
therefore, the relatively small size of the Soviet Naval Infantry is a
misleading indicator of the Soviet Union's capacity for amphibious
assault.

Even so, the Soviet Union in no way approaches the United
States in its ability to project this kind of power ashore. Compared
to the 190,000 strong US Marine Corps, the Soviet Naval Infantry
force is quite tiny; it has few long-range ships, and virtually no
organic air support. As yet, the Soviet Navy does not have a
Western-style intervention force. Instead, the main effort is on the
development of a capability for local amphibious operations in close
support of the ground forces and, very possibly, for the seizure of
fleet exits from the Baltic and Black Seas and elsewhere. As we
shall see later, Soviet amphibious forces have certain peacetime
functions as well.

FLEET DISTRIBUTION AND OCEAN ACCESS

A glance at the map (see Figure 4) shows that geography has been
unkind to the Soviet Union as far as her maritime aspirations are
concerned. She has the longest coastline in the world but it is so
configured that the Russians have to maintain what is in effect four
separate and self-contained fleets; in Mahan's terminology, there
fore, the Soviet Union cannot concentrate her naval force with ease
Mutual support between these four distinct fleet areas, in fact
takes up a good deal of the Soviet Navy's maritime effort. Transfer
ring ships from one area to another is a complicated business requir
ing long sea voyages, the use of inland waterways or the exploitation

Fleet Headquarters
A. Severodvinsk (Northern Fleet)
B. Kaliningrad (Baltic Area Fleet)
C. Sevastopol (Black Sea Fleet)
D. Vladivostok (Pacific Ocean Fleet)

Main Soviet Fleet Choke Points
1. Barents Strait
2. Greenland–Iceland–United Kingdom Gap
3. Danish Straits
4. Strait of Gibralta
5. Turkish Straits
6. Suez Canal
7. Tsushima (Korea) Strait
8. LaPerouse Strait

FIGURE 4   *Soviet naval fleet areas and ocean access points*

Source: Naval War College Review, September 1980.

of the very difficult North Siberian route. The requirement to make each fleet area as self-sufficient as possible aggravates the Navy's resources problem since it necessarily leads to duplication problems in the naval supply system, for instance.

It is difficult to give precise indications of the way in which Soviet naval assets are distributed between the four fleet areas because this is particularly subject to change and competing interpretation. Broadly, the Northern Fleet has by far the largest number of ballistic missile firing and attack submarines, followed by the Pacific Fleet with the Baltic and Black Sea Fleets a long way behind. The distribution of major surface combatants is more equal. The Black Sea Fleet supports the Soviet Mediterranean Squadron and generally has rather more than a third of the total, with the remainder being distributed evenly around the other fleet areas. The Baltic Fleet generally has the fewest aircraft in total of the four, but the highest number of strike aircraft since the other three have more ASW, transport and training aircraft. All four fleets are well endowed in minor combatants and naval auxiliaries. In short, they are all powerful in their own way, well adapted to their particular climatic and geographic circumstances and as self-sufficient as they can be made.

The enormous programme of industrial and military investment in the Northern Fleet Area and the large number of ships, submarines and aircraft deployed there make it arguably the most important of the four. The Kola Peninsular, in particular, now has a population of over 800,000 (compared to about 15,000 in 1920) and a well-developed industrial complex which includes support facilities for the merchant and fishing fleets as well as for the Navy. Severodvinsk on the White Sea is the headquarters of the Northern Fleet and also has a huge submarine construction yard. Altogether the Northern Fleet Area is one of the biggest concentrations of military power in the world.

The Soviet Pacific Fleet is based at Vladivostok but makes extensive use of Sovietskaya Gavan, Magadan, and Petropavlovsk on the Kamchatka peninsular. The Pacific Fleet's SSBN force operates out of the latter port, while most of the larger warships are based at Vladivostok, Sovietskaya Gavan and the newer port of Korsakov on the southern end of the island of Sakhalin. Altogether between one-half and one-third of the ships and submarines of the Soviet Navy are to be found in its Pacific Fleet, a proportion which has tended to rise in recent years.[36]

The other two main fleet areas, in the Baltic and Black Seas, are well endowed in ports and, especially, naval construction yards. But both suffer acutely from the second of the two major geographic disadvantages confronting the Soviet Navy, namely difficult access to the high seas. To get into the Mediterranean the Black Sea Fleet has to transit the NATO-controlled Dardanelles and from there it has to leave through either the Suez Canal or the Straits of Gibraltar. Even if these three straits were not in hostile hands (as they now all are) they would still be very vulnerable to interdiction. The same goes for the Baltic Fleet whose initial transit needs to be through the Danish Straits and then either south through the English Channel or north between Scotland and Norway.

The Pacific Fleet can only reach the open oceans by the again rather easily blockaded Tsushima and La Perouse Straits. Although Soviet submarines can make use of the icebound waters of the north and the Northern Fleet has a certain room for manoeuvre in the Arctic and its marginal seas, access to the Atlantic requires penetration of the Barents Strait between Norway and Spitzbergen and then the Greenland–Iceland–United Kingdom (GIUK) Gap. There is also the problem of the weather. The Baltic Fleet suffers badly from this with its ports icebound through much of the year. The Pacific Fleet can only keep going through the winter by dint of a considerable ice-breaking effort at Vladivostok and Petropavlovsk. Even then it has frequently to contend with heavy fog and storms. Although, thanks to the peculiar workings of the Gulf Stream, the Northern Fleet bases are open throughout the year, operating conditions are often very bad indeed.

Marine geography of this kind not only constrains naval operations, it also affects policy. The Soviet Union's determination to maintain its access to the oceans has led to difficult relations with Japan, especially over the ownership of the Lower Kurile Islands, to long drawn-out negotiations with Norway (especially over the possible installation of oil rigs and the like in the Barents Strait), to constant dealings with Turkey and to several attempts to set up naval bases in new areas.

Long and attentive periods of courtship of Egypt and Somalia eventually led to the Soviet Navy's establishing significant base facilities at Alexandria and Berbera respectively. The Russians were able to use both places for supply and fleet repair purposes and opened up airfields and communications facilities nearby. These major efforts were supplemented by less ambitious but still important arrangements with other countries such as Syria, India, Ethiopia,

Vietnam (where, ironically, the Russians have been able to use the facilities built by the United States at Cam Ranh Bay) and, reportedly, in Kampuchea. The effect of these arrangements has been to make naval operations in distant waters much easier and partially circumvents the natural hindrances of Russian geography. However relations with the locals have often proved quite tricky and led in the case of Alexandria and Berbera to the eventual closure of facilities with much economic, strategic and political loss to the Soviet Union.[37] It is very apparent from all this that geography puts the Soviet Union at a considerable disadvantage relative to its Western adversaries.

COMMAND AND CONTROL

The command structure of the Soviet Navy has two parallel hierarchies: the professional and the political (see Figure 5). This state of affairs reflects the general way in which power in the Soviet Union is shared between the Party and other groups. The Navy's professional and governmental head is the Defence Minister, currently (1982) Marshal Ustinov, to whom the Navy's Commander-in-Chief is directly responsible. Since the Revolution, this has been the general pattern apart from the three distinct periods in which the Navy had a separate Ministry (most recently between 1951–3). Admiral of the Fleet of the Soviet Union, to give him his full title, Sergei Gorshkov has been Commander-in-Chief of the Navy since 1955, an astonishingly long period of command which affords much continuity in direction. The Commander-in-Chief is the spokesman for and representative of the Navy within the system, a position now analagous to the British First Sea Lord since the recent abolition of the post of Minister for the Navy. In the United States the equivalent responsibility is shared between the Chief of Naval Operations and the Secretary of the Navy. The institutional significance of his post, and his long period of tenure, makes the extent to which Admiral Gorshkov himself was the architect of the Soviet Navy very apparent.

Below the Commander-in-Chief comes his first deputy. He has a particular responsibility for the Soviet Navy's Administrations, namely Personnel, Logistics, Intelligence, Combat Training, the Medical Services, the Naval Infantry, AVMF, Coastal Defence and Coastal Air Defence. Then comes the Chief of the Main Naval Staff who is responsible for operations and training. Below the main staff,

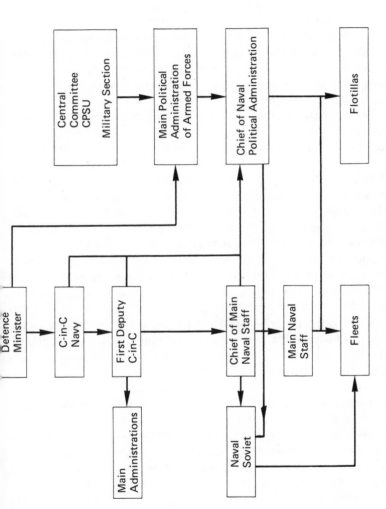

FIGURE 5   *Command structure of the Soviet Navy*

are the four fleets (Northern, Baltic, Black Sea and Pacific) and the flotillas (on the Danube, the Dnieper, the Amur and the Caspian Sea). By the word 'fleet' is understood naval forces, an independent air formation, land elements, coastal and base defences (including coastal artillery, and infantry) and a hydrographic service.

The Naval Soviet is an interesting survival of the Tsarist Navy's Naval War Council and is a higher consultative body without powers of decision or command. It has advisory and admonitory functions, reviewing morale and the state of combat training. It is also significant for being the place where the naval professional and political leadership come together.

The political administration has its own distinct hierarchy and is ultimately responsible to the Military Section of the Central Committee of the Communist Party of the Soviet Union. As far as the Navy is concerned, its main representative is the Chief of the Naval Political Administration (who also has his own first deputy and deputy head). Nowadays, he is responsible for discipline, general conditions of service and has a significant welfare, training and combat readiness role. He is the chief of the *Zampolits* discussed later. The fact that he now owes allegiance to the Commander-in-Chief of the Navy, his first deputy and the Chief of the Main Naval Staff indicates the extent to which the old commissar role has dwindled as a result of the general acceptance of the principle of 'one-man command'. But for all that, the Chief of the Naval Political Administration can still report upwards independently and so remains a force to be reckoned with. Like all his subordinates he has naval rank and wears a uniform. Moreover Admiral V. M. Grishanov's tenure of this post has been almost as long as Gorshkov's of his.

According to some authorities, the activities of the commissars partly explain why the Soviet command structure of the Second World War was so rigid and slow to react to the unexpected. 'Even in 1944–5,' wrote Admiral Ruge, 'the larger German ships could count on being able to bombard Russian positions on the coast for four days before they had to expect massive air attacks.'[38] This no longer appears to be the case however. In February 1972, for instance, a lone *Hotel* submarine encountered mechanical trouble in the North Atlantic. Within three days, seven Soviet ships had gathered round and within one week ten more, including rescue tugs, an oiler and a submarine support ship were fast approaching.[39] This was a remarkable instance of the way in which the Soviet system of command and control can react quickly and efficiently to an unexpected situation and can co-ordinate naval activities around the world. The *Vesna* exercise in 1975 also showed the extent to which the activities of the Soviet Navy could be orchestrated from a centralised agency in Moscow, producing, for instance, attacks on different warships in different oceans at exactly the same time. Admiral Gorshkov in fact made it clear that the Soviet Navy needs, and has, a global system of communications which can co-ordinate submarines, aircraft and widely dispersed and highly mobile surface combatants so they can be wielded as a cohesive whole, even from the other side of the world.[40] This fits in with Gorshkov's stress on the importance of winning with the first salvo, as we shall see, but such possibilities of centralised direction may lead to the man on the spot having too little freedom to act as he thinks fit. Like any other Navy, the Soviet Navy has to weigh up the relative advantages of centralised direction and local initiative, and it may not always get this right.

SOVIET NAVAL PERSONNEL

In July 1976, the Minister of Defence told graduating officers: 'However awesome and sophisticated the weapons, the outcome of a battle, operation or war as a whole is, in the final analysis, determined by people.'[41] This is a useful reminder that people matter and that an effective assessment of the Soviet Navy's strengths and weaknesses requires analysis of its personnel. There are about 443,000 officers and men in the Soviet Navy (including the AVMF) spread between the four fleets, three-quarters of them being conscripts.

Although it is plainly dangerous to press notions of national character too far, Soviet sailors do reflect the society from which they come. Russia's historical experience encourages a sense of positive patriotism, a prevalence of what the West would generally regard as old-fashioned military attitudes, a generalised fear of attack and a deep suspicion of foreigners. To a greater or lesser extent the conscript will exhibit these characteristics when he joins and the naval political authorities will encourage and develop them. The conscript will also tend to share in national traits induced by the climate (which, in the countryside, has always led to long periods of indolence interspersed with short periods of desperate industry, a pattern seen in Soviet military activity), by the traditionally autocratic nature of the regime and by its quite low standards in creature comforts (which means that Soviet sailors will put up with poorer living conditions on board than will their Western counterparts, a matter of some benefit to Soviet ship designers). Taken together these social forces tend to produce a conscript who

> will submit readily to military authority, adapt easily to the close and shared living conditions of a barracks or a ship, recognise early his responsibility to the unit, and respond effectively to group motivation and control. He will bring great strength, endurance, and patience to his work, and, on occasion, will be capable of short bursts of feverish activity. On the other hand, the Navy finds that he needs constant motivation, direction, and supervision to overcome his tendency to idleness, his apathy, his plodding approach to work, his reluctance to exercise initiative, and his unwillingness to discipline himself, or to depend on himself. He seems to lack the ability to organise his fellows and his work spontaneously and effectively. For a modern sailor he is technically underdeveloped, crude, and haphazard in his work. Given authority, he is likely to be bureaucratic and to exercise his power arbitrarily and harshly.[42]

To a certain rather generalised extent the conscript will have had some military training at school, and possibly some as well through the activities of DOSAAF (the All Union Volunteer Society for Assistance to the Army, Air Force and Navy). He joins the Navy for a period of three years and will often spend a considerable proportion of that time in the same ship doing the same job. He specialises much more than do his Western counterparts. There is also a very strong tendency for him to 'go by the book', a characteristic sometimes translated as 'exactingness', to such an extent that initiative, innovation and the delegation of authority are positively discouraged. Technically, most Soviet sailors are competent but no more than that; accordingly junior officers in the Soviet Navy will often have to do maintenance jobs that, in the West would be left to senior rates and petty officers.

Discipline is stern, both afloat and ashore and is reinforced by steady programmes of political indoctrination. After a Soviet naval squadron visited East Africa in 1969, for example, *Morskoi Sbornik* claimed: 'The Kenyans were amazed that Soviet sailors, unlike British and American sailors, left not the slightest sign of chaos after their visit. The Soviet sailors were serious and behaved as if they were people of another planet.'

On visits to foreign ports, small groups of five or six sailors are shepherded around by a reliable rating; they have little money to spend and usually speak only Russian. They visit the obvious tourist attractions, buy a bottle of *Coca-Cola* or some other such symbol of Western decadence and generally behave themselves in a scrupulously correct, if rather unproductive fashion. Both ashore and afloat, in fact, Soviet sailors give every indication of being acutely aware that they are regarded as an elite by their countrymen and as ambassadors by everyone else.

All, however, is not sweetness and light in the Soviet Navy. Demographic patterns inside the Soviet Navy mean that relatively more and more non-Europeans, like the Muslims of Central Asia, who often have only the most rudimentary grasp of the Russian language and outlook, will have to be enlisted in the Navy. This seems very likely to lead to ethnic tensions, cultural disruptions and at the very least an increased training and education burden for the naval authorities. The Russian Navy also has a long tradition of mutiny and unrest (the Battleship *Potemkin*, the 1917 Revolution, the Kronstadt Mutiny of 1921) recently exemplified by the apparent rebellion in the destroyer *Storezhevoy* in the Baltic in 1975. Apparently, dissent remains something of a problem in the Soviet Navy. According to General Alexei Yepishev (the head of the Soviet armed forces' political wing) recent recruits to the army and navy 'show elements of political naïveté, pacifism and a carefree attitude when assessing the threat posed by our class enemies'. While there is no reason to doubt that Soviet sailors are proud of their service, reliable and enthusiastic, they have their limits, like sailors everywhere.

Soviet naval officers are a class apart, to an astonishing extent, in an allegedly classless society. The great majority of them are trained, sometimes from as early as seven years old, at the Nakhimov Naval School on the banks of the Neva in Leningrad, hard by the famous cruiser *Aurora*. Generally, they are the sons of Party and government leaders or, more especially, of naval officers. The Nakhimov School produces an exclusive naval officer caste in a way that is distinctly reminiscent of the Tsarist Army's Imperial Cadet Schools.

After this, the officer cadet goes to one of the eleven or so specialist naval academies, the most prestigious of which is the Frunze Naval Academy in Leningrad. Graduating as a commissioned officer some years later, he will then go to his first ship, staying with it for a long time by Western standards – up to six years if it is a major combatant. The Soviet Navy believes in learning on the job. 'Long ocean voyages', said Gorshkov in 1976, 'are the best school for enhancing naval training and special and tactical training of personnel.'[43] Accordingly, while the newly joined young officer may be extremely inexperienced at first (often having no sea-time at all when he joins) he is intensively trained from then on, with intrusive supervision from above, 'socialist criticism' from below and with political officers monitoring his performance from the side. This regime tends to make him cautious, very specialised and reluctant either to change things or to delegate his newly won authority. Thereafter he will progress up the naval hierarchy in the normal way, with periods of further staff training. Throughout his career, however, affiliation to the Communist Party will be an important advantage.

In connection with this, the Soviet Navy is unique in having (alongside the professional hierarchy) a kind of parallel command structure of 'political officers' under the 'Political Directorate of the Navy'. The function of these *Zampolits* is to ensure that the Navy is politically healthy and well motivated. Unlike the political commissars of former times, however, they are subordinated to the operational commander of each unit. As well as being responsible for political indoctrination, they also assume the functions of the chaplain, personnel, welfare and recreation officers of Western navies.

These days the *Zampolits* are often naval officers who have chosen to specialise in political work and gone through the Kiev Higher Naval Political School. Otherwise, they come to the Navy from civilian life, through the Lenin Military Academy in Moscow. Both the switch in emphasis in their function and in their individual origins make them more acceptable to the professional officers than they used to be. But the fact that the *Zampolit* reports on his contemporaries and seniors, and to an extent gets between the officer and his men doubtless still makes him an occasional source of irritation.

It is, and always has been, notoriously difficult to assess the quality of another country's military personnel, and this is particularly true of the Soviet Navy. They clearly have their strengths (good motivation and endurance) and their weaknesses (low levels of initiative and technical competence). Which of their many characteristics proves to be decisive will depend critically on the particular circumstances in which Soviet naval personnel are put to the test.

THE SOVIET MERCHANT MARINE

Like Mahan, the Russians take a very comprehensive view of sea power. 'Maritime transportation, fishing and scientific research on the sea', said Gorshkov, 'are part of the Soviet Union's naval might.'[44] Accordingly, the build-up of Soviet sea power has occurred across the whole spectrum of maritime activity.

From about 1963 the Soviet Union has shown considerable interest in ocean mining, starting with a research programme into the formation and possible extraction of ferromanganese nodules on the sea bed, both on her extensive continental shelf and in the deep ocean. Although she is technologically less advanced than the West, she fully appreciates that about 75 per cent of her extensive continental shelf has good oil and gas prospects and she has apparently initiated a programme of rapid exploration and exploitation.[45] This is generally supported by a very considerable oceanographic effort from the world's largest fleet of marine research vessels. The extent of this effort was made clear as early as the International Geophysical Year of 1957–8, when the Soviet Union successfully completed a larger oceanographic programme than did any other nation.

Marine research has also played an important part in the phenomenal development of the Soviet fishing industry. The reasons for this effort are very clear. First, the Russians have always liked eating fish and catching their own saves foreign exchange; secondly, given the climatic and administrative difficulties of modern Soviet agriculture, it actually requires less effort to produce a pound of fish than a pound of beef, even if that fish comes from the other side of the world. Realising this, the Soviet government deliberately set about creating what is now one of the largest and most modern fishing fleets in the world, comprising some 4,500 vessels (of which 760 or so are large stern, factory or freezer trawlers) totalling in all some 7 million tons. This is the product of a very high level of capital investment at home, much purchasing of foreign-built fishing boats (especially from Finland and the VEB Volkswerft yard in East Germany) and an ambitious programme of marine education and training.

Over the last twenty years the quantity of fish landed has increased enormously and by 1976 the Soviet catch was second only to that of the Japanese. Since then the Russians have suffered through the progressive fencing off of many of their main fishing grounds. Their fishing methods are characteristically collective: Soviet fishing boats operate in vast co-operative flotillas (quite unlike their intensively individualistic Western counterparts) with freezing and processing vessels in close attendance. They tend to suck areas empty rather indiscriminately and are frequently accused of over-fishing. The Russian willingness to fish in distant waters for long periods of time and their reluctance to waste foreign exchange by buying supplies, means they operate with a much larger number of support vessels than do Western fleets. Since assessments of fishing efficiency usually involve dividing the catch by the number and tonnage of the vessels engaged, this makes Soviet productivity look lower than the West's. But this is to miss the point. The Soviet fishing fleet is a selfconsciously *national* fleet which is operated for the benefit of the Soviet Union as a whole and not just for the trawlermen themselves. For this reason the economics of Soviet fishing are different from anyone else's: it makes *national* sense for the trawlermen to take their own supplies with them even though they could buy what they need quite cheaply from the locals. This is equally true of the operations of the Soviet merchant shipping fleet.

The expansion of her mercantile fleet, in fact, has been another of the Soviet Union's most impressive maritime achievements since the war. Russia has no tradition of commercial sea-faring: in 1913, for instance, 85 per cent of her very small merchant fleet was foreign built and only some 15 million tons of cargo was carried. There was little attempt to build up the Soviet merchant fleet during the interwar period and half the existing fleet was sunk during the Second World War, the remaining half being in a very bad state of repair by 1945. In March 1946, however, the Soviet authorities embarked on an ambitious programme to refit ships, improve facilities and build up their cargo-carrying capacity. Construction of new merchant ships really took off in the mid-1950s, however, when yards used for destroyer and cruiser construction were turned over to commercial use. This resulted in spectacular growth, especially from 1962 to 1966. As a result, the Soviet merchant fleet of about 1,700 ships of 21 million deadweight tons is now some five times larger than it was in 1950. In 1979 it carried 226 million tons of cargo, fifteen times the 1913 level.[46]

Although these figures are impressive, their significance should not be exaggerated, as it often is in Western analysis. In January 1980, according to Lloyd's figures, the Soviet fleet represented only some 3 per cent of the total world trading tonnage of 675 million tons deadweight.[47] The increase in Soviet cargo-carrying capacity in fact has simply kept pace with the dramatic increase in the country's general international trade: it has not lessened Soviet dependence on foreign shipping very significantly. Thus in 1979 about 44 per cent of the Soviet Union's trade was still carried in foreign ships. This was not a very significant advance on the equivalent figure of 47 per cent for 1965. The Soviet tanker fleet (one of the most important types of merchant shipping from both the strategic and the economic points of view) has actually shrunk as a proportion of the world's total and Soviet progress in other key areas like automated container ships and roll-on/roll-off (Ro-Ro) ships has been quite modest. The Soviet merchant fleet is not generally considered to be very well balanced, having a disproportionately large number of small, unsophisticated, slow, general-purpose cargo ships most appropriate for short-haul coastal work between Russia's rather underdeveloped ports. The great increase in her commercial construction output should also not disguise the fact that a large proportion of her ships are either entirely foreign built (coming especially from East Germany, Poland, Yugoslavia, Japan and Western Europe) or have important foreign components (particularly engines).

Even with these qualifications, however, the Soviet merchant fleet does represent a threat to Western shipping interests. With aggressive rate-cutting tactics, the Russians have been able to elbow their way into some of the more lucrative routes, especially in the United States–Europe–Australia–Japan trades. A report by the General Council of British Shipping in 1976 showed that Soviet freight rates were then some 25 per cent below the agreed conference rate on North America routes, 30 per cent below the North America–South Africa routes, and on some Far Eastern routes initial Soviet undercutting was by a factor of no less than 60 per cent.[48] It is also true, though, that once the Russians have effected their entry into a conference system they tend to behave thereafter like anyone else.

Their strong trading position mainly comes from the fact that their merchant fleet is based in a different type of economic system and, like their fishing fleet, derives a lot of advantages from this. Soviet shippers have large reserves of finance to fall back on, have low labour costs and are not as badly hit by insurance and capital depreciation as their Western counterparts. Although the extent to which their various activities are integrated into some kind of maritime master-plan should not be exaggerated, Soviet shippers plainly benefit from the fact that they are part of a centralised economy which can discriminate in their favour in the national interest, can support uncommercial tactics and which encourages them to act more collectively than their highly individualistic and mutually competitive Western rivals. The success of the Soviet Union's shipping policy, in fact, is quite as much a function of particular Western weaknesses as it is of her own strength and determination. Moreover the more she gets involved in the merchant shipping business, the more she herself will become vulnerable to pressure. Recently, the Soviet merchant shipping industry was very badly affected, for example, by the US East Coast Longshoremen's boycott of its ships in the wake of the Soviet invasion of Afghanistan.

The principal reasons for the Soviet Union's very evident desire to expand her merchant shipping are economic. By carrying more of her own trade she saves foreign exchange, and by carrying other peoples' she earns it: this improves her balance of trade position and better enables her to import the Western technology she needs to make economic progress.[49] Imperatives of this kind occasionally override the commercial interests of shippers. This explains why the Soviet merchant marine sometimes does things which do not make economic sense in Western terms – a phenomenon which leads some observers to underestimate the importance of the Soviet Union's economic motivation relative to other political and strategic considerations. The Soviet Union does, of course, have non-economic reasons to develop its large merchant marine, but the dominance of these in Soviet concerns should not be exaggerated.

Even so, the merchant fleet is clearly a very useful supplement to the logistics fleet operated by the Soviet Navy itself and is a vital source of supply, replenishment and military sea-lift. In 1976, for example, about 60 per cent of fleet oiling was done from merchant ships.[50] This reliance partly derives from the deficiencies of the Navy's formal logistics fleet which currently comprises some 85 underway replenishment ships, 135 fleet support vessels and about another 450 auxiliaries of various kinds.[51] Numerically this force lags far behind its American counterpart. The Soviet Navy's ratio of fleet support ships to combatants of 1:42 contrasts badly with the 1:15 figure for the US Navy.[52] Also, the Soviet Union has only fairly recently begun to develop an organic fleet train capable of sustaining naval operations in distant areas, with such ships as the *Boris Chilikin* class (15,000 tons) and the newer and much larger

Berezina class (36,000 tons, with helicopters, SAMs and ASW weaponry). Overall, its reach is much shorter still than that of the US Navy. Its operating procedures are far behind Western standards of efficiency, although they have markedly improved in recent years. The US Navy, for instance, usually replenishes itself underway, as fast as possible, and does so inside a defensive screen: the Soviet Navy, on the other hand, still tends to do it with its ships completely unprotected and virtually dead in the water. The technical excellence of the *Berezina* suggests that the Soviet Navy could develop this capacity much more if it really wanted to: its failure to do so suggests that the task of replenishment at sea is still accorded a relatively low priority. Nevertheless the limited size and reach of the support fleet, its generally indifferent performance, its cumbersome administration and its still rather limited access to shore facilities must all considerably inhibit the Soviet Navy's ability to conduct sustained military operations on the open oceans.

The Soviet Union's concentration on the building and operation of passenger ships increases her capacity to carry numbers of men far above that provided by their amphibious warfare ships. Ro-Ro ships, and the many Soviet ships with heavy lift booms and long hatches could easily transport artillery, aircraft, tanks and so forth, if required. Many of the ships incorporate features like sophisticated communications equipment, photo laboratories, protection against nuclear/biological/chemical attack and so forth, which suggests that their original design was at least partially affected by their potentialities for sea-lift.

In a more general way the merchant fleet helps the Soviet Union win friends and influence people. Merchant ships encourage mutually beneficial trading links, advertise the prosperity, power and sophistication of the Soviet Union and can often move about with far less restriction than warships. During the Vietnam War, Soviet merchantmen demonstrated the way in which they can serve economic and strategic purpose simultaneously, when they took arms to North Vietnam on the outward journey (a common and very effective method of influence-building) and wool from Australia to Europe at special discount rates on the way home. The Soviet Union has also been able to use its fishing fleet to improve relations with many Third World countries by negotiating fish deals of various kinds. Nevertheless there have been difficulties as well: Equatorial Guinea, Senegal and Sierra Leone conspicuously failed to renew lapsed joint fishing ventures with the Soviet Union which they felt were too little in their favour. Although merchant and shipping fleets may produce closer contact between the Soviet Union and the Third World they do not always lead to better relations, a point Western commentators are apt to forget.

Finally, these fleets also perform a variety of ancillary roles of strategic significance. Soviet trawlers and merchant ships are useful gatherers of information about Western naval activities and can be moved about (because of a command and control system centred on Moscow) more or less at will to participate in exercises, search and rescue missions, political visits and the like. The huge marine research fleet doubtless provides information about the sea bed and ocean currents that is as useful to Soviet submarines as it is to fishermen. The merchant navy is also a uniformed, disciplined service which builds up a pool of experienced seafarers which would act as a naval reserve should the need arise. The close connection between the Soviet Navy and the merchant marine is also symbolised by the fact that merchant ships frequently carry naval personnel on training and acquaintance missions of various kinds.

SOVIET NAVAL DESIGN AND CONSTRUCTION

The Russian capacity to construct warships has always been subject to drastic changes in fortune. In one sense, it started at the beginning of the eighteenth century when Peter the Great worked in the shipyards of Western Europe and employed foreign shipwrights at home. But less enlightened rulers followed him and much was lost. This stop–go pattern of development, a characteristic of Russian naval construction ever since, was partly the result of the shaky political and economic order in the country as a whole. Although in 1914, for instance, the Russians were able to produce some very impressive ships, their shipyards were vulnerable because of Russia's spotty industrial performance and low level of political stability. Defeat in war, revolution and civil war more or less destroyed Russia's shipyard capacity. Stalin's subsequent ruthless drive for industrialisation, however, meant a slow recovery was possible in the late 1930s, but this was all devastated once more in the Second World War. The Leningrad yards were under constant attack and came virtually to a standstill. Nikolayev and other Black Sea yards were occupied by the Germans and then destroyed when they withdrew.

Recovery in the post-war period has been slow but steady. There was also a marked shift from naval to civilian construction in the 1950s in the Khruschev era. This has only partially been reversed since then: the Navy has yet to recapture all its old cruiser yards, for instance.[53] There have, however, been massive programmes of modernisation and expansion and the Soviet shipbuilding industry has never been stronger than it is now. The Soviet Union has eighteen large shipbuilding complexes which either could or do construct naval vessels, and extensive use is also made of the shipyard capacity of Poland, East Germany, Finland and various Western countries. Major surface warships are produced at the Nikolayev and Zhdanov yards on the Black Sea. To a certain extent these are also built at the huge general-purpose United Admiralty yard complex at Leningrad. The Severodvinsk submarine yard on the White Sea is the biggest such yard in the world and can probably outproduce the United States, Britain and France combined – and the Russians have another four smaller submarine yards as well.

A glance at the map (see Figure 6) shows that the Soviet Union has made a major endeavour to disperse its shipyards to render them less vulnerable to attack. The creation of the Komsomolsk yard on the Amur river and the Gorki complex in central Russia is characteristic of this. To make their construction facilities safer, the Soviet authorities are willing to pay the penalty of having to move uncompleted hulls to the sea via inland waterways. Even so their shipyards remain vulnerable not least to the weather. Their heavy concentration in the almost closed Baltic and Black Seas would also be a grave disadvantage in war unless the Soviet Union commanded the exits to the oceans beyond.

As befits a planned economy, all Soviet shipbuilding is centrally organised by the Ministry of Shipbuilding Production which runs separate research institutes for the various consumers (the fishing industry, the Navy and so forth). This tends to result in a more settled allocation of industrial resources and more orderly patterns of construction than currently apply in the West.[54] In some respects, though, the Ministry acts rather like a Western shipbuilder. It gives guarantees and has to make deficiencies good out of its own budget, not the Navy's. This may explain some of the Soviet Navy's more peculiar habits, particularly the tendency of its warships to tow each other around and to spend long periods at sea anchorages apparently hibernating with all systems shut down. They may be doing this to keep within the conditions of the Ministry's original guarantee.

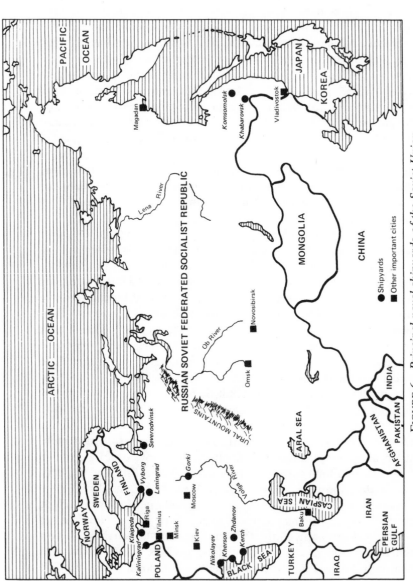

FIGURE 6 *Principal naval shipyards of the Soviet Union*

TABLE 2   *US and Soviet shipbuilding deliveries, 1961–1975*

Type of ship	USSR	US
Ballistic missile submarines	54	38
Attack submarines	177	57
Major surface combatants (3,000 tons and more)	57	117
Major surface combatants (1,000–3,000 tons)	83	2
Minor surface combatants (incl. amphibious)	1,175	71
Underway replenishment ships	4	25
Other support ships	199	17
Total	1,749	327

Source: Joint Chiefs of Staff, *Soviet Shipbuilding Deliveries, 1961–1975*, 20 May 1976.

The output of this shipbuilding capacity, as measured in naval deliveries over the period 1961–75, shows the Soviet Navy to be ahead of the United States in all categories but major warships of more than 3,000 tons and underway replenishment ships.[55] Over the past twenty years, the total tonnage allocated to destroyers has declined, that of cruisers has remained relatively constant and the air-capable ships' share has risen dramatically[56] (see Table 3). Adding this altogether, the surface fleet as a whole has stayed about the same in total tonnage terms, but has fallen in number from about 182 to about 130. Of course, neither of these measures can accurately indicate the Soviet Navy's fighting power, which has risen considerably over the period, but they do give a crude idea of the relative effort and industrial resource put into each category of ship and into the surface navy as a whole. What these figures do make clear, however, is the astonishing rise in the relative tonnage devoted to submarines.

As far as ship design is concerned, the Russians have made much use of foreign expertise from Peter the Great's time onwards. In the 1930s and 1940s Soviet naval design showed much Italian, French and German influence; in 1937, Stalin is believed even to have requested battleship and carrier blueprints from the United States government. After the Second World War, a centralised administration was set up in East Berlin to co-ordinate exploitation of German naval ideas, an exercise which had an impact on everything from Soviet submarine construction and propulsion technology to the AA fire control systems of the *Chapaev* and *Sverdlov* cruisers.

Even so, the Russians have frequently shown a marked originality

TABLE 3   *The Soviet Navy: proportionate numbers and tonnages over 20 years*

	Aircraft carriers		Cruisers		Destroyers		Blue-water surface navy		Submarines		Coastal forces	
	No.	Tons in 000s	No.	Tons in 000s	No.	Tons in 000s	No.	Tons in 000s	No.	Tons in 000s	No.	Tons in 000s
1961	–	–	25	343	157	399	182	743	409	438	1194	304
1971	2	30	22	251	100	297	124	578	394	792	1161	327
1981	5	141	40	390	87	254	132	785	371	1,430	1200	450

Source: Approximate data derived from *JFS*, 1961, 1971, 1981.

in their ship design too. In 1912, for instance, they produced a fast battleship design conceived by Vladimir Yourkevitch that astonished the world and proved to be some twenty years ahead of its contemporaries. As has already been noted, the Russians have also demonstrated comparable capacities for startling innovation in the period since 1945. As a rule, the Soviet Navy does not however operate on the bolt-from-the-blue principle of its main Western adversary, but incorporates new ideas in an incremental step-by-step manner. Whereas the United States produced *Polaris* submarines as her first SSBNs for instance, the Soviet Union only reached this point through a series of cumulative stages starting with the *Zulu* adaptations of 1955/6. This is undoubtedly part of the reason for the 'continuing picture of cancellations, adaptations and expedients' which some analysts have drawn of Soviet naval design.[57]

There are other reasons for this though. Uneven development has partly reflected significant changes in attitude towards what were the Soviet Navy's main tasks. But it has also been the product of a distinctive approach to the whole problem of ship design, in which emphasis is given to the idea that the hull of a warship is a versatile platform for the placement or removal of weapons more or less at will. Soviet ship constructors tend to bolt as many weapons and sensors onto the hull as it will accept at any one time and still stay upright, an approach which encourages experiment and adaptation. Since this practice has apparently led to some ships like the *Skory*, *Kotlin* and *Kynda* being top heavy in a way disturbingly reminiscent of Admiral Rozhestvenski's new battleship of 1905 which was apparently warned not to fly too many flags lest it capsize, the reasons for this are worth exploring. It reflects a more permissive safety philosophy, a lower concern for living conditions below deck and a tendency to have separate directors and guidance radars for each launcher (unlike Western navies which are happy to accept a lower number of multi-purpose radars). These radars tend in any case to be heavier and bulkier than their Western counterparts because they are less sophisticated technically and are often naval adaptations of land systems.[58] Finally, Soviet ship designers prefer to offer as many weapon options as possible, even if this does make for redundancies, mutual interference and difficulties in command and control.

For such reasons as this the Soviet warship is often markedly different to its US Navy counterpart. Usually fitted with fin stabilisers, it may well be a better sea-keeper, and will almost certainly have more weapons and sensors per displacement ton than American equivalents. The *Kara*, for instance, has no less than thirty radar and other electronic systems of various kinds. Whereas the US Navy's *Belknap* class of cruiser carries eight weapon systems in 6,750 tons, the *Kresta I* has thirteen in 6,140. Soviet ships in general have less reload capacity and lower standards of endurance and habitability.[59] Soviet submarines as a rule, are bigger, faster and noisier than their Western counterparts.

However, it is dangerous to try to infer Soviet naval purposes from the design of their warships, at least beyond a certain rather basic level, because design characteristics can often be legitimately interpreted in quite different ways. But it does seem true to say that on the whole Soviet warships were once best fitted for one-shot sea denial tasks in European waters. More recently, however, there has been significant evidence of convergence in design between Soviet and Western naval construction. The missile silos of the *Kirov*, for instance, were integral to the hull, rather than bolted on to the outside, which was hitherto the normal practice. Taken together, such evidence implies that the Soviet Navy is better fitted for sustained operations on the high seas than it used to be and more nearly approximates the Western (or rather the American) model. Even so, the confident independence of Soviet naval design is now quite clearly exemplified by the distinctively 'Russian' look to many of its warships and submarines. It is also now in a much better position than ever before to base its growing design expertise on a solid and viable shipbuilding industry.

OTHER NAVIES OF THE WARSAW PACT

For the sake of completeness this brief *tour d'horizon* of the Soviet naval inventory must be concluded by a look at the navies of Bulgaria, Romania, East Germany and Poland. The first two are both very small (comprising some 10,500 men each) and are exclusively coastal in their orientation. The Romanians have three ex-Russian *Poti* corvettes and a number of small combatants, including some hydrofoils obtained from China. Much the same goes for the Bulgarians who also have four rather elderly *Romeo* and *Whiskey* submarines in their fleet. Neither navy is of any real strategic significance, even in the context of Black Sea operations.

Although the East German and Polish navies are also quite small (at about 16,000 and 22,500 men respectively) and largely coastal in aspiration, they are, nevertheless, more important to the Soviet Union than either Bulgaria or Romania. Both countries provide useful ports along the Baltic shore for the Soviet Navy to use, both do a significant amount of naval and merchant ship construction for the Soviet Union and both participate regularly in local exercises (especially amphibious ones). Interestingly, both navies also share in the Soviet Union's apparent preoccupation with mine warfare. The East German Navy, for instance, in its *Kondor I* and *II* classes has no less than 50 mine-sweepers – compared to Britain's 38 and France's 32. For all these reasons the small navies of these two countries can be expected to co-operate in the Soviet Navy's Baltic operations and, moreover, their contribution may be of some military significance.[60]

7 The Missions of the Soviet Navy

CONTROLLING THE SEAS

'Command of the sea' is one of the oldest notions in maritime strategy. Put briefly, it means getting a position in which one can to a greater or lesser extent use the sea for one's own purposes and prevent the enemy from using it for his.[1] It is, and always has been, the central feature of conventional maritime strategy. Without question, the commanders of the Tsarist Navy adhered to the concept: indeed, according to Gorshkov, they practically invented it since a Lieutenant-Captain Berezin apparently put pen to paper on the matter some twenty years before Mahan, Colomb and other Western prophets of the faith. Berezin certainly summed up the main arguments when he wrote:

> When a war begins, involving the fleets, attaining dominance at sea is usually the first and principal task. If the forces are greatly incommensurate this task is solved by direct blockade of the roads or the harbours where the hostile squadrons are, and then of the whole shore; in absence of such incommensurability it is necessary to gain this dominance by inflicting defeats . . . on the hostile fleet and only then establish a blockade seeking to destroy the sea trade of the enemy and all his transport by sea.[2]

By and large, the Tsarist Navy accepted this as a point of principle, although practice lagged a long way behind theory. This type of thinking survived the Revolution, if in a somewhat watered-down form and found expression in the generally orthodox teachings of Professors Gervaise and Petrov at the Voroshilov Naval War College and the Frunze Naval Academy.

But by the end of the 1920s a new faith was arising to challenge the tenets of the old. Petrov and Gervaise were denounced and fired. The 'New School' as it soon became known, persuaded the Soviet Navy to abandon its residual aspirations to behave like any other navy in seeking to control the seas. 'Down with Command of the Seas!' declared A. P. Alexandrov, one of the school's leading lights. Instead the Soviet Navy should content itself with the efficient conduct of 'minor war' in coastal waters. Torpedo boats, mines, submarines and aircraft properly and massively used would be enough to protect the coastline against foreign attack and support army operations to the limited extent necessary. According to the New School, this was the only kind of naval power the Soviet Union needed.

The New School's rejection of the whole concept of the command of the sea seems to have been generally accepted for a whole variety of reasons, some fundamental and some not. There were some ideological objections to the idea of command of the sea, partly because of its historic associations with European colonialism and partly because it implied that navies had a role distinct from that of armies which seemed to conflict with the idea of singleness of purpose so central to Leninist military theory. At this time, there were also widespread doubts in all the principal maritime countries about the future of the battleship, a vessel which was then generally regarded as a supreme expression of power at sea. People were saying that the battleship was now so vulnerable to submarines and to aircraft that it would not be able to perform its traditional functions; in consequence many of the things that blue-water navies used to be able to do would now be beyond their capability, including their habitual aspirations for ambitious levels of sea control.

There was, finally, the more mundane point that post-Revolutionary Russia was industrially and navally weak and seemed likely to remain so indefinitely. For the moment at least, this state of affairs forced the struggling Soviet Navy to settle for relatively modest missions. Thus in 1921, Admiral Dombrovskiy, the Soviet Navy's Chief of Staff declared: 'Defence of the borders of the state from the side of the water boundaries is the cornerstone of our present day naval policy; *for the time being* we will relinquish the broader tasks'.[3] The New School argued that it would be quite demoralising for a necessarily weak Soviet Navy to have to go on adhering to a concept of maritime operations which gave all the advantages to the strongest fleet.

However by the end of the 1930s it was clear that the rehabilitation of the old ideas was well under way. Industry had recovered
sufficiently for 'the Soviet Union (to) set out on the course of creating a high seas fleet capable of resolving tasks at a significant distance from their bases. Powerful capital ships were laid down; the
fleets received new cruisers, destroyers, long-range submarines, and
other ships.'[4] Despite this, the Soviet Navy's attempt to secure even
quite limited degrees of sea control in the Second World War was
half-hearted to say the least. This especially applied to the surface
ship which made hardly any effort to contest naval mastery with its
German adversary. Accordingly, as one German officer of the time
has since concluded:

> In spite of submarines and frequent air attack, the German sur-
> face ships were masters of the sea, operating against the flanks of
> the Soviet Army and guaranteeing sea transport from and to all
> Baltic ports still in German hands.[5]

The Russians' reluctance to use their large ships offensively meant
they lost many opportunities to do real harm to the German cause,
particularly towards the end of the war when the odds were very
much in the Soviet Union's favour. This may have been a function
of the poor quality of the Soviet naval command in the wake of
Stalin's purges. Gorshkov himself atttibuted it not to any rejection
of the concept of command for ideological reasons, but to a failure
to build a properly balanced fleet. In particular, the potentialities of
maritime aviation were neglected. No carriers were built and,

> we did not even have any fighter aviation which could provide
> cover for warships at sea far from our coasts . . . Thus even our
> big surface fleet . . . actually was doomed to operating solely in
> our coastal waters, protected by fighter aviation from shore.[6]

The problem was aggravated by poor liaison between ships and
land-based air forces which often led to heavy losses even in areas
where aircover was theoretically available. Such disasters as the sinking of a destroyer task force in the Black Sea on 5/6 October 1943
by German dive bombers made Stalin forbid the operational use of
large surface ships without his express permission.

After the war, the Soviet Navy built heavy cruisers, ocean-going
submarines, destroyers and may even have contemplated the con-

struction of aircraft carriers. This all implied a continued acceptance of the tenets of orthodox maritime strategy. But Stalin's death in 1953 ushered in a new and ambiguous period in the history of the Soviet Navy – an era in which it is widely supposed to have turned its back once more on the idea of controlling the seas and to have developed instead the notion of Sea Denial. By this, the Soviet Navy would not aim to control the seas (even local ones) for its own use but would merely prevent anyone else from using it for theirs.

This new orientation was signified by the Soviet Navy's heavy concentration on narrowly defined tasks of homeland defence, especially against Western carrier task groups. Although the fleet of the 1950s and 1960s looked large and powerful, its capacity for assertive operations on the open oceans was in fact very restricted. Furthermore, an emphasis on sea denial would also explain Khruschev's widely reported attacks on the usefulness of large surface warships, carriers included, and the nature of Soviet naval construction. Sea denial weapon systems like submarines, raiding warships, land-based aircraft, inshore combatants and mine-warfare vessels were emphasised. The Soviet Navy's major warship construction programme was much reduced and was apparently intended to produce ships fitted for a first and single strike, at the expense of a capacity for sustained maritime operations. Many of their weapons had no reloads, their crew accommodation was poor and their endurance was limited. Altogether, Soviet warships seemed to be just of the fire-and-forget sort required for sea denial. Both the naval material and the operating concepts of this period in fact suggest that the Soviet Navy had few aspirations for Sea Control as understood in the West.

But, from the start, it seemed unlikely that the Soviet Navy would content itself for long with these humble conceptions. As early as 1964, the Naval lobby persuaded Marshal Sokolovskiy to concede in an important *Red Star* article that the Soviet Navy's acquisition of submarines, missiles and nuclear weapons 'permits a shift from carrying out wartime missions along the coast in co-operation with the Ground Troops to independent and decisive operations on the broad reaches of the oceans'.[7] The ideal that the Soviet Navy could have its own 'independent' missions was a significant and early achievement for the naval lobby in this period of relative humility. Many Western observers have emphasised the centrality of carriers to ambitious maritime operations and concluded from their absence in the Soviet Navy's line of battle that its preoccupations were exclusively local and defensive.[8] The logic of this argument is far from unassailable however for even in the West there has been a fair amount of scepticism about the cost effectiveness of carriers as components of a modern, balanced and assertive fleet. In any case, the Soviet Navy *has* generally been interested in carrier development, at least of a sort. Moreover, throughout this period the Soviet Navy showed itself determined to move forwards in order to compensate for the extending strike ranges of Western carriers and SSBNs. The way in which the defence perimeter has been gradually extended to encompass more varied threats and wider stretches of ocean shows that sea denial is not, as it is so often portrayed, a distinct alternative to sea control: the difference between the two is a fuzzy matter of degree.[9] Describing the Soviet Navy of the late 1950s and 1960s as a sea denial navy should indicate merely that it was a sea control navy of modest means and aspirations. It should not be taken to imply that the Soviet Navy had a concept of maritime strategy that was generically different from the West's. Since the term 'sea denial' often seems to bear this inaccurate implication, it is probably better to avoid it, as in fact do the Russians themselves.

In the following decades Soviet ideas about sea control increasingly resembled orthodox thinking in the West. Gorshkov was at pains to emphasise how important what he called 'dominance at sea' actually was. 'History', he wrote, 'does not know of a more ancient and hardier concept.'[10] His argument was that only with such dominance could a fleet gain control of shipping, deploy its forces and prevent the enemy from interfering with its operations; it was a means to an end, a way of creating a 'favourable operational regime' for it to use the sea for its own purposes and prevent the enemy from using it for his. Sinking the enemy's fleet may not in itself be significant; it is what may happen afterwards as a result of such encounters that matters. To Gorshkov, in fact, command of the sea was 'a vehicle for creating the definite preconditions that will allow fleet forces and means successfully to accomplish particular tasks in definite regions of the theatre in a concrete time period'.[11] Although some Western maritime strategists have been more absolutist about this (notably Mahan), most have considered command of the sea to be 'relative, incomplete and imperfect'.[12] Soviet views on the matter in fact do not appear to be significantly different from those of the West.

Gorshkov made it clear that the strategic consequence of naval dominance has often been decisive for success in peace and war. Sea power has been historically important for the positive rather than the negative or defensive contribution it can make to the security of the state. A country strong at sea can use that strength for positive purposes. In peacetime it can exploit the sea as a medium for commercial enterprise (a point given much emphasis in *The Sea Power of the State*), for deterrence and for naval diplomacy. In war, naval supremacy can confer every advantage. Gorshkov pointedly reminded his readers that in the Korean and Vietnam wars, the US fleet struck land targets with devastating effect, sent ground forces ashore and kept them supplied and supported almost with impunity because no serious effort was made to contest it at sea.[13] This experience showed that countries which neglect the positive as well as the negative potentialities of the use of the sea fare badly, as has even Russia from time to time. Hence the absolute need for the Soviet Union to be a sea power of the first rank.

Nevertheless, as a good Marxist, Gorshkov showed himself to be well aware of the effect that social, political and technological change has had on the nature of naval dominance. The advent of nuclear weapons and missiles made it more difficult to gain and to keep sea supremacy.[14] It was likely to be more restricted in area and more fleeting in time than it used to be. But it was still fundamental to the conduct of warfare at sea.

> From all this it follows that such a category of naval arts as the gaining of dominance at sea retains its topicality and therefore the elaboration of it in all its aspects relevant to the present, forms one of the most important tasks of naval science.[15]

In short, Gorshkov's writings suggest that the Soviet Navy intends to achieve a working level of sea control that will enable it to conduct maritime operations decisive for the outcome of the war. We can now turn to the subordinate question of how he and the Soviet Navy think this level of control should be achieved. The first thing that needs to be said about this, is that they do not seem to expect this to be a distinct type of naval activity. Although both in theory and in logic, control has to be secured before it can be exercised, Gorshkov plainly thought that these apparently sequential tasks would generally be carried out together. In fact, he pointed out that this was usually the case in both the World Wars. Sometimes the destruction of the enemy's forces at sea was a distinct operation and almost an end in itself – as in the case of the Taranto and Pearl Harbor raids. But 'such operations were nearly always constituent parts either of the struggle for oceanic communications or landing operations' (thus the battles of Midway, Matapan, the Philippine Sea, the pursuit of the *Bismarck* and so forth).[16] Time, technology and operational circumstance made it increasingly unlikely that navies at war would first meet in combat simply to secure command and then (and only then) seek to exercise it to the extent they were successful. Gorshkov seemed to imply that in a war, the Soviet Navy would move directly into the business of using the sea for whatever purposes it required (strategic defence and offence, the launching of amphibious attacks, assaulting NATO shipping and so forth). Encounters with opposing Western forces would not be sought as a matter of course, and largely for the sake of it, but would instead be dealt with simply as they occurred and to the extent they were found necessary.

Over the past two decades, the Soviet Navy has clearly been deployed and exercised in ways which would help it to achieve and exercise useful levels of sea control. In 1962, after the chastening experience of the Cuba missile crisis, Gorshkov ordered the Navy to 'Sail upon the Oceans of the World' and this has certainly been done. Traditionally, Soviet maritime activity was confined to the Arctic, Baltic and Black Seas and to the Seas of Okhotsk and of Japan. Going outside this maritime area put a big strain on the Soviet Navy and led to breakdowns in equipment and collisions.[17] But progress since those early days has been rapid and substantial. There was a dramatic surge in the 1965–70 period when ship days in the Pacific, Atlantic and Mediterranean went up by 400 per cent and when the Soviet Navy also developed a significant operational presence in completely new areas like the Indian Ocean and the Caribbean. The build-up in out-of-area ship days steadily continued to 1975 but has levelled off since then. The US Navy, on the other hand, started the period as a dominating blue-water sea control navy on a global scale. Its out-of-area ship day levels were far higher than those of the Soviet Navy. In 1969, for instance, they were still nearly three times as high: about 115,000 ship days to the Soviet Navy's 40,000. Since then they have declined absolutely and relatively to a position of rough equivalence to those of the Soviet Navy.[18]

Many of these ship days come from formal naval exercises, which have also shown a startling increase in scope and range over the past twenty years or so. Hitherto, the Soviet Navy had confined its exercise activity to its own local waters. Only in 1961 did it venture into the Norwegian Sea, for instance, when eight warships, four submarines and some support ships conducted exercises there in the summer. The extent of the advance was soon made very clear to the West. In *Okean–1970*, no less than 200 ships engaged in the Soviet Navy's 'first world-wide coordinated naval exercise . . . for testing and further improving the level of combat skill of the Navy and operational preparedness of staffs'. Many recently constructed ships like the *Kresta Is* and the *Moskvas* tried out their paces for the first time. The hostile 'Southern' fleet was well and truly beaten by the Murmansk 'Northern' fleet in a variety of anti-carrier, ASW and amphibious operations. 'Now on the chart of the World Ocean,' declared Gorshkov proudly in *Red Star*, 'it is difficult to come upon regions where the ships of the Soviet fleet are unable to sail.' [19]

Anti-carrier operations also featured heavily in the more modest exercises of 1971 and 1972, but from 1973 ASW exercises took the limelight, together with intermittent and localised amphibious exercises. The high point was *Vesna–1975*. For the first two weeks in the April of that year, upwards of 220 ships and submarines of the four fleets, a number of merchantmen, many aircraft operating from Warsaw Pact territory, the Yemen, Somalia, Guinea and Cuba, and probably *Cosmos 723* and *724* satellites were deployed for global operation. After two days of intensive reconnaissance and surveillance, there was a sequence of simultaneous and centrally controlled strikes on hostile shipping (naval and civilian) around the world, particularly by aircraft and submarine. The high level of coordination and the geographic extent of this exercise were particularly significant. 'In my view,' concluded the US Secretary of the Navy, 'this Soviet naval exercise clearly demonstrates the fact that the Soviet Navy is capable of operating effectively in all oceans of the world.' [20] Although rather to the surprise of many people there has been no such maritime spectacular since, the Soviet Navy has nevertheless continued to develop its capacity for the kind of blue-water operation needed for a navy with sea control aspirations.

The physical composition of the Soviet fleet shows the same preoccupations. Gorshkov has emphasised the need for the Soviet Union to have a balanced fleet capable of a wide diversity of tasks. In 1967, he put it this way:

By a well-balanced fleet we mean a fleet which both in composition and armament is able to complete the missions assigned to it
in rocket-nuclear war and in wars without nuclear weapons, and
also to guarantee state interests on the sea in peacetime.[21]

Earlier scepticism about the useful future of large surface ships has
been replaced by a cautious optimism that they now have sufficient
mobility and means of defence to survive while 'conserving the ability to solve combat tasks'.[22] Accordingly a substantial number of
large surface ships is now accepted as a vital constituent of a properly balanced fleet, even though the bulk of the Navy's firepower in
a war with the West would probably still be delivered by the AVMF
and a notably versatile submarine force. Gorshkov also criticised the
Soviet Navy's past practice of designing ships specifically to counter
elements in the Western fleets. Instead he advocated and eventually
produced ships capable of a wide range of general purposes. This
shift in policy resulted, as we have seen, in the ship modernisations
of the 1970s, the weapons complement of the *Kievs*, and the design
philosophy behind such versatile ships as the *Kirov* and *Sovremenny*
classes. So far at any rate, the Soviet Navy has not deployed fleet
carriers, the most versatile ships of all – but this may be simply a
matter of time. The fact that surface combatants and auxiliaries now
take up a far higher proportion of the Soviet Navy's out-of-area ship
days than they used to is further evidence of a new emphasis on the
attainment of a general-purpose maritime capability, rather than a
capacity to execute a narrow range of specifically defined and generally defensive missions in local waters.

Traditional conceptions of maritime strategy have tended to stress
the idea that a decisive encounter on the high seas between the
opposing battlefleets was the best and most satisfactorily complete
way of reaching a decision as to who was to control the sea, to what
extent, where and when. Soviet naval theory as enunciated by Gorshkov generally accepted this idea. Gorshkov pointed out that decisive victories of this sort were of value in that they made it much
easier to use the sea and to undermine, perhaps permanently, the
enemy's capacity to resist.[23] But he also made it clear that battles of
this sort were increasingly likely to be a part of operations intended
actually to use the sea in some way. He argued that the importance
of fleet versus fleet operations had actually declined relative to
those of fleet versus shore and that this would be especially true of
those naval battles which had little effect on land operations.[24] Cer-

tainly the stress on preparing for some decisive encounter on the high seas could easily be overdone, as he thought it was in the First World War.[25] Nevertheless the requirement actually to defeat enemy forces at sea in mortal combat remains a high priority for the Soviet Navy for, as Gorshkov declared, 'the battle always was and remains the main means of solving tactical tasks'.[26]

The Soviet view of what that battle would be like stresses its great dispersion: there would be no grand shoot-out between battle groups in line ahead, but a widespread encounter over many thousands of square miles of ocean. This is partly because of the increased range of naval weaponry – especially with the advent of the naval missile. But dispersion is also a function of the increased diversity of the means of attack. Both in its writings and practice, the Soviet Navy has emphasised the rising attack potential of submarines and land-based aircraft. Its exercises commonly feature orchestrated attacks by submarines and aircraft, in combination with surface warships, although until recently at least these latter have tended to play a notably subordinate role. If fleet carriers do appear in the Soviet order of battle, however, there may well be a switch in emphasis, which would take Soviet thinking more into line with US Navy practice.

The stress on orchestrated mass attack also needs, and judging by *Vesna–1975* and other such indications, evidently has, an extremely sophisticated and resilient communication system which can co-ordinate widely dispersed naval forces over enormous distances.[27] In war, this type of centralised direction may be a source of weakness if Soviet communications are interfered with or if things do not go the way the Soviet naval command expects them to. In fact, given the diverse range of requirements for the different weapons deployed by Soviet naval formations (which is generally greater than that in its Western counterparts) effective tactical command and control may well turn out to be precarious.

The hugely increased destructive effect of naval weaponry will in the Soviet view make battle a much faster and more savage affair than it used to be, with the great stress being on the advantage derived from winning the first salvo. Manoeuvre and speed will increase and so will the importance of surprise. Because of all this, Gorshkov urged his commanders to demonstrate 'initiative in the use of new tactical moves not known to the enemy' and recommended 'spirited offensive tactics'.[28] Such ideas explain the relatively heavy armament of Soviet ships and their operational tendency in exercises and times of tension to deploy surface attack groups in close attendance on their likely Western targets (especially carriers) which are plainly intended to achieve a first strike at almost any subsequent cost. This may also explain the tendency in Soviet exercises for the 'enemy' to be very passive, not practising evasive manoeuvres or defensive tactics. Indeed, the 'enemy' is often not even in an advanced state of readiness when the blow falls.[29] However, more recently, the Soviet Navy has begun to produce ships whose defensive armament makes them more capable of sustained operations in a hostile environment and Soviet tactics will doubtless increasingly reflect the greater staying power of both ships and formations.

This tendency to regard the strike as 'increasingly tantamount to a battle' makes particular sense when the Soviet attitude to the operational use of nuclear weapons at sea is considered. It seems from the naval literature that Soviet leaders have relatively fewer inhibitions about the use of these weapons than have their Western counterparts. 'A special feature of the sea battle', declared Gorshkov, 'is that it has nearly always been waged to destroy the enemy. The equipping of the forces of the fleets with nuclear weapons', he added, 'is further accentuating this feature.'[30] However analysts have detected in Soviet military doctrine in general a greater sympathy over the past decade or so to the idea of a war between great powers which may stop short of the nuclear threshold. If this in fact is the case, one can expect naval science to follow suit. The armament of Soviet ships, submarines and aircraft moreover, certainly shows they could give a very good account of themselves without going nuclear.

DEFENCE AGAINST MARITIME ATTACK

Russian history as it was and as it is processed by Gorshkov and others shows how necessary it is for Russia to defend herself against maritime attack while the forces threatening her are still at sea. But when the Russian Navy was weak, this was not possible. Such was the case during the Crimean War, the Revolutionary and Civil War periods and the Second World War when 'not a single successful anti-landing operation was undertaken, with delivery of powerful and successive blows on the enemy, from the points of assembly to the area of disembarking of the invasion force on a coast'.[31] This inability to resist foreign attack at sea meant that the war on land went much less well than it need have done. In fact the Civil War period showed that a capacity for maritime resistance might actually prevent such a campaign from starting in the first place. Gorshkov pointed out that in 1918 the Soviet Union was ringed by enemies with intervention on their minds. 'It should be noted', he wrote, 'that . . . [troops] . . . were disembarked from the sea and operated where the Soviet Republic had no naval fleet (that is, Murmansk, Vladivostock and the Black Sea ports). In the Baltic where quite a strong fleet was maintained, the interventionists hesitated to make a landing.'[32]

The Soviet Union was frequently unable to offer this kind of maritime defence because the Army-dominated leadership did not always see how important it was. Instead, the Generals often conceived of coastal defence in the narrowest terms, thinking of it as a localised means of guarding the maritime flanks of the Army. A fairly recent example of this inability wholly to grasp the blindingly obvious was provided by Marshal Sokolovskiy and his colleagues in their definitive statement of Soviet military strategy.[33] The first edition was bitterly attacked by Admiral Alafuzov and others who pointed out the value of the Navy in countering attempted landings. Rather grudgingly, ther second edition of the Sokolovskiy book conceded that

> the enemy may attempt to land large seaborne assaults, in which connection readiness to break up assault operations remains an important requirement of our naval, ground and other types of armed forces.[34]

Despite the Army's apparent reluctance to recognise the potentialities of maritime defence, it has always been the chief preoccupation of the Soviet Navy. In fact, in this as in so many other ways the Soviet Union merely built on the naval foundations of Tsarist Russia. For instance, in the last half of the nineteenth century, after the chastening experience of the Crimean War, the Imperial Navy devoted much thought to how it could defend St. Petersburg and the Gulf of Finland against superior Western battlefleets. It was very interested in monitors, minefields, submarines and torpedoes in this connection, a technological solution which also appeared in the philosophy of the New School in the interwar period. The idea here was to disperse Soviet naval power between such a large number of submarines, aircraft and torpedo boats that an incoming invasion force would be subject to an attack of increasing diversity and intensity the nearer it came to Soviet territory. The hardest blows of this mosquito fleet would fall in coastal waters as the enemy approached the shoreline. But there were other thinkers like Petrov and Gervaise of the Old School who put forward a more ambitious alternative to this: they wanted the Soviet Navy to offer a more active defence outside coastal waters and advocated the retention of a core of heavy ships for the purpose. For a while these views were dismissed and the narrowest conception of coastal defence was adhered to even 'when our fleet had already become capable of waging combat operations beyond its coastal waters'.[35] Stalin's pre-war naval construction programme, with its battleships and large cruisers, marked the end of this period of stagnation, though as we have already seen, this last minute conversion came too late to allow the Soviet Navy to cover itself in glory during the Second World War.

After the war, the Soviet Navy once more devoted itself to the task of defending the country from maritime attack, its collective mind doubtless concentrated by the prospect of a conflict with the Western maritime powers who had so recently demonstrated their extraordinary capacity for amphibious assault on a truly oceanic scale. The solution was to prepare a defensive perimeter up to about 500 miles from the Soviet coast within which invading forces would come under increasingly severe attack as they headed for Russia. Beyond and at the outer limits of this perimeter, defending forces would be restricted to land-based bombers, long-range submarines (*Zulus*) and a few heavy ships (*Sverdlovs*, *Chapaevs* and various destroyers) whose exact function was not very clear. Closer in, the stress would be on huge numbers of medium-range and coastal submarines (*Whiskeys* and *Quebecs* respectively), more and more aircraft, a swarm of minor combatants, especially torpedo boats, dense minefields and last but not least, powerful batteries of coastal artillery. The idea was that each of the four fleet areas should be essentially self-supporting and this required the vast number of submarines (about 1,200) which the Soviet government claimed to be building in 1948.[36] Judging by the way this submarine force was deployed, the Soviet Navy regarded the Black and Baltic Seas as its most vulnerable fleet areas. Its anti-invasion task would not necessarily end if the enemy did get ashore. Then the Soviet Navy would switch to those operations against the enemy's local maritime supply lines which it had conducted with reasonable success in the Baltic and Black Seas during the Second World War.

The Soviet Navy's assiduous development of small missile-firing warships like the *Osa*, *Komar* and, later, the *Nanuchka* and its continuing maintenance of large offshore defence forces shows that defending the Motherland against maritime attack remains a high priority. Nevertheless, there are several indications that its perceived importance slipped for a few years following the death of Stalin in 1953. What brought it back into prominence, if in rather a different guise, seems to have been the progress made by the West in the development of carrier aviation. For instance, at the time of the Suez operation in 1956, the *Seahawk* was the main strike aircraft of British carriers, an aircraft which had an effective range of only 200 miles and which fired 3-inch rockets. A carrier's strike capacity was therefore limited to the Soviet Union's coastal zone and would probably have been exerted against naval bases, airfields and the like. By the end of the decade, however, the British were test flying the *Buccaneer*, an aircraft able to carry nuclear weapons, with an operational range of 1,000 miles. The same kind of increased threat, only much more so, was offered by the US Navy. Whereas between 1946 and 1952 the Americans had built no new carriers, from that time on the US Navy's determination to win a strategic mission for itself resulted in the appearance of fast new attack carriers with aircraft like the *A-3D Skywarrior*. Operating from the Norwegian Sea, the eastern Mediterranean and the western Pacific, these carriers seemed increasingly capable of delivering devastating nuclear strikes against the Soviet Union's industrial heartland. Naturally this refocused Soviet concern on the requirements of maritime defence. Thus, wrote Sokolovskiy,

> From the outset, one of our Navy's most important tasks will be to destroy the enemy carrier strike forces. The enemy will attempt to deploy these formations in the most important theatres near Socialist countries so as to deliver surprise nuclear strikes on major coastal targets ... and possibly on targets much further inland. For example, in the NATO exercise *Autumn–60* a carrier strike force deployed in the Norwegian Sea simulated the delivery of 200 nuclear strikes on targets on our coasts and deep within our territory ... It is essential to attempt to destroy the attack carriers before they launch their aircraft; we must destroy the protective forces, the auxiliaries and the carrier bases.[37]

Western carrier task groups were the epitome of conventional maritime power at that time. Since the Soviet Navy had none itself it could only counter this threat by an outflanking operation with radically new concepts and weaponry. The apparent solution to its problem was the naval missile with a nuclear warhead. The first move was to fit the *Scrubber* SS-N-1 missile to a dozen or so *Krupny* and *Kildin* destroyers. In somewhat slower time, the *Kynda* missile cruisers were constructed, the first appearing in 1962. Later still came the *Kresta I*. In the air, naval bombers like the *Badger* were fitted to carry the *Kipper* ASM and others were especially equipped for a reconnaissance and missile-targeting role. SS-N-3 *Shaddock* missiles were fitted to a number of *Whiskey* submarines and new classes of missile-firing submarines like the *Juliett*, *Echo I* and *II* appeared in the early 1960s as well. The main advantage of the missile was that it allowed submarines and aircraft to engage the carrier, in Sokolovskiy's words, 'without entering the task force's anti-submarine and air defence zone'. The naval missile could also carry a nuclear warhead and, as Sokolovskiy also wrote, 'the attack carrier is an extremely vulnerable target for nuclear strike . . . Now any surface ship can be destroyed with a single missile or torpedo with a nuclear warhead.'

In its exercises, the Soviet Navy has developed various tactics of massed and orchestrated attack by aircraft, submarines and surface ships, whose cumulative effect is intended to overwhelm the carrier task group's defences by sheer weight and diversity of numbers. In *Okean–1970*, for instance, a simulated carrier task group passing through the Greenland–Iceland–United Kingdom Gap was attacked by 10 missile armed surface ships, 30 submarines and 400 aircraft sorties, operating in waves.[38] Torpedo attack submarines would doubtless add their mite to such actions as well.

Initially, the Soviet Navy may have expected this operation to take place within range of Soviet fighters based on land. This would provide Soviet surface ships with a measure of protection against Western carrier-based aircraft. But this became steadily less feasible as the strike range of Western carriers outstripped that of Soviet land-based aviation. This meant that surface ships found themselves increasingly at risk to pre-emptive strikes beyond the range of their missiles while Soviet strike, reconnaissance and targeting aircraft became more vulnerable to Western carrier fighters. The Soviet Navy seems to have tried to get round this problem by the construction of ships with an effective SAM defence, by the development of shorter-ranged missiles which did not require mid-course guidance by aircraft and by a relatively increased emphasis on submarine attack.

The idea of hitting the carrier before it reached its launch position obviously required Soviet anti-carrier operations to move forward as the range of possible Western strikes increased. Recent exercises suggest that the Soviet Navy is working to establish a 1,500-mile defence perimeter around Soviet territory, passing through the Greenland–Iceland–United Kingdom Gap, the Sicilian straits and enclosing a sizable chunk of the north-west Pacific. Extensive anti-carrier operations within this defensive perimeter have been a regular feature of Soviet naval exercises over the past twenty years or so.[39] A typical forward anti-carrier group of the mid-1960s would have included at least one cruise missile submarine (perhaps a *Juliett*, *Echo II*, or later, a *Charlie*) with maybe a couple of torpedo attack submarines. *Kresta Is*, *Kyndas* or even *Nanuchkas* would supply the SSM firepower and Tu-16 *Badgers* the ASMs. Information about the carriers would be provided by trailing *Kashins* or *Kotlins* and Tu-95 *Bear D* aircraft.[40] As we have seen, new aircraft, ships and submarines have since been produced to replace or supplement these older platforms. Soviet carriers have joined in these exercises too, but so far only as simulated targets, as the *Kiev* did on several occasions in 1979.[41] But the Soviet Navy has also adopted the potentially dangerous expedient of simulated attack on real US Navy carriers; during the 1973 Arab–Israeli war, for instance, the three US Navy carriers in the Eastern Mediterranean (the *J. F. Kennedy*, *F. D. Roosevelt* and *Independence*) were all menaced by surface attack groups and cruise missile firing submarines to the south of Crete. The Soviet Mediterranean squadron also targeted the assault carrier *Iwo Jima* in the same way. This was significant as the *Iwo Jima* could not possibly have posed a direct threat to the Soviet Union and the incident shows that not all anti-carrier operations need be regarded as part of the maritime defence task.[42]

In fact quite a few such operations are conducted beyond the Soviet Navy's putative 1,500-mile defence perimeter. As early as February and March 1963, large numbers of Tu-95 *Bears* conducted wide-ranging operations to fly over US Navy carriers, and several of these incidents occurred well forward of any such line. On 22 February 1963, for instance, four *Bears* ostentatiously flew over the carrier *Forrestal* south-east of the Azores: on 16 March, another group covered the *Constellation* 600 miles south-west of Midway Island.[43] Since then anti-carrier evolutions of one sort or another have often been conducted in places like the central Atlantic, the Philippine Sea and the Indian Ocean where the carriers could not really be thought to represent a direct threat to the Soviet homeland.

This suggests rather strongly that anti-carrier operations are no longer to be seen as exclusively, or perhaps even primarily, part of the Soviet Navy's coastal or strategic defence missions. Instead, they are part and parcel of its bid to contest control of the oceans with the US Navy.[44] There are other politico-strategic explanations for these operations too. Not unnaturally Soviet leaders argue that US Navy carriers are the spearhead of a determined Western endeavour to control the seas, encircle the Soviet Union and interfere with the progress of the revolution in the Third World:

> To gain domination on the high seas and use its armed forces to create strong points in various parts of the world – it is towards this goal that the United States has been striving ever since the war, proceeding from the expansionist objectives of its imperialist foreign policy course . . . the [US] Navy, which has always been closely linked with the implementation of foreign policy, is being made into the primary strike echelon of the American armed forces . . . All this shows what a tremendous role – one which determines the success of any naval actions – is played by aircraft. All recent practical measures testify that the concept of creating naval air power is being allocated particularly crucial importance for the fulfilment of the long-term strategic task of winning dominance at sea.[45]

Given these perspectives on Western naval developments, it is perfectly understandable that the Soviet Navy should seek to counter them – and very possibly emulate them too.

The likely success rate of such attacks is extremely hard to gauge and is probably unknowable until they are carried out for real, but the difficulties are probably greater than is often thought to be the case. Almost by definition large ships like carriers have extensive active and passive defences which make them more resilient than small ones to conventional attack. The blip that represents them on Soviet radar screens, moreover, may well be made to prove quite undistinctive; and unless the Soviet Navy has a nearby submarine, surface ship or aircraft to act as a tattletale that will give the game away, it may therefore have to attack every blip in a task group as though it were the carrier – an expensive undertaking.[46] Certainly the further away from the Soviet homeland the operation takes place, the more difficult it would be for the Soviet Navy to prevail in sustained conflict. Its surface ships would require extensive support from an auxiliary fleet much more capable of keeping them supplied in a hostile environment than it appears to be at the present moment. The narrowness of the choke points through which the Soviet Navy has to get to and come back from the high seas would be an operational disadvantage even for its submarines. Extensive oceanic reconnaissance would be needed as well.

There seem to be two possible solutions to the problem. The Soviet Navy may one day create equivalent battle groups (of *Kirovs* and carriers?) of its own to fight the US Navy on more equal terms or, more immediately, it may consciously try to avoid the need for sustained operation by relying on surprise attack by carrier attack groups whose subsequent survival would not be regarded as particularly crucial. Hence its constant trailing of US carriers and its determination 'to pose a permanent counter under the protection of peace'.[47] (Arguably, this practice could be used to explain why US Navy carriers are targeted even when temporarily out of range of the Soviet Union, all apparently in the name of national defence.)

For such reasons as these, the success of Soviet anti-carrier operations depends critically on things like the degree of surprise achieved, Soviet readiness to use nuclear weapons pre-emptively, the effort both sides devote to the task on the day and on the area in which the conflict takes place. There are in fact too many variables in this equation for short and simple answers. As Admiral Moorer, the then Chief of Naval Operations reported: 'Victory in a Mediterranean encounter in 1973 would have depended on which navy struck first and a variety of other factors. Victory would have depended on the type of scenario which occurred.'[48]

It is almost as difficult to assess the relative importance the anti-carrier task now assumes in Soviet eyes. In the era when US Navy carriers exerted one of the most severe strategic nuclear threats against the Soviet Union, countering them was clearly regarded as very important indeed. According to one estimate, the 'anti-ship' function (of which the anti-carrier component was but one part) enjoyed some 30 per cent of the total Soviet investment in new combatants as late as 1960–5.[49] Subsequently the proportion has declined quite drastically to about 10 per cent in the 1970–5 period; no new classes of surface ship with a principal anti-ship function were embarked on and most of the effort seemed to be concentrated instead on tasks associated with the maintenance of the nuclear deterrent at sea. This might have been the result of feelings either that other tasks were intrinsically more important, or that the carrier problem had been solved, or simply a reflection of the relative decline in US carrier power – or of all three. But as we have seen modifications to existing ships and the construction of new ones have demonstrated increased attention to making them capable of fighting sustained operations; the effort devoted to submarines like the *Charlie II* and the *Oscar* and aircraft like the *Backfire* also indicate a driving concern for the outcome of the surface battle. The matter is now more complicated by the fact that it is rather difficult, and perhaps ultimately pointless, to try to separate anti-carrier operations undertaken in the name of maritime defence from those subsumed by the more generalised mission of sea control. Either way, defending the Soviet Union and its global interests against threats from the surface of the sea have a perceived importance in Soviet eyes second only to strategic attack and defence.

STRATEGIC DEFENCE

In 1964 Marshal Sokolovskiy wrote in *Red Star* that, 'The first priority mission of naval operations in the oceanic and sea theatres will be the destruction of atomic missile submarines.' The absolute importance the Soviet Navy attaches to the task of defending the homeland against submarine launched ballistic missile attack is stressed by a large number of Western observers, Michael MccGwire and Robert Herrick among them. Indeed it has often been described as the Navy's primary mission.[50]

It is easy to see why the Soviet Navy and many Western observers should think this way. The worst threat facing the Soviet Union, like any other country, is that of nuclear attack. With the advent of the SSBN, the maritime component of this multidimensional threat has become strategically much more significant and potentially far more destructive. If the Soviet Navy were able to reduce this threat substantially, it would clearly be a major contribution to Soviet security. As Gorshkov wrote:

The imperialists are turning the World Ocean into an extensive launching pad . . . of ballistic missiles, of submarines and carrier aviation trained on the Soviet Union and the countries of the Socialist community. And our navy must be capable of standing up to this real threat.[51]

The Soviet Navy's attempt to do this is partly through offering a counter-deterrent against the Imperialists in the shape of its own SSBN force, and partly through active measures against Western SSBNs. No task could be more crucial. In Gorshkov's words, action against the West's strategic nuclear systems 'with the aim of disrupting or weakening to the maximum their strikes on ground objectives' has become the most important of the Soviet Navy's fleet versus fleet tasks.[52]

The emphasis on post-war survival and ultimate success in Soviet military writing increases the Navy's incentive to try to limit the damage the West could do to the Soviet Union by destroying all the Western SSBNs it can. This makes particular sense for the Soviet Union given that country's well-known penchant for extreme measures of protectiveness at almost any cost. Secondly the Soviet Union would also like to avoid the situation where a largely intact Western SSBN force might be used to blackmail it into relative submission towards the end of a less-than-absolute war. By whittling away at Western SSBNs in fact, the Soviet Navy might be able to reduce the effectiveness of this Western vehicle for last-ditch strategic leverage, and so make a major contribution to the 'successful' outcome of such a war. It has even been argued that this kind of stealthy symbolic conflict beneath the surface of the oceans might actually be the main component of a limited war between the superpowers, but one whose result might nevertheless prove decisive.[53] Finally there is the more worldly point that the proposition that the Navy should be support so that it can defend the country against sea-based nuclear attack is a persuasive one in the Soviet Union, and works to the Navy's advantage. The Soviet Navy therefore has an institutional interest in making as much of this mission as it can. Historically it has proved to be the Navy's most effective means of being more than merely the 'faithful helper' of the Army.[54]

Soviet naval writing and experience shows that the anti-SSBN mission requires above all else a balanced response of all the arms, which is not necessarily restricted to the Navy itself. Gorshkov acknowledged the contribution that the other services might make to this mission and stressed that the Soviet Navy's campaign against Western SSBNs would be a team effort involving ships, submarines and aircraft and would depend critically on its ability to control the relevant air and sea space.[55] Soviet thinking on this is quite different from that which often seems to apply in the West, where the hunters (SSNs) and the hunted (SSBNs) are pictured playing their deadly game in sinister isolation. As befits a nation with a collectivist ideology, the Soviet Navy appears to believe in the pack rather than in the lone wolf. 'The essence of the problem', it was stated as early as 1961,

> is to create effective means for the distant destruction of submarines from the air which will make it possible to employ for their destruction the most effective modern means of destruction – missiles with nuclear charges launched from submarines, aircraft and ships, and possibly also from shore launching mounts.[56]

For the next few years traditionalists in the Soviet Navy argued for a balanced fleet in general and for the surface ship in particular, stressing their value in ASW operations. For this reason, Soviet naval construction since the early 1960s has seen the production of many large ships like the *Kresta II*, *Kara*, *Moskva* and *Kiev* whose principal weapons fit appears to be for ASW operations.

Radicals pushed instead for a concentration on aircraft and submarines for the proposition that the best weapon against the submarine *is* the submarine appears to have been as generally accepted in the Soviet Navy as it has in most other countries' navies. There have been many reports and much speculation about Soviet submarines attempting to trail Western SSBNs as they leave their bases or pass through geographic choke-points. References to the task also appear in Soviet naval literature, as in Captain First Rank B. I. Rodonov's 1977 remark: 'One of the basic missions of nuclear-powered torpedo submarines is achieving a constant tracking of nuclear-powered submarines with ballistic missiles with the aim of destroying them at the outbreak of a nuclear war.'[57] Although there are some indications that the Soviet Navy is not as good at this as it is sometimes claimed, the open literature offers little guide about how prevalent or effective this practice is, but the argument that this is what Soviet torpedo-firing SSNs (and the deep-diving *Alphas* in particular) have been largely designed for is at least superficially a quite persuasive one.

However current Soviet practice in general ASW also stresses co-ordinated action by submarine, ship and aircraft. The heart of the ASW effort appears to be the 'search–strike' group of between two to five ASW ships, supported by land-based ASW aircraft (mainly the Il-38 *May* and the Tu-142) and ship-borne helicopters which locate, track and attack submarines with torpedoes. The surface ships would attack with torpedoes, ASW rocket launchers and torpedo-dropping missiles like the SS-N-14. Given the stress on the value of submarines for ASW in Soviet literature, *Victors*, *Tangos* and *Alphas* would also be valuable members of the team, although details of their performance in this role are conspicuously absent from the public domain. Certainly large numbers of these submarines take part in Soviet ASW exercises.[58]

Soviet thinking about operations against the Western SSBN force indicates that attacks on the system as a whole are contemplated as well as the more familiar stalking of individual submarines. It is by no means inconceivable that the Soviet Navy might attempt to 'sanitise' likely SSBN patrol areas by saturating them with nuclear warheads delivered by submarine launched ballistic missiles (the SS-NX-13 of the *Yankees* possibly) or by missiles fired from shore such as the SS-18.[59] The idea of these attacks would be to incapacitate Western SSBNs so they could not fire their missiles: actually sinking them would be something of a bonus. The West can also expect the Soviet Navy to compensate for the difficulty of destroying SSBNs themselves by attacking their support structure instead, their bases, communications aircraft, control centres and so on. This has always been a feature of Soviet writing on the subject. In 1964, for instance, Colonel V. P. Zhukov included within the task of maritime reconnaissance aircraft the requirement for 'searching for transports carrying special weapons needed by rocket submarines and directing naval strike forces to them: determining the location and identity of navigation and communication facilities needed by submarine rocket carriers'.[60]

Finally the increasing range of Western SLBMs meant that the submarines firing them were able to do so from positions further and further away from Soviet territory. The *Polaris* A-1 missile of 1961 had a range of 1,200 nautical miles, the A-2 of 1962 1,600 nautical miles and the A-3 of 1964 2,500 nautical miles. The range of the *Poseidon* C-3 missile is also about 2,500 miles. This forced the Soviet Navy to move forward in order to deal with Western SSBNs. Their difficulty in doing so led Michael MccGwire to argue that the Soviet Navy very evidently was *not* straining at the leash to become a blue-water navy.[61] He pointed out that it had actually to operate further from the Soviet Union than these ranges suggest in order to destroy SSBNs before they fired their missiles, and/or to prevent the United States using them as a strategic reserve. The decision to move forward in this way was evidently taken at the

Twenty-second Party Congress in October 1961 but the prac-
ticalities defeated the Soviet Navy until about 1963/4 when operations in the 1,500 mile undersea defence area began in earnest, an
operation taking Soviet ASW teams into the Norwegian Sea and the
eastern Mediterranean. MccGwire suggested that the second phase
aimed at the *Polaris* A-3 began about 1968; this involved the Soviet
Navy in operations even further forward, against SSBN bases in
Europe, Atlantic transit routes and possible patrol areas as far away
as the Indian Ocean. This forward policy required high levels of
operating experience, shore facilities, the development of a fleet
train and a need for bases for reconnaissance aircraft. 'The primary
determinant of the Soviet Navy's forward policy', MccGwire concluded, 'was the strategic defence of the homeland against the threat
of attack from distant sea areas.'[62] It was the only satisfactory
explanation for the Soviet Navy's dramatic move forward in the late
1960s, the Soviet Union's courtship of Egypt, Somalia, Ethiopia,
West African states and so on. Political influence-building was a
subsequent bonus, not an initial justification for forward deployment: it was something the Soviet Navy did with ships that were
there for another reason.[63] Moreover, MccGwire went on to say that
it was also grappling with the even more difficult task of countering
the West's very long range *Trident* submarines: 'All the evidence,
including Gorshkov's own statements, indicates that the Soviet
Union is striving to meet this demanding operational requirement.'[64]

However, this whole argument has come under severe attack from
those who point out the inherent difficulties of anti-SSBN operations, doubt the extent to which Soviet naval operations in areas like
the Mediterranean and the Indian Ocean can really be attributed to
this mission and who suggest instead that the Soviet Navy had other
reasons for moving forward at this time. According to the members
of the Center for Naval Analyses in the United States, for instance,
there was an undoubted stress on strategic defence in 1960–5, but
the West, bemused by the scale of Soviet expansion from then on,
has exaggerated both its permanence and its effectiveness – and,
moreover, has dangerously neglected the Soviet Navy's potential for
other missions such as sea control, coercive naval diplomacy and
strategic strike.[65] In fact this mission has perceptibly lost priority
since 1965, a decline symbolised in Soviet naval literature by a
corresponding increase in the stress put on the invulnerability of
SSBNs. 'Contrary to a widespread but unfounded impression, it has

not been the primary task since then', James McConnell has concluded.[66]

The main reason for this decline in emphasis was the Soviet Navy's gradual acceptance that in the current state of the art, the task was substantially beyond it, and, for that matter, beyond any other navy too. Although both sides have devoted huge efforts to research in ASW methods, they have so far failed to come up with any technological breakthrough which could, in the current phrase, render the oceans transparent. At most, such solutions are on the distant horizon and, almost certainly, would be effectively offset by the deployment of long-range missiles like the D-5 and SS-N-8 in *Trident*, *Delta* and *Typhoon* submarines.[67] It is very difficult to see how Soviet ASW groups which, as we have seen, feature aircraft and surface ships rather prominently could seriously expect to operate in *Trident* patrol areas off the coast of the United States. Even the task of trailing the SSBNs is in practical terms considerably more difficult than it looks in theory, assuming the SSBN could be reliably 'picked up' in the first place. SSBNs could probably outrun diesel-powered trailers relatively easily and given maintenance/cruise cycles, the need to put more than one SSN onto every hostile SSBN, and other maritime requirements which SSNs would doubtless be needed for (such as operations against US Navy carriers) the Soviet Navy simply does not appear to have enough hunter–killer submarines to make this mission enough of a practicality for it to be regarded as a top priority.[68]

In fact the Soviet Navy appears to be much more vulnerable to strategic ASW than does the US Navy. The West is generally considered to be ahead in most aspects of ASW technology and it produces quieter nuclear-powered submarines.[69] The *Yankee* component of the Soviet SSBN force, on its way to the broad oceans, has still to transit geographic narrows where it would be more vulnerable to ASW ambush. Moreover, as we shall shortly see, the Soviet Navy may well believe that Western forces – especially submarines – would seek to attack the Soviet *Delta* force. For all these reasons, Soviet ASW efforts may well be directed at Western hunter–killers rather than at Western SSBNs. The more this is the case the less the Soviet Navy's capacity for strategic defence.

Soviet naval exercises, especially those since 1973, have certainly featured ASW operations prominently: they were an important element of *Vesna–1975* and probably the main theme of the spring exercises of 1976 and 1977. The bulk of the effort seems to have

been undertaken in waters near the Greenland–Iceland–UK Gap –
an area appropriate for operations against both SSBNs and
hunter–killer submarines.[70] Both the location and the character of
these ASW exercises are inherently ambiguous. Probably we shall
only know that the Soviet Navy is definitely after Western SSBNs as
a major priority if/when it deploys ASW teams into *Trident* operating areas.

On present evidence it seems fair to conclude that the Soviet
Navy does expend considerable effort on strategic defence but has
rather low expectations of success. Working on a characterisation
which has 'annihilation' (meaning 80–90 per cent loss of enemy
forces), 'smashing' (70 per cent), 'defeating' (50 per cent), 'substantially degrading' (30 per cent), and 'degrading' (10–15 per cent),
James McConnell argues that Soviet naval writing implies an expectation of a maximum of 15 per cent success.[71] It is very hard to
gauge what significance the Soviet Union would attach to this performance. On the one hand it might be considered worth the effort
simply by virtue of the fact that it might reduce damage to the
Soviet Union to a certain extent or give the Soviet Navy more
politico-strategic leverage in a less-than-absolute conflict. On the
other hand, the 85 per cent of Western SSBNs which would by the
same measure succeed in their mission would surely still be regarded
as a totally effective deterrent force, and the putative loss of the
remainder might be thought to make little real difference, either in
terms of negotiating power or of the death and destruction inflicted.

To conclude, the Soviet Navy's main motivation in its strategic
defence effort against Western SSBNs is probably to maintain as
many options for the future as possible, rather than to attempt to
build up a strategic ASW capacity in the present. By exploring all
the possibilities seriously it prepares itself for future eventualities,
particularly for the chance that there may some day be a technological breakthrough in submarine detection. In the meantime,
and as a bonus, these efforts may effect some reduction in possible
damage to the Soviet Union; they increase the Navy's political
effectiveness in less-than-absolute conflicts with the West, and they
enhance the Navy's institutional standing inside the country.

STRATEGIC STRIKE

Since the mid-1960s strategic strike, that is the use of sea-based
nuclear weapons against land targets, has been the main mission

priority of the Soviet Navy. Up to then, as we have seen, it had been some type of maritime defence: against the threat of amphibious attack, Western strike carriers and, finally, Western SSBNs. This important shift was achieved at the Twenty-third Party Congress of 1966. At that time in *Izvestiya* Gorshkov declared: 'Nuclear powered submarines equipped with ballistic missiles have now become the main force of the Navy.' [72] Since then the same point has constantly been made in Soviet naval writings. The policy was announced on the eve of the successful deployment of *Yankee* class submarines. The fact that over 40 per cent of the Soviet Navy's constructional effort from 1966 onwards has been devoted to the building of SSBNs confirms the absolute importance this task has in Soviet eyes. (There is some evidence, incidentally, that suggests that this mission priority was forced on a reluctant Navy by the Soviet Government. [73] In this case, writings on the subject by Gorshkov and others may have been aimed at unreconstructed salt-horses inside the Navy, at least as much as it was at unbelievers outside.)

Soviet strategists believe that the use of nuclear weapons in the early stages of a major war will essentially decide its outcome. According to Sokolovskiy 'the initial period of a contemporary nuclear-missile war, obviously, will be a major and decisive period which predetermines the development and outcome of the entire war'. [74] We have already seen why Gorshkov thought it such a good idea to deploy these decisive weapons at sea in SSBNs (see above). The effect of so doing meant that:

> Today a fleet operating against the shore is able not only to solve the tasks connected with territorial changes, but directly to influence the course and even outcome of a war. In this connection the operations of a fleet against the shore have assumed paramount important in armed conflict at sea.

In fact, 'the constantly growing ability of nuclear fleets to achieve ever more decisive objectives in a modern war' has greatly increased the importance of the Soviet Navy in Soviet defence and has also led to fleet versus shore operations becoming steadily more important than those of fleet versus fleet, a trend Gorshkov saw operating throughout the present century. [75] Operations against the shore were now much more important than operations against the enemy's navy, except in so far as the second was a precondition of the first.

Although none of this seems significantly different from orthodox Western thinking on the subject, the same certainly does not apply to Soviet concepts about nuclear deterrence as a whole. Soviet strategists believe that a recognised ability to fight a war through to a successful conclusion makes the best deterrent, whereas Westerners generally are content to make it clear to an aggressor that the costs of his action would outweight the benefits. Soviet deterrence will not necessarily have 'failed' if a war breaks out: it will only have done so if the Soviet Union does not emerge as the 'winner'. Because of this Soviet strategists show a particular interest in weaponry and policies which will either reduce damage to their own side or which will otherwise lead to their coming out of the war in a better state, socially, economically and strategically, than their adversary.[76] This explains the Soviet Union's determined efforts to create an effective system of civil defence and their willingness to devote a lot of resources to the very difficult business of destroying Western SSBNs. It is also said to lead to the Soviet Navy's adopting a 'withholding strategy' with its own SSBNs.

Put briefly, the idea is that missiles carried by the Navy's SSBNs would not be launched but would instead be kept back as a strategic reserve capable of devastating its adversary in the final stages of a general war. Such a reserve would help the Soviet Union in any bargaining about the conduct or conclusion of the war that might take place; accordingly it would be the final decisive means to meaningful politico-strategic victory.[77] The argument that the Soviet Navy would seek to defer its strategic strike in this way leans on two different types of evidence. First it seems to emerge from the way in which Soviet naval writers seem to process history. Gorshkov, for instance, argued that naval power actually determined the final events and politico-strategic outcome of many wars in which the bulk of the action had already taken place on land. Into the category comes the Great Northern War (1700–21), the War of American Independence (1775–83), the Crimean War (1853–6), the Russo-Turkish War (1877–8), the Sino-Japanese War (1894–5) and the Russo-Japanese War (1904–5). Given the overwhelming belief in the Soviet Union that the Red Army won the Second World War, more or less single-handedly, Gorshkov had to be extremely circumspect about making similar observations on that conflict, but he seems to have done his best.[78] The same argument was certainly made about Admiral Jellicoe's cautious conduct of the Battle of Jutland in the First World War; whereas once Soviet military historiography simply contented itself with attacks on the British Admiral's indecision, Gorshkov was concerned to show how right Jellicoe was not to endanger a good strategic position by seeking precipitate and unnecessary local victories over the enemy. The mere existence of a superior British fleet, Gorshkov concluded, would lead eventually to the defeat of Germany. He maintained: 'History gives us examples of how navies, by their presence or even by virtue of their existence in the possession of one of the belligerents, have had a definite and sometimes very substantial influence on the outcome of an armed struggle ... merely by posing a potential threat to keep the war going.' [79]

It is easy to read into this kind of naval history the proposition that naval power in general and its strategic strike capacity in particular should not and would not be expended prematurely but should instead be held back until such time as its use, or threatened use, would have a decisive effect on the outcome of a war. Perhaps the existence of a large, unused and inviolate SSBN force would enable the Soviet Union to secure a victory won on the ground of Europe, or elsewhere, or (unthinkable thought) to reduce the strategic consequences of defeat.

The implications of this line of argument for the Soviet Navy are fairly clear: it would need to build up a strong force of SSBNs and be prepared to keep them safe, possibly for the duration of a less than absolute conflict with the West. Because the same possibilities are open to the West as well (a point sometimes overlooked) the Soviet Navy also has every incentive to whittle away at the enemy's SSBN force, if it can.

The second indication that the Soviet Union has a withholding strategy of this kind comes from the pattern of its SSBN deployments. Typically, rather less than 15 per cent of the Soviet Navy's *Delta* and *Yankee* forces, currently something like nine or ten submarines in total, are deployed on their war stations at any one time, with the *Deltas* staying back in the Barents Sea and Sea of Okhotsk by virtue of the very long range of their missiles. These proportions are much lower than applies to any of the Western navies, the US Navy in particular, which achieved a 72 per cent deployment rate for its *Poseidon* submarines in 1979.[80] If the Soviet Navy intended to use the SSBN force pre-emptively in the early stages of a nuclear exchange, the argument goes, would it not deploy more of them at sea?

But there are competing explanations for this low level of deployment. It may be a case of 'reculer pour mieux sauter' – of the Soviet Navy's keeping few SSBNs 'up front' simply in order to be better able to send out a surge of them if and when the need arises. Alternatively, the Soviet Navy may in fact be deploying all the SSBNs it can: the low rate may easily be a function not of choice but of circumstance. Geography and the climate make refitting SSBNs a much more demanding task for the Soviet Navy than it is for Western navies. Its nuclear submarine repair yards at Leningrad (two of them), Gorky, Komsomolsk and Severodvinsk are all frozen up for much of the year; additionally, at the first four yards an absence of dry dock facilities and low water depths have to be contended with. There may be special bureaucratic and institutional difficulties in refitting nuclear submarines as well.[81] The same deficiencies would similarly explain why the deployment rate of nuclear-powered cruise missile or torpedo-firing submarines is also low compared both to Western levels and to the equivalent ratio for the Soviet Navy's diesel submarines. Finally, as Paul Nitze, a former Secretary of the US Navy, reported:

> the Soviet Navy did not know how to recruit and maintain the number of crews necessary to keep all of these nuclear power plants going. They have the same problem we do. It is not only a question of quantity of manpower, but also of the quality of manpower needed to keep these things in operation.[82]

Clearly the proposition that the Soviet Navy deploys so few of its SSBNs simply because it has no choice for technical, bureaucratic and manpower reasons would cast some doubt on the proposition that it is in fact working to the concept of the 'deferred strike'.

Nevertheless, a policy of deferred strike would almost certainly increase the Soviet Navy's need to protect its SSBNs against Western attack since they would become strategically more important as the war went on. Consequently, Western forces would have growing incentives (and, perhaps, more opportunities) to attack them. Thus it may well be more than coincidental that a 'pro-SSBN mission' seems to have come to the fore about the same time as the 'withholding strategy'.

As we have already seen, there is much support inside the Soviet Navy for the idea that 'The struggle against missile-armed submarines and the efforts to destroy them before they employ their weapons has become one of the foremost missions of navies.'[83] It follows from this that the operation of Soviet SSBNs depends on the Soviet Navy being able to defeat Western attempts to sink them.

The Navy, wrote Gorshkov in 1975, 'must work out methods for enabling submarines to overcome the counteraction of ASW forces'.[84] SSBNs could not look after themselves. 'The First and Second World Wars showed the fallacy of the view that the submarine by virtue of its concealment after emerging from its base can itself ensure its own invulnerability.'[85] The rest of the Navy, in Soviet terminology, had to give the SSBNs enough 'combat stability' for them to 'solve their tasks'. This kind of sea control in short was a precondition for the Navy to carry out its task of strategic strike.

With the advantage of hindsight, it is not difficult to see why the Soviet Navy put such stress on this requirement. In the West, from the late 1960s onwards there has been much research and analysis of the possibilities and the perils of strategic ASW. Western navies have invested heavily in large area underwater surveillance systems, ASW mines like CAPTOR, ASW patrol aircraft like the P3C and the *Nimrod*, ASW ships of all shapes and sizes and, above all perhaps, in sophisticated ASW-capable submarines. Much of this huge ASW effort could be directed against Soviet SSBNs.

The Soviet Navy's solution to the problem was typically complex and multidimensional. In the first place much stress was put on the development of SLBMs of such range that the firing submarines need not leave local waters. *Deltas* are intrinsically safer and more cost effective than *Yankees* because they do not need to break out into the open oceans to reach their launch positions. *Yankees* in consequence are being phased out as SSBNs in favour of *Deltas* and perhaps *Typhoons*. Nevertheless, while *Yankees* remain a significant part of the Soviet Navy's SSBN inventory, the Soviet fleet must also have the possibly demanding task of helping them fight their way out into the open oceans.

The real advantage of very long range SLBMs is that they allow the SSBNs to operate in local waters which the Soviet Union can more easily turn into secure sanctuaries. Such seems to be her intention for the Barents Sea and the Sea of Okhotsk. These safe areas are heavily mined, criss-crossed with acoustic surveillance systems, and covered by intense air patrols. The configuration of their sea-beds is doubtless well known to the Soviet Navy.[86]

The Navy places much less emphasis than does the West on stealth as a means of defence for its SSBNs (whether they are in these sanctuaries or trying to break out of them), doubtless because Soviet submarines are generally noisier. Instead it seems to rely on a complex system of active defence comprising air, surface and sub-surface action. Taking these in reverse order, Soviet submarines would certainly be on guard against intruding Western hunter–killer submarines, detecting them by using active sonar (even though this means revealing Soviet submarines as well) and perhaps sinking them with or without the help of aircraft and surface ships. They would also take action against any Western surface ships involved directly or indirectly in the strategic ASW task.

Soviet naval writers also lay great stress on the necessity for command of the air in the task of providing 'combat stability' for their SSBNs. Air superiority may be supplied either by land-based or sea-based aircraft, and would allow the Soviet Union to attack Western ASW aircraft, and very possibly their bases as well, protect her surface ships from Western air strikes and attack Western ships. Also, as we have already seen, the AVMF contains a large component specifically dedicated to the ASW task.

Surface ships are the final layer of this multidimensional system of defence. 'Surface ships', wrote Gorshkov, 'remain the basic and often sole combat means of ensuring deployment of the main strike forces of the fleet – submarines.'[87] In Gorshkov's view, the unwisdom of neglecting the contribution surface ships can make to the effective operation of submarines was clearly demonstrated by the fate of the German Navy in the Second World War. Because the Germans ignored the potential flexibility and versatility of sea power and constructed a 'narrowly specialised' and one-sided force based on submarines, 'the German fleet proved no match for the Anglo-American fleet'.[88] Gorshkov has plainly taken this parallel and its warning to heart. It is perhaps one that should be heeded more in the West as well.

Surface ships have a variety of tasks in this pro-SSBN role. They would certainly be deployed directly against Western hunter–killer submarines, something for which most of them are especially well equipped. Ships with a substantial command-and-control, air defence or surface strike capacity (such as the *Kirov* and some of the more recent Soviet cruisers and large destroyers) would protect Soviet ASW ships and submarines against Western air and surface attack. Finally, it is by no means inconceivable that surface ships would be involved in connected operations to seize territory adjacent to these SSBN sanctuaries (Northern Norway? Svalbard? the Japanese Islands?) either to facilitate Soviet departures or to harass Western arrivals. The idea that this is the main war task of the Soviet surface fleet may explain the Soviet Navy's tendency to keep some of its best ships back in times of tension; indeed the whole burden of the argument is that in the event of major conflict with the West the great bulk of the Soviet Navy would operate in relatively local waters.

Analysts of the Soviet Navy are constantly warned of the dangers of 'mirror-imaging', that is assuming that Soviet equipment and concepts of war are essentially the same as those of the West. Conceivably they may, in fact, be wholly or partly different from what most Westerners expect. This may especially apply to the complex and uncertain business of strategic strike. The fact that the Soviet Navy had SLBMs long before it had a delineated strategic mission of the sort understood in the West, and discussed above, reinforces the impression that they, unlike the West, may have other uses for their SSBNs as well.

There is some evidence to support the notion, for instance, that SSBNs might be used not so much as part of an integrated national system of nuclear deterrence but against land targets of particular interest to the Navy. After all, at the time when the *Yankee* submarines were being developed, Rear-Admiral Isachenkov (deputy commander-in-chief of the Soviet Navy for Shipbuilding and Armaments) reportedly stated: 'Ballistic rockets are basically assigned to the destruction of coastal targets such as naval bases and industrial centres.' [89]

More generally, analysts such as James McConnell have concluded that the Soviet Union actively began from 1975 to prepare her forces for a nuclear war confined to the territory of her East European allies, Western Europe and other areas of contention around her strategic perimeter. They deduced this from the growing number of suggestions in Soviet literature that a nuclear war might not after all, engulf the homelands of the superpowers. Such a proposition (which, incidentally, preceded and could be held to justify NATO's decision to modernise its theatre nuclear forces) can be supported by Soviet observations about possible targets for their SSBNs which can certainly be interpreted to mean that they are at least partly intended for 'tactical' targets in Western Europe, China, Japan or for US bases on foreign soil. In the autumn of 1976, moreover, the Soviet Navy once more demonstrated its extreme reluctance to throw anything away by deploying six old *Golf 2* diesel submarines into the Baltic, an area from which they could launch their 600 nautical mile missiles against many theatre targets in north and central Europe. The use of these submarines (or, indeed, of

SS-20 missiles fired from advanced positions in Eastern Europe) would not necessarily invite American retaliation against the territory of the Soviet Union itself, and would therefore be entirely consistent with the existence of a Eurostrategic option of this kind.[90]

Alternatively, or additionally, Soviet SSBNs may be used against naval targets at sea. It has been suggested that they have an important function in strategic defence. As we have already seen, they might launch their missiles against those areas of ocean where Western SSBNs patrol in the hope that this kind of saturation would destroy or at least effectively disarm any of them that happened to be there. This would be an expensive undertaking, admittedly, but one which makes a certain kind of sense, given the Soviet Union's known propensity for protectiveness.[91]

There is also the possibility that ballistic missile firing submarines down to and including the *Yankees* might have been partly intended for use against high-value surface targets, like Western carrier task groups. Some public statements seem to confirm this possibility. Thus in April 1970, *Izvestiya* declared that Soviet SLBMs could be used against 'major land bases, ships at formation and those which are laid up, and industrial centres'. A little later N. Shablikov, in the newspaper *Zarya Vostoka*, stated that: 'Submarines armed with ballistic missiles are capable of destroying ships at a distance of hundreds of kilometres and of delivering blows from beneath the water at strategic enemy targets at greater distances.'[92] Such a function would seem to be technically perfectly feasible, especially in view of the characteristics of the SS-NX-13 missile which the *Yankee* was, arguably, originally designed to carry. But other missiles like the SS-N-4, SS-N-5 and SS-N-6 seem quite adequate for this task.

This hypothesis also offers explanations for a number of otherwise rather odd things about Soviet SSBNs in general and *Yankees* in particular: why *Yankees* were produced even after the period when *Deltas* were available: why so few *Yankees* are out on patrol at any one time: why the *Yankee*'s design emphasised speed at the expense of noise (whereas SSBNs with a strike mission need to be quiet but not necessarily fast). This kind of evidence has led one recent analyst to conclude: 'However much Gorshkov brags about his strategic strike forces, the Soviet Navy's basic wartime mission definitely is not submarine-launched strategic nuclear strikes at the United States.'[93]

But there are explanations for these puzzles besides Soviet SSBNs being tasked with non-strategic missions. Moreover, given the finite number of SSBNs allowed the Soviet Union under arms control agreements with the United States and their particular value for retaliatory nuclear strike against strategic targets, it is inherently unlikely that the Soviet Union should allocate them to what it seems to regard as secondary missions, many of which could be perfectly well undertaken by land-based missiles of one sort or another. Even so the hypothesis is an interesting and useful one. It should alert Western observers to the idea that the Soviet Union does not *necessarily* see things the same way as the West; Soviet SSBNs might, after all, be used in ways the West does not expect. Moreover it highlights the way in which the Soviet Union avoids tying itself down to specifics about its military intentions – not so much in order to confuse the West as simply to maintain its options. Soviet leaders have clearly grasped the essential versatility and flexibility of sea power, especially in the nuclear age.

AMPHIBIOUS WARFARE

In the Civil War period the Soviet Union's experience of amphibious warfare and of other forms of attack from the sea was mainly from the point of view of the victim. The Western powers intervened in the Baltic, the North, the Black Sea and in the Far East, and by virtue of their sea power were able to exert much influence on events ashore. According to Gorshkov, the new Soviet state rapidly saw the need to develop defences against that kind of threat, and to develop an equivalent capacity for itself. 'For the first time in the history of naval art,' he claimed somewhat obscurely, 'the thirties in our country saw the elaboration of the theory of the marine landing operation which was tested in the course of combat operations.'[94] However, not enough ships and equipment were produced to turn theory fully into practice.

During the Second World War amphibious operations were important to the progress of the land campaign on the Eastern Front, and, along with attacks on German supply lines, were the Soviet Navy's main contribution to the Soviet victory. They also did much to establish Gorshkov himself on the path to a successful naval career; then a mere captain, he distinguished himself in amphibious operations around Odessa in the late summer of 1941. But the scale and success of Soviet efforts in this area were quite dwarfed by the equivalent performance of the Western maritime powers. During the war they demonstrated an impressive capacity for amphibious operations at a strategic level and, as we have seen, the post-war Soviet Navy took as its top priority the task of defending the Soviet Union against this threat.

All the same, both the threat and the need for the Soviet Navy to build up such a capacity itself were taken much less seriously from the mid-1950s onwards. Sokolovskiy accepted that joint operations were important, but still put them at the bottom of the list. 'Although support of the land forces will not be one of the Navy's main tasks, considerable effort must be expended in this direction ... The fleet will ... have the task of carrying out landings on the enemy's coast, and safeguarding the crossing of straits and large water obstacles by the land forces.'[95] Apparently, the view was that, with the advent of nuclear weapons, large-scale amphibious operations were hardly feasible, and smaller-scale ones could perfectly well be 'accomplished by airborne assaults or by the armed amphibious personnel carriers of ground troops'.[96]

This de-emphasis on the need for an amphibious capacity was probably a part of Khruschev's general scepticism about the future validity of the traditional maritime functions and it seems more than coincidental that the reactivation of the Naval Infantry in 1964 came at about the same time as Khruschev's departure from office. Certainly by 1970 there was every sign that the importance of an amphibious capacity was generally accepted once more. As Admiral Stalbo, one of the Soviet Union's leading writers on maritime strategy, put it later:

> We would stress that the basic reasons which forced the warring sides to resort to amphibious landings [in the Second World War] have not only been maintained under modern conditions, but have been considerably enhanced. Because of this, amphibious landings have not lost their importance to the slightest degree.[97]

This impression is reinforced by the stress put on amphibious exercises since the mid-1960s, operations such as *Baikal I* and *II* (1966–7), *Sever* (1968), *Oder-Neisse* (1969), *Okean* (1970), *Iug* (1971) and so forth.

The reasons why the Soviet Navy attaches the importance it does to amphibious warfare can be inferred from the naval literature, exercises, Soviet experience in the Second World War and the way this experience has since been processed as naval history. The predominance of the land forces in Soviet strategic perceptions is illustrated by the attention given the very basic point that wars are fundamentally struggles for territory. It follows from this that naval operations against land targets are, almost by definition, the most important kind there are.[98] In this case, the centrality of the Army and the land battle to Soviet strategy can be used to the Navy's benefit. As Gorshkov pointed out:

> The experience of the Great Patriotic War once again confirmed the validity of the basic tenet of our military doctrine that victory over a strong opponent can be gained only by the common efforts of all branches of the armed forces. The experience also showed that, in a struggle even against a continental adversary, an important role is played by the Navy.[99]

Soviet experience of amphibious operations in the Second World War shows what kind of assistance the Navy should be able to offer the Army. Then sea power could protect the maritime flank of the Army; it could shore up tottering positions by running in supplies and reinforcements, as it did in the Oranienbaum position near Leningrad in 1941; by putting troops ashore behind the enemy's lines it could hold up or disrupt his advance, as the Soviet Army was able to do against Romanian troops heading for Odessa and German troops driving for Murmansk. As a last resort the Navy could evacuate troops from doomed positions (Odessa, Sebastopol, etc.) or even employ its own personnel as ordinary military units – as it did in the defence of Leningrad.[100] This kind of help could easily prove decisive if things were going badly on land. According to the German Admiral Friedrich Ruge, for example, 'the exercise of sea power in the closed Black Sea and the Sea of Azov had a considerable effect on the operations on land and may have saved the Soviets from complete defeat'.[101]

Of course the reverse of all these things was true too: the Navy could (and in the Second World War certainly did) offer considerable help to the Army in its victorious advance, by launching raids, by sudden and unexpected strikes from the sea, by outflanking operations and by keeping the ground forces supplied and reinforced. Sometimes, in fact, an amphibious assault could even be the precondition for a significant land campaign, as in the Kerch–Feodosiya landings of December 1941, and during the final Crimean campaign. Altogether, in Gorshkov's words: 'The Soviet

Navy made a significant contribution to achieving a victory over a strong enemy, ensuring the stability of the strategic flanks of the ground front and comprehensive support of our troops defensively and offensively.'[102]

The presumption is very strong that the Soviet Navy should and could be prepared to do all these things again if the need arose – even in the nuclear age. Various Soviet writers have admitted that nuclear weapons could be used with considerable effect on forces attempting large-scale amphibious landings, but have recommended palliatives such as an emphasis on surprise and deception, the dispersal and camouflage of transports and landing ships and so forth.[103] They have pointed out, moreover, that land operations in a nuclear environment seem likely to be more dispersed, fluid and decentralised than usual: this lack of density makes enemy territory more rather than less vulnerable to a successfully launched assault from the sea. Soviet writers have also argued that amphibious forces can use nuclear weapons themselves, against the enemy's defences. Soviet amphibious exercises are often conducted in a simulated nuclear environment, sometimes with the shore defender using them, sometimes the attacker. In *Okean–1970*, for instance, landings in the Baltic area were only started after the defender had suffered a nuclear bombardment. The same thing happened more or less at the same time in an assault on the Rybachii Peninsular near Murmansk with the nuclear fire support being apparently provided by submarines.[104]

But even if they have involved nuclear weapons, these exercises suggest a tactical rather than a strategic concept of amphibious warfare. They are modern versions of the localised and limited landing operations of the Soviet Navy during the Second World War: they do not suggest that the Russians as yet have serious aspirations for the kind of oceanic amphibious capacity exhibited by the Western allies in that war, and subsequently. With no organic air support, few amphibious warfare ships of the *Ivan Rogov* type and virtually no experience of this larger kind of operation, the Soviet Navy's amphibious reach is currently quite limited.

It concentrates instead on more limited capacities such as those regularly exercised in the Baltic. In the early 1960s amphibious exercises were conducted along the Estonian coast at the entrance to the Gulf of Finland. Since then they have gradually crept westwards and now frequently take place on East German territory, an area which is both near and geographically similar to Denmark.

Danish islands like Bornholm and Zealand are often involved in these exercises willy-nilly: Danish warships have been rammed and, as the Copenhagen newspaper *Aktvelt* recently reported: 'NATO experts claim the Eastern Bloc countries are now working with a completely new boundary for their defence, namely a boundary between Hanstholm and Southern Norway'.[105] In the summer of 1981 the increasing range of these activities was demonstrated by an exercise in which the *Ivan Rogov* led an amphibious assault force 220 miles across open sea, helped defend it against a variety of naval and air attacks en route and safely delivered some 2,000 Naval Infantry, together with all their tanks and heavy equipment, at the end.[106]

The purpose of such operations would, of course, be to offer direct support to the Ground Forces as they advance westwards. But they seem to have other, more particularly naval, objectives too, such as the seizure of strategically significant islands, naval bases, ports and straits. It seems very likely that the Soviet Navy would try to close off the Baltic from Western intervention by dominating the passages around the north of Denmark. By this means it would control the Baltic more securely and so, with even greater confidence, be able to help the Army. Possibly control of these straits could even lead to Soviet Baltic fleet units breaking out into the North Sea and beyond. In this case these small-scale landing operations could be seen as part of Russia's historic battle for access to the high seas.

The Soviet Navy has similar capacities in its other fleet areas too. The Northern Fleet often conducts equivalent operations near the Norwegian border and is sometimes said to have designs on northern Norway, Spitzbergen and, more remotely, on Iceland. Amphibious requirements seem to have a particularly high priority in the Pacific Fleet, at least judging by the high share of amphibious warfare ships it normally has. These ships and the men they carry may be intended for use either against offshore islands or mainland targets in support of Soviet Ground Forces in a war against China: or to secure the various straits around Japan in conflict with the West. In these fleet areas, too, even a limited capacity seems to serve a whole variety of naval and military objectives.

Amphibious operations have always been regarded as some of the most difficult tasks that navies can perform. After their own bitter experiences in this area, the Russians have every reason to know how demanding this function can be. They clearly appreciate the need for specialist and highly trained landing troops (the Naval Infantry) who can act as a spearhead to be followed by regular army units coming along closely behind. Polish and East German units are frequently involved in these 'Brothers-in-Arms' exercises too. The need for specially built and operated amphibious warfare ships, 'landing craft and disembarkation devices', is equally well recognised.[107] Gorshkov remarked that 'American intervention in Vietnam also showed that ship armament continues to hold an important place in the arms system of the modern fleet.'[108] Accordingly all the four fleets are provided with gun-ships such as the *Sverdlovs*, *Kotlins* and *Skorys* which would be used to provide fire support in landing operations. Finally, there is also much stress in the naval literature on the need for air support. In the Second World War, Gorshkov observed, 'Dominance in the air in the area of an operation was an essential prerequisite for its success even if the enemy predominated in naval strength. By the end of the war, airborne landings had become an obligatory constituent part of naval landing operations.'[109]

Exactly the same is clearly held to be the case now: airborne troops (often Czech in nationality) frequently participate in Baltic exercises, seizing enemy airfields and the like. The stress given in Soviet naval literature to the importance of aircover, and the absence of strike carriers in the Soviet fleet, when taken together, suggest that Soviet amphibious operations will only take place within the range of friendly land-based airpower. It reinforces the impression that, for the moment at least, amphibious operations are still regarded as being mainly of tactical importance and are unlikely to be conducted outside waters relatively close to the Soviet Union.

However, Gorshkov put some emphasis on the value the Western powers have derived from their amphibious capacity in 'Local Wars of Imperialism', such as the Korean and Vietnamese conflicts. He catalogued in rather persuasive detail the size and importance of US Navy air strikes, artillery bombardments and landings, and pointed out how very important seaborne military shipments were to the conduct of campaigns ashore.[110] Interestingly, Gorshkov offered little comment about all this, apart from some low-key and ritualistic remarks about the disgraceful use to which this power was put; no doubt he expected the figures to speak for themselves. His dead-pan analysis perhaps suggests that the Soviet Navy would like to develop this kind of intervention capacity for itself one day.

MARITIME INTERDICTION

The Russians have long been interested in the idea of using their Navy to mount a sustained assault on the enemy's merchant and military shipping. In the nineteenth century, for instance, this naval function influenced warship construction (with the production of fast raiding cruisers like the *Admiral Kornilov* class) and was much debated by naval writers. The main fruit of this appeared in the mid-1880s: *Russia's Hope*, a kind of textbook on cruiser warfare which took Britain as an illustrative enemy and which was widely translated and read abroad.

But the emphasis which the Soviet Navy gives this task now is a matter of considerable controversy amongst Western experts. Many believe it to be a major mission of the Soviet Navy; a few have even stated it to be a top priority.[111] Uri Ra'anan, for instance, has detected in Gorshkov's writings an 'almost obsessive preoccupation with the potential of naval warfare against maritime arteries, particularly submarine warfare'. Many professional Western naval men are similarly concerned. For instance, Admiral William Crowe, US Navy, recently argued that the Soviet submarine force could seriously impede Western trade and the flow of troops and military equipment to her allies. This, and the United States' increasing dependence on raw materials from abroad, meant, he thought, that 'any extended disruption of our sea lines of communication would have an enormous impact on our domestic productivity and national security'.[112] The presumption is that the Soviet Navy must realise this as well as we do. Both Herrick and MccGwire, on the other hand, readily concede that the Soviet Navy will almost certainly indulge in this kind of attack, but argue that other missions such as strategic attack and defence are held to be far more important.[113] James McConnell believes the emphasis of maritime interdiction has very markedly declined and was never very high in the first place. He quotes Admiral Filanov in 1965: 'Ocean communications in the initial period . . . will not play any vital role, especially as the major ports and naval bases of the belligerents will most probably have been destroyed by nuclear missile strikes.'[114]

To summarise, this mission was probably not held to be as important in the Soviet Navy of the immediate post-war period as most Western opinion thought it was. Among the reasons for thinking this are the building of medium-range *Whiskey* submarines rather than long-range *Zulus*, which we have already noted (see page 112), and the Soviet Navy's pattern of submarine deployment. If they seriously intended to raid Western maritime communications, Soviet naval leaders would surely have deployed the bulk of their submarines in the Northern fleet area which was far and away the best fitted, geographically, for the task. But no such emphasis took place, an omission which strongly suggests that maritime interdiction had low priority.[115]

Its perceived importance was certainly low in the Khruschev era, for maritime interdiction is a task particularly relevant to a sustained conventional conflict between East and West, something about which Khruschev was very sceptical. The Soviet consensus seemed to be that a major war would inevitably 'go nuclear' and would not last for long. Thus, as Admiral Stalbo put it in 1969:

> A diminution in the importance of combat on ocean lines of communication is one of the natural developments of nuclear missile war. As a result of the use of nuclear weapons against ground targets, enemy losses can turn out to be several times larger than the losses from the most successful operations against his shipping . . . Finally, the devastation that will be caused by the mass use of nuclear weapons against targets located on the territories of the belligerents will sharply reduce all spheres of consumption and in certain cases may even exclude the need for it.[116]

But by the time this was written there had already occurred something of a renaissance for maritime interdiction. In all the versions of Sokolovskiy's *Military Strategy* it was given some prominence: 'Among the primary missions of the Navy in a future war will be the disruption of enemy ocean and sea shipping and the interdiction of his communication lines.'[117] Between 1971 and 1976, it moved up the priority order of naval capabilities from fifth to third in the Great Soviet Encyclopaedia's entries for the Soviet Navy, an improvement sometimes seen to be reflected in other naval writing.[118] Certainly maritime interdiction figured quite prominently in the *Vesna–1975* exercise, as we shall see shortly. Nevertheless it is fairly clearly *not* a primary function of the Soviet Navy. The Russians would certainly indulge in this activity as they do not believe in allowing their enemies 'a free ride' anywhere and realise the West's vulnerabilities in this area. But they would not do it if this means they were less able to carry out other tasks, like strategic strike, which they think more important.

In truth, the emphasis given the task depends quite critically on particular sets of circumstances, the composition of which is hard to predict in advance. The advantages of maritime interdiction, and the consequent stress given it, will be substantially determined by the kind of war it figures in. Soviet naval writers are certainly well aware of the support maritime interdiction can offer the Ground Forces in the prosecution of a land campaign: this is particularly true of the more tactical kind of maritime interdiction which is aimed at *military* shipping in the actual theatre of land operations. This was certainly what the Soviet Navy tried to do in the Second World War. As Gorshkov pointed out: 'Destroying in the war years some 1,300 enemy vessels in the shipping lanes, our fleet had no little influence on the course of the armed struggle on the Soviet–German land front where the fundamental question of the outcome of the war was decided.'[119] Although the execution of this mission in the Northern, Baltic and Black Sea areas was frequently faulty, partly through the absence of aircover, partly through an excessive caution in the use of heavy ships and partly through sheer inefficiency, its potential value was very clearly appreciated after the war. It offered the prospect of sapping the enemy's current ability to fight the land battle and undermining his strategic reserve. A submarine force active in the Mediterranean and missile-armed aircraft operating out of the Black Sea, for instance, might well prevent Western reinforcements and military supplies from reaching Turkey by sea.[120] Similar operations in northern waters would greatly weaken the Western position on NATO's northern flank.

What, however, is true tactically could also be true strategically. If the Soviet Navy were able seriously to inhibit United States reinforcement shipping across the Atlantic, this would clearly have a substantial impact on a sustained conflict in Europe. Gorshkov argued that the German Navy did not concentrate enough resources on the task of undermining the enemy's military–economic potential in this way. The Germans' error 'was to develop the struggle for the Atlantic communications on a wide scale only several years after the start of the war, when it had become clear that their plans on land had failed'.[121] Gorshkov plainly believed that this task was a constituent of the Soviet Navy's growing stress on 'fleet versus shore' operations, and a crucial one, too. He wrote that 'the disruption of the ocean links of communications, the special arteries feeding the military and economic potentials of ... [enemy] ... countries has continued to be one of the most important of the Navy's missions'.[122]

The Soviet Navy shows that it knows how very vulnerable the West is to this kind of attack because of its dependence on shipping for reinforcements, military supplies, food and other strategic commodities. Such vulnerabilities increase the likely cost effectiveness of this method of attack. Even in the Second World War, Gorshkov has remarked, the size of the Allies' anti-submarine effort was wholly disproportionate to the number of German submarines deployed. With the advent of nuclear propulsion and modern surveillance and attack systems, this ratio was likely to be even more in favour of the submarine.[123] For this reason a campaign of maritime interdiction based on the submarine might be of benefit to the Soviet Navy not merely for the Western ships and cargoes it sank, but for the distracting and diversionary effect it might have on the West's maritime forces themselves. It might force the West to pull ASW forces away from such other tasks as hunting Soviet SSBNs or protecting its own SSBNs and surface forces. If it meant that the West devoted more resources to the defence of maritime communications than the Soviet Union committed to their attack, such a campaign could hardly fail to work to the overall strategic advantage of the Soviet Navy. Indeed this might be the main purpose of the exercise.[124] Maritime interdiction, in other words, would be an integral part of a fully rounded strategy: it would not be an isolated activity undertaken simply for the sake of the actual damage it did.

It is also quite conceivable that a limited campaign of maritime interdiction would be of considerable politico-strategic value to the Soviet Union in situations of less-than-absolute conflict with the West. An ability to harass the West's maritime communications (its oil shipping, possibly?) might, in some circumstances, give the Soviet Union some strategic leverage. Some analysts have seen an analogy between this and a period in the 1860s when a previous display of such a capacity was apparently intended to deter the Western powers from interfering in an earlier Polish crisis. It has also been argued that the very obvious maritime interdiction component in *Vesna–1975* was partly designed to contribute to the political de-coupling of Western Europe and the United States, by reminding the Europeans of the fragility of their Atlantic communications.[125] Finally, Gorshkov made some play of the value the Western powers have derived from local wars of Imperialism through their capacity to mount a military blockade of the revolutionary masses ashore.[126] Naturally, an equivalent Soviet capacity could easily be thought desirable as a means of redressing the balance.

Assuming that the Soviet Union does, in fact, think a campaign of maritime interdiction worth the effort, how would it be conducted and with what forces? Soviet literature makes it clear that the submarine would be the main vehicle for such an attack. The Soviet Navy evidently expects such a submarine campaign to be effective but there are obvious difficulties in the way. Although the Soviet Navy has a very large number of cruise missile and torpedo-firing submarines, as we have seen, a great many of them would be permanently involved in other naval functions: being nearly ten years behind the West in ASW technology,[127] the Soviet Navy doubtless anticipates a fairly high rate of submarine loss as well. Geography offers the Soviet Navy little help: access to the high seas is difficult from all four fleet areas. Even in the best of them, the Northern Fleet area, Soviet submarines would be much further away from the Atlantic shipping than was the German U-boat force of the Second World War. Raiding submarines would also have to contend with the West's ASW barriers. Soviet naval literature includes very detailed analyses of the equipment and techniques employed by the West in these barriers.[128] Their diagrammatical reconstruction of the Greenland–Iceland–UK Gap defences, and the more advanced lines due north of Norway, show that they appreciate that Soviet submarines would have to run a potentially formidable gauntlet of patrolling ASW aircraft of high effectiveness, hunter–killer submarines, undersea detection systems, deep mines of the 'Captor' type and a variety of large ASW-dedication surface warships. Even in the Atlantic they would encounter considerable difficulty in the face of Western ASW efforts. Whether the West decides to send its shipping across in protected convoys or in 'defended sea lanes', Soviet submarines would still have to penetrate some rather effective defences, once in the open oceans.

Moreover there are strong indications that the Soviet Navy believes that attack on the West's ports would be at least as cost effective as attack on shipping still at sea. Arguably, this was actually the main method of maritime interdiction envisaged by Sokolovskiy.[129] Certainly the point is much discussed in the Soviet literature. In 1967, for instance, Captain First Rank Marinin menacingly argued: 'Whereas merchant ships located in ports beyond the range of enemy aircraft were considered safe in past wars, today,

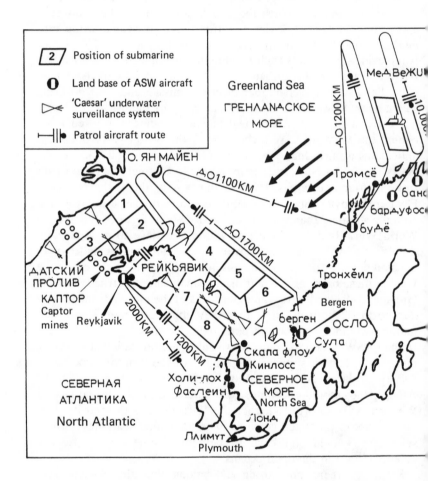

FIGURE 7   *Western ASW barriers – the Soviet view*

Source: Military Electronics/Countermeasures, July 1979, p. 64; originally
published in *Morskoi Sbornik*, November 1976.

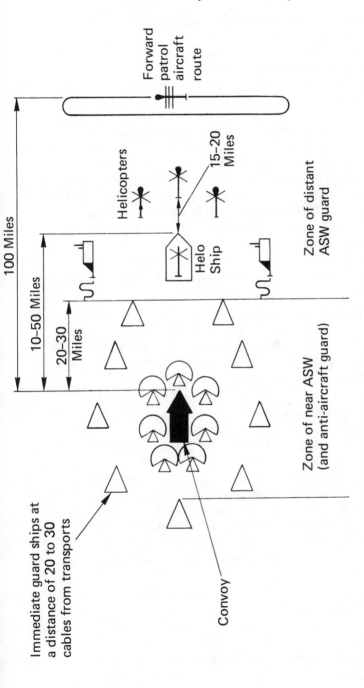

FIGURE 8 *Western convoy tactics – the Soviet view*
(The wording is a literal translation of the Russian)

Source: Military Electronics/Countermeasures, July 1979, p. 64; originally published in *Morskoi Sbornik*, November 1976.

with the development of nuclear weapons, they will be more vulnerable than merchant ships at sea.'[130] As a less dramatic alternative, the Soviet Navy's long-standing capacity for mine warfare could prove most disruptive if applied against European harbours and port approaches. Many Western observers believe this to be the weakest and most vulnerable part of the West's system of maritime communications.

There are also plenty of indications that land-based aircraft would be an important constituent of a Soviet campaign of maritime interdiction. In *Vesna–1975*, for instance, *Backfire* bombers flew from the Kola peninsular in this role for the first time. Long-range reconnaissance aircraft operated extensively over the West's most obvious commercial routes. The Indian Ocean was covered by Il-38 *Mays* and Tu-95 *Bear Ds* from Somalia and the Soviet Union. Il-38s operating from the Siberian coast patrolled the North Pacific: Tu-95s out of Cuba, Guinea and Northern Russia covered the Atlantic. In the same year V. F. Zemshov reminded his readers that:

> Missile-carrying naval aircraft are capable of launching powerful nuclear-missile strikes against highly manoeuvrable formations of surface combat ships and enemy convoys in distant regions of the sea and oceans and also against his ports and naval bases at stand-off ranges.[131]

The Soviet Navy does not, of course, expect the West to stand idly by in the face of this kind of air assault. Necessarily unescorted *Backfire* bombers out of the Kola peninsular sweeping over the top of Norway on their way to attack the West's Atlantic shipping must expect opposition from Western land and carrier-based fighters en route (there and back) and possibly over the target: the targets would have their own defensive surface-to-air missiles as well.

A possible attack might go like this: 40 *Backfire* bombers set off from airbases near Murmansk, heading for an important Atlantic convoy. They do not fly in close formation, instead:

> relying on their inertial and satellite navigation systems to bring them together at the rendezvous point.

The bomber stream is escorted out past the Norwegian coast by *Mikoyan MiG-23 Flogger* fighters. Once well out over the Norwegian Sea, the fighters depart, and the bombers turn south, to pass midway between Scotland and Iceland. The *Backfires* fly in a loose stream at their optimum cruise speed of just under 500 knots, climbing as they burn down their fuel loads. As they near the gap between Iceland and the Faroes, they dip down to 8,000 feet to avoid any possibility of radar detection. Once clear, they climb again to their optimum cruising altitude, a little below 30,000 feet.

Moscow transmits a revised aircraft rally point, based on latest satellite and submarine reports. Some aircraft fail to appear, for one reason or another, but 36 *Backfires* meet and form up for the run-in and attack. Following their leader, still keeping radio silence, they select full afterburner on their twin NK-144 turbofans, climb to 45,000 feet, and accelerate to 1,000 knots or more. A few minutes later, the leader breaks radio silence. The convoy is in sight on the radar, he orders his formation to turn 20° to port in order to intercept.

At virtually the same moment, the SPS-49 air search radar of one of the screening *Oliver Hazard Perry* class frigates (FFG-7) registers the massive raid at a range from the convoy center of 250 nautical miles. With the radar operator calling jamming strobes all over the scope, and no IFF (identification, friend or foe), no one has any doubt about the raid's identity or intent. But what can be done about it?

Within six minutes, the *Backfires* have identified their targets and have set their missiles. The range has closed to 150 nautical miles, and the missiles are released. The *Backfires* turn to return home, with a few of their number remaining within radar range long enough for the damage assessment.

Some of the missiles fail to perform as intended, but more than 60 (each plane carries two) approach the convoy in the space of minutes. The guided-missile frigates among the escort belch standard SM-1 missiles until their foredecks are burnt black, but they can get only a fraction of the AS-6s. More than 30 survive to plunge into convoy ships. Several ships are sunk, and several more have much of their vital cargo destroyed.

The *Backfire* force does not get home unscathed, of course. Alerted by reports from the convoy, NATO interceptors based in Iceland and Scotland await the bombers along their return route. With support from long-range Soviet interceptors, heavy use of their own electronic countermeasures, and a high speed dash to minimise exposure time, the bombers break through, but only after three are lost. It is not a cheap victory for the Soviets, but it is a victory all the same.[132]

The extent, or indeed the possibility, of Soviet victory would also depend on whether the West had been able to attack Soviet airbases in northern Russia, perhaps by means of carrier strikes. The Soviet Navy's success in maritime defence, therefore, may have important consequences for its capacity for maritime interdiction. The same kind of multidimensional approach is evident in the Soviet Navy's attitude to the role of surface ships in maritime interdiction. Its campaigns of the Second World War were fought by all the arms – aircraft, submarines, minor and major combatants – although naval writers freely concede that the latter were used much less effectively than they should have been.[133] The role of surface ships, though, may not be in the direct attack of shipping but in various other vital supportive tasks. They would doubtless have an important role in helping submarines break out through the West's ASW barriers, for instance. The need for this kind of assistance is stressed in Gorshkov's writings on several occasions: 'Throughout the war not a single attempt was made to counter the anti-submarine forces of the Allies in an organised way from operating with total impunity.'[134] The implication here, and elsewhere, is that an effective campaign of maritime interdiction can only be waged by a properly balanced fleet and naval air force, and not by submarines alone.

THE PROTECTION OF SHIPPING

In his account of the Russian Civil War, Gorshkov put some stress on the way the Western powers were able to keep the counter-revolutionary forces going much longer than would otherwise have been the case, simply by virtue of military supplies brought in safely across the sea.[135] The tactical protection of shipping in the military theatre of operation, he considered, directly met the needs of the Ground Forces and had a major influence on the outcome of the land battle. The same was true during the Second World War when the Soviet Navy kept military shipping going in and out of threatened places like Sebastopol, Odessa and Novorossisk in bitter campaigns which required convoy operations against submarines, air defence against constant German air attack and much mine clearance. Without it the Soviet Navy's defensive and, later, offensive power would have been much reduced. For this reason Marshal Sokolovskiy representing the interests of the Army, freely conceded the military value of the naval protection of military shipping.

This function is still reckoned to be very important. The poor state of the Soviet road and rail system means that a surprising amount of military supplies would still have to go by sea in the event of a war. The large Soviet offshore defence forces have the protection of this local shipping as their top priority. As the Army advances, a cloud of minor combatants is expected to move forward as well, guarding the Army's maritime flank and its supply routes. The help offered by the Soviet Navy would not just be in the direct defence of shipping against air, surface or sub-surface attack but would be indirect as well. In the event of a sustained conflict in central Europe, for instance, the Soviet Army would rely quite heavily on sea supply, especially since its rail and road logistics system in Eastern Europe would probably be subject and vulnerable to Western air attack. For this reason, the safety of Soviet shipping in the Baltic would be important to Soviet success on land. The threat of Western naval attack on Soviet shipping would dramatically decline, if the Soviet Navy were able to control the Baltic. The seizure of strategically important parts of Denmark would help the Soviet Navy do this. In such a way Soviet amphibious and sea control capacities are 'justified' by the indirect contribution they make to the progress of the land battle. The nature of the Soviet Navy's exercises is entirely consistent with this putative chain of reasoning.

Much the same case is made for the Soviet Navy's contribution to a land war with China. It would plainly be dangerous for the Soviet Army to rely exclusively on the fragile and still quite limited Trans-Siberian railway for the movement of its supplies into the theatre of operations, and for local land and rail communications for their transport within it. Coastal shipping would be as important here as it would be in the Baltic, Black or Northern Seas and would need to be protected. But in this case, military supplies arriving in the Far East by sea (from European Russia) would need to be protected in transit from there as well. Certainly it would need to be guarded against naval and air attack in the East and South China Seas. Arguably a concern for the safety of this West–East shipping was one of the Soviet Navy's major reasons for moving into the Indian Ocean from the 1960s.[136] Soviet Naval deployments in this area in 1979 seemed to reflect a concern for the protection of military and other shipping going to Vietnam, especially during that country's war with China.[137]

The growing Soviet involvement in the affairs of the Third World, of course, increased the need for distant protection of this kind. It has led to the Soviet Navy guarding military supplies (and sometimes troops), and going into countries like Ethiopia, Angola, Mozambique and Vietnam, where the Soviet Union is acting in support of friendly regimes. In Ethiopia, for instance, the Russian General Petrov directed a mixed force of Cubans and East Europeans in the Ethiopian Civil and Somali Wars. The supply routes back to the Soviet Union were long, fragile and vital: they called for a degree of naval protection. This kind of military role is rather new to the Soviet Union, but familiar to the West through its involvement in local wars of Imperialism. Gorshkov was well aware of the advantages the West derived from this capacity: 'Seaborne military shipments in local wars have played a very important, sometimes decisive role.'[138] All the signs are that the Soviet Navy is seeking to emulate the West in this respect although its performance so far has been relatively modest.

Some interesting examples of such an effort occurred in 1973 before and during the Arab–Israeli War of that year. In April and July 1973 the Russian Navy sea-lifted several thousand troops and about 60 tanks from Morocco and took them to Syria: they were carried from Oran to Tartus in two *Alligator* amphibious warfare ships and provided with an escort which included SAM equipped cruisers and a destroyer, to protect them from Israel's air and submarine attack. The cruise took eight days. In the summer of 1973 troops were also sea-lifted into South Yemen.[139] When the war came, the Soviet Navy became involved in a competitive re-supply operation with the United States: while the Americans helped the Israelis with tens of thousands of tons of military supplies, the Russians did the same for the Egyptians and the Syrians. The Soviet Navy found itself facing a real rather than a potential threat; Soviet merchantmen were sunk and damaged in Syrian ports by Israeli FPBs and generally menaced by Israeli naval predominance in the eastern Mediterranean. To counter this the Soviet Navy escorted its merchantmen in and out of the war zone, used its *Alligator* and *Polnochny* amphibious warfare ships to unload equipment away from congested and threatened ports and established a defensive blockade line between Cyprus and the northern port of Lebanon. Against the more dangerous though less likely threat of the US

Navy's Sixth Fleet attacking Soviet shipping, the Soviet Navy took the precautionary measures already noted.[140] In all these ways, the Soviet Union has behaved increasingly like a traditional Western maritime power, determined to use the sea and to defend its ability to do so.

This protective function is also growing as a simple consequence of the expansion of the Soviet merchant and fishing fleet. The Soviet Navy quite clearly has accepted that it must guard this shipping because so much national effort and prestige is tied up in it. 'With the growth of the economic power of the Soviet Union,' Gorshkov remarked, 'its interests on the seas and oceans are expanding to an ever greater degree, and consequently new requirements are laid on the Navy to defend them from imperialist encroachments.'[141] When Ghana seized some Soviet trawlers in 1969, the Soviet Navy moved to protect them in a way distinctly reminiscent of traditional Western practice.[142] As the Soviet merchant and fishing fleets grow, then so will this very familiar naval function.

NAVAL DIPLOMACY

All the naval roles analysed so far have been related to fighting wars, and the Soviet Navy, like any other, devotes most of its time to preparing itself for them. But it has other important tasks in peacetime as well. These are mainly to do with its use as a diplomatic instrument to defend or extend the political interests of the Soviet Union around the world.

This was not an important role of the Soviet Navy through the 1940s and 1950s, although Soviet warships made appearances from time to time at naval occasions, like the Coronation Review of 1953, and conducted a few ceremonial visits, such as the important but ultimately abortive one to Syria in 1957. Generally, Soviet leaders were only too aware of their naval limitations. According to his own recollection, Khruschev once advocated sending the Russian fleet to counter US naval activity in the Mediterranean and the Far East but, 'in the end Malinovskiy came out against it on the grounds that it would be ineffective and far too expensive. I now believe Malinovskiy and the General Staff were absolutely right to oppose me on that score.'[143]

Nevertheless, from this period on the Soviet Union became increasingly concerned about its interests beyond the seas. 'As a

major world power with extensively developed international con-
tacts,' declared Foreign Minister Gromyko in 1969, 'the Soviet
Union cannot regard passively events which though territorially
remote, nevertheless have a bearing on our security and the security
of our friends.' [144] Accordingly the Soviet Union has slowly transformed itself from a regional to a global superpower and has shown
an increased propensity to become involved in political events far
beyond its shores and, if necessary, to bring power to bear in support of its own interests. As a result the recognised functions of the
armed services were modified in the early 1970s: no longer were
they exclusively concerned with the defence of the Motherland.
Now they were also expected to have important external uses in
support of a forward foreign policy intended to safeguard state
interests beyond the seas.

Since the Navy was the only service with the necessary reach this
move forward worked to its special advantage. As Gorshkov
pointed out, navies with their mobility, flexibility, high standard of
readiness and general controllability have always been seen as
important vehicles of distant diplomacy. Russian history confirmed
this, he thought, and so did the widespread use of Imperialist fleets
for such purposes. The stress given this kind of naval diplomacy in
Gorshkov's writings suggests that he considered it not just a bonus,
or something one does with a navy when it has no war to fight, but
actually a justification for having a large fleet in the first place. In
this, Gorshkov was at one with his counterparts in the main Western
navies. [145]

Support for naval diplomacy is by no means unconditional inside
the USSR however. In a defence establishment still dominated by
Army interests a degree of dissent is probably inevitable. Almost
certainly there will be people who stress its difficulties and costs,
and who argue that, for the Third World to be able to distinguish
easily between good socialist gunboats and nasty Western ones, the
Soviet Navy will have to act with great circumspection. Also the US
Navy still has the edge in deployed sea power of this kind – largely
through its monopoly in strike carriers: perhaps rather than risk
defeat, it would be best for the USSR not to contest the issue at all?
Nevertheless, the current consensus seems to be that untroubled
peace and absolute war are not mutually exclusive opposites, but
two conditions at different ends of a spectrum of interstate relationships. Further, the USSR should be able to prevail over as wide a

range of these particular mixes of peace and war as possible – and this will require an effective capacity for naval diplomacy. In fact in some ways the Soviet Navy's peacetime functions seem a good deal more assertive than its wartime ones.

The Soviet Union has used its navy for a diversity of political tasks ranging from courtesy visits at one end of the scale to an evident readiness to fight limited wars at the other. As Gorshkov remarked: 'Official visits and the working calls of our ships to foreign ports make a substantial contribution to the improvement of mutual understanding between states and peoples and to the enhancement of the international authority of the Soviet Union.'[146] Accordingly the number and geographic variety of these visits have greatly increased over the past fifteen years or so, especially in the Caribbean area, the Mediterranean and the Indian Ocean. These visits are carefully planned, tightly controlled and highly stylised in format. A lot of them are simply intended to improve relations with the governments and peoples of the countries visited, but the political impact of these visits is very hard to assess. The population at large is doubtless impressed by the sight of naval power in all its majesty, by the troupes of dancers and choirs the ships specialising in this kind of activity seem often to carry, and by the quiet, polite, almost bloodless propriety of the Soviet sailors ashore. On the other hand, real communication is hampered by the fact that Soviet sailors have virtually no money to spend, seldom speak the local language and are usually shepherded in little groups around the least contaminating local sights by reliable NCOs. Governments are probably impressed and depressed by these things too, but the extent to which their subsequent behaviour is affected mainly depends on whether Soviet naval diplomacy is supplemented by the promise of more lasting political and economic benefits.

The Soviet Navy is also used to help local allies with supportive deployments and the carriage of military and other supplies as it did during the Arab–Israeli wars of 1967 and 1973, the Bangladesh War of 1975 and the various conflicts in the Persian Gulf, South East Asia and the Horn of Africa. Cuba has been a leading recipient of this kind of naval aid as well. Since 1956 the Soviet Navy has also transferred nearly 500 ships to various Third World countries, an act which often forges links of reasonable permanence since the recipients will usually require supplies and operating assistance for some time afterwards. Finally, friendships can be cemented by co-operative exercises such as those with Cuba, Vietnam and the Soviet Union's Warsaw Pact allies.

The Soviet Navy wants to impress adversaries just as much as allies or neutrals. Gorshkov showed himself to be well aware of the advantages of this kind of maritime deterrence:

> Demonstrative actions by the fleet in many cases have made it possible to achieve political ends without resorting to armed struggle, merely by putting on pressure with one's own potential might and threatening to start military operations ... Thus the fleet has always been an instrument of the policy of states, an important aid to diplomacy in peacetime.[147]

In the Soviet view, this kind of demonstration of strength deters the West from doing things it might otherwise have done; it allows the Soviet Union to negotiate from strength and avoid having to make unnecessary concessions. In a more general way it prevents the West from having a free and uncontested ride. Thus Vice-Admiral N. I. Smirnov wrote in 1969 on Soviet naval purposes in the Mediterranean:

> Already the very presence of Soviet ships in the Mediterranean does not allow the American Sixth Fleet to carry out the aggressive ideas of the Pentagon with impunity. They cannot throw their weight around so ceremoniously as before.[148]

By having a constant naval presence and by occasional acts of confrontation at sea, where circumstances warrant them, the Soviet Union, in fact, shows the West that it is a global maritime power whose views and interests cannot be ignored. The whole tenor of Gorshkov's writings is that the Soviet Union must be great at sea in order to prevail, and that her maritime power must exist and be seen to exist by friends and adversaries alike. For this among other reasons, the Soviet Navy closely accompanies Western fleets wherever they go, a perpetual reminder of the power, interests and presence of the Soviet Union. In the early days Soviet ships and submarines often made their point very crudely with games of maritime chicken, simulated attacks and other dangerous manoeuvres which occasionally led to collisions and sinkings. Now that their presence is accepted, they are more restrained: they have become part of the maritime scenery.

Since the mid-1960s the Soviet Union has also devoted increasing thought to the question of its Navy being involved (possibly as the USSR's main agent) in limited and local wars. In the words of Admiral Stalbo in 1968: 'Soviet military doctrine also recognises the possibility of local wars arising, conducted without the use of nuclear weapons.' Increasing attention has been paid to the possibility of limited conflict, as well, even between the historically mutually antagonistic social systems of world socialism and Western imperialism. Combat at sea could easily play a vital part in conventional conflict with the West, China or Third World adversaries.[149] This does not mean that the Soviet Union will actively seek these conflicts, but merely a recognition that a clear capacity to fight them is a crucial constituent of its peace and wartime power.

The inherent flexibility of Soviet sea power and its capacity to serve a whole variety of differing strategic interests was impressively demonstrated in 1979 by the very successful world tour of the carrier *Minsk* and its deployment group. The *Minsk* was certainly an effective vehicle for transmitting impressions to countries like Mozambique and the South Yemen about the strength of the Soviet Union and its desire for friendly relations. Its presence also signalled the West about Soviet concern for the outcome of events in the troubled Persian Gulf and South East Asia regions, although the ship's apparent rerouting away from a potentially provocative visit to Cam Ranh Bay may have indicated a desire not to make this signal too pointed. The eventual arrival of this high-value evidently combat-effective ship in the Far East made it a significant component of the multi-level system of general maritime deterrence directed against China, Japan and the United States, in that area.[150]

The Soviet Navy evidently regards its surface ships as a particularly important instrument for this kind of naval diplomacy. The striking rise in their out-of-area deployments in the decade after the mid-1960s is a clear indication of Soviet sea power's growing politico-strategic utility which, thanks also to the dramatic fall in US Navy out-of-area ship-days over the same period, is now more or less equivalent to that of the West. While this is true numerically, however, the complete absence of strike carriers and its very limited capacity for amphibious operations still put the Soviet Navy at a very considerable relative disadvantage in terms of quality. Soviet ships still tend to spend a high proportion of their out-of-area time swinging uselessly at anchor, but their diplomatic tactics have been increasingly sophisticated. One analyst fairly described their use during the Angolan Civil War crisis (November 1975 to February 1976) for instance as 'multiple in purpose, restrained in execution, artful in their timing and quite clearly political in their objectives'.[151]

The activity of the Soviet Mediterranean Squadron over the years illustrates the growth in Soviet skill, confidence and purpose particularly well. The Soviet Navy first sought to establish an admittedly rather sporadic presence in the Mediterranean in 1956. In that year it achieved a mere 100 ship-days; by 1960 this total had risen to 5,600,[152] a remarkable achievement reflected in an equivalent rise in transits through the Turkish Straits. Although there were temporary setbacks after the loss of base facilities in Albania in 1961 and Egypt in 1972 and 1976, the Soviet Navy gradually achieved approximate parity with the US Fleet, at least in numerical terms.

Broadly this effort seems to have been intended to serve three purposes. The first was general: it was to establish the fact that the Soviet Union was a Mediterranean power with legitimate interests in the area and a perfectly natural intention to win friends and influence people. Egypt was a particular target for the Soviet Navy, doubtless because of that country's importance in the Arab world and the relative lure of its base facilities. These attractions were sufficient to warrant a succession of naval visits from the mid-1960s and the arrival of Admiral Gorshkov himself on two occasions. The Egyptians were reluctant to yield as much as the Soviet government wanted, however, and the whole campaign had to be conducted with great tact to have a hope of success. The Navy was very useful for this careful kind of diplomacy because it was able to convey a very diverse range of messages to the Egyptian people and government. For instance, the inclusion of the depot ship *Magomet Gadzhiev* (named after a naval officer from one of the Soviet Muslim republics) in the first official naval visit in 1966 was a rather subtle signal of particular fraternity: on the other hand, the exercises conducted off Alexandria in May 1972 (in which the helicopter carrier *Moskva* played an important part) paraded Soviet power in a manner which the Russians doubtless hoped the various Egyptian dignitaries watching them would find impressive and persuasive. Because the Soviet Navy could be used in so many different ways, it was to prove an extremely versatile instrument of state policy, though it has to be said that political advances during this period owed at least as much to Israeli intransigence during the War of Attrition as they did to the activities of Soviet ships.

Nevertheless a Soviet naval presence in the Mediterranean was recognised, accepted and sometimes welcomed. It gave the Soviet government more political options and also helped in the second of the three objectives it had in the area, namely the provision of aid and succour to local allies. In June 1963 a large arms deal concluded between the Soviet Union and Egypt included two submarines, two destroyers and over thirty *Osa* and *Komar* fast patrol boats and began a long period in which the USSR supplied naval *matériel* to various countries of the Middle East. The Soviet Navy also helped train the Egyptians and others in the use of their new vessels. (In the Arab–Israeli war of 1973 the Israelis recognised Soviet concepts of operation in the way their Arab adversaries used their naval forces – the small scouting forces about 15 miles in advance of the main party of missile boats, the reliance on surprise and massed numbers to compensate for aiming errors, and so forth.)[153] For some years after 1967 the Soviet Navy also kept some of its warships at Port Said in a way perhaps intended to deter the Israelis from attacking the area. As the 1973 war approached the Soviet Navy helped to pull the Arabs together in a variety of ways which, as we have seen, included taking a number of Moroccan troops to the battle area by sea. When the war began, as we have also seen, the Soviet Navy rapidly became involved in an operation to move well over a million tons of crucial military supplies to the Egyptians and Syrians; the obvious need to do this, and to protect the operation against Israeli attack, meant that the Soviet Navy had to move into an active war zone for the first time since 1945. This ability to offer effective aid to local allies supports Soviet influence in the Mediterranean, and the Third World generally. It was one of the Navy's most valuable contributions to Soviet policy.

Finally, Soviet naval activity in the Mediterranean was also directed at the task of countering the US Sixth Fleet, either for the threat it posed to the Soviet homeland itself or to Soviet interests in the area. Soviet naval activity during the Arab–Israeli War of 1967 was the first example of a Western fleet being countered in this way in out-of-area waters. Given the gross disparity in deployed strength, it was naturally a modest and low-key debut, restricted largely to a leisurely expansion of the naval forces in the area and to the constant shadowing of the US Navy's strike carriers. The Soviet

Navy was similarly restrained during the Jordanian crisis of 1970 when its object was, once more, to signal Soviet interest in the proceedings ashore and to deter the United States from intervention. Again it was a question of reinforcement and 'tattle-tailing'. According to the Commander of the Sixth Fleet:

> Both sides operated in a normal and restrained manner. There was none of the nonsense of their ships running in and around our men-of-war at close range. It was evident the Soviets were under the direction of a seasoned seaman who not only knew well the capabilities and limitations of his equipment, but also was sensitive to the potential seriousness of the situation.[154]

Three years later, the Soviet Navy gave its most impressive performance in the Mediterranean so far. Its squadron there was the largest to be assembled, reaching a total of 95 ships on 31 October 1973, a force which included 23 submarines and 40 surface warships (among them, *Kresta II* and *Kynda* cruisers and 8 amphibious warfare ships). But even this was much less than Admiral Gorshkov could have deployed had he wanted to. The Black Sea Fleet could have sent in many more cruisers and destroyers had the need arisen: the fact that it did not may have been an indication of restraint. Offering such messages of reassurance was certainly an important part of the Soviet Navy's general campaign during this crisis: the Mediterranean squadron showed itself to be a useful instrument of diplomacy because, like most naval forces, it could demonstrate good will as effectively as it could resolve. By not doing things it could have done, by calling off menacing manoeuvres and by positive gestures of co-operation, the Soviet Navy showed that in some circumstances it could be a force for peace.

As usual, the Mediterranean squadron covered the Straits of Gibraltar and of Sicily, and shadowed major US Navy formations closely. But it also showed a greater propensity to menace its American adversary: as already noted, the Soviet Navy formed itself into surface attack groups against each of the Sixth Fleet's carrier task groups and against the amphibious task group centred on the assault carrier *Iwo Jima*. As Admiral Murphy (Commander-in-Chief of the Sixth Fleet) subsequently reported:

> On 26 October, the Soviets began large-scale anti-carrier warfare (ACW) exercises against TF 60 with SSG and SSGN (guided mis-

sile submarines, diesel and nuclear) participation: this activity was conducted for the 6 days following 27th October ... The US Sixth Fleet and the Soviet Mediterranean Fleet were, in effect, sitting in a pond in close proximity and the stage for the hitherto unlikely 'war at sea' scenario was set. Both fleets were obviously in a high readiness posture for whatever might come next, although it appeared that neither fleet knew exactly what to expect.[155]

More ominously still, there were sufficient indications that the Soviet Union was preparing to intervene in events ashore to justify at least in the eyes of United States decision-makers the calling of a Defence Condition III general nuclear alert. Preparatory moves in the Soviet Union's airborne divisions were the most worrying feature of these admittedly ambiguous indications, but there were reports also of portentous movements in the Soviet Navy's amphibious warfare forces and even more alarming suggestions that the Soviet Navy had unloaded nuclear warheads for the Egyptian army's *Scud* surface-to-surface missiles at Alexandria.[156]

In short, the Soviet Navy during the Arab–Israeli War demonstrated new levels of professional expertise and a greatly increased readiness to take the US Navy on at what the Soviet leaders regard as the Americans' own game, that is of projecting power ashore. This, taken with a more forward foreign policy and a construction policy giving more emphasis to general-purpose warships, strengthens the argument of those who believe the USSR is gradually developing an interventionist capacity. But even if this is not the case, the Soviet Navy over the past twenty years or so has still become a uniquely flexible and effective instrument of Soviet foreign policy.

There is, nevertheless, one final argument, associated in the past particularly with Michael MccGwire, that the Soviet Navy's evident diplomatic utility was something of a bonus, and that the main justification for the construction of a balanced blue-water fleet and for its forward deployment in peacetime was not general political-influence building but instead directly strategic. MccGwire explained the Soviet Navy build-up in the Indian Ocean, for instance, largely in terms of its seeking to counter threats to its maritime communications with the East and the possible deployment of Western SSBNs in the area.[157]

Other analysts vigorously contested the idea that strategic defence was the Soviet Navy's only or even main objective in such cases. They argued that there was no real threat from the Indian Ocean either to the Soviet homeland or to its maritime links with the East: they pointed out that Soviet forces in the area did not seem to be particularly well fitted for ASW – a rather surprising omission if one of their main tasks was to hunt down Western SSBNs. 'Since the mid-sixties and increasingly in the seventies,' concluded Dismukes and McConnell instead, 'political considerations have dominated Soviet motivations for operating their general-purpose navy in the forward area.'[158]

There is, however, in any case, a danger in taking such arcane disputes too far: sea power is infinitely flexible and versatile. Simply by being in an area the Navy makes a whole range of political and strategic options available to the Soviet Union. Which of these options turns out to be the most useful, or the most used, depends on circumstances which even the Soviet government cannot prophesy in advance. In short, we should probably not seek single and specific explanations for the construction of a force so obviously capable of serving a diversity of purposes.

IN SEARCH OF PRIORITIES

Up to a certain point it is possible to detect changes in the order of priority of the various missions the Soviet Navy has been capable of performing since 1945. In the late 1940s and 1950s, the main stress was on the defence of the homeland against Western amphibious and carrier attack. For a while thereafter, operations against Western SSBNs moved to the forefront. Since the mid-1960s the Soviet Navy appears to have concentrated its energies on the manifold requirements of strategic strike and, increasingly, on making its influence felt around the world in situations short of absolute conflict with the West.

For a number of reasons it is unwise to try to carry the analysis about Soviet naval priorities much further than this. In the first place, navies have often been used for wartime purposes quite at variance with their peacetime intentions. Secondly, the Soviet Navy, contrary to the common impression, is no more a static unitary organisation with a single set of operational concepts than any other navy. Instead, it is a constantly evolving web of different interest groups with different and doubtless competing ideas about naval priorities. For this reason, the relative perceived importance of the various tasks may seem ambiguous, unsettled and often contradictory. The apparent stress put on the necessity of defending Soviet SSBNs, for instance, seems at odds with the rather low expectations of Soviet success against Western SSBNs, identified above. (In a way this is reminiscent of the British Air Staff of the interwar period which argued on the one hand that the bomber would always get through but on the other that the defence of Britain against German bombers could be effected by large numbers of fighters.) In short, the Soviet Navy is probably as unsure about the precise order of its priorities as the West is.

The problem is made worse by the absence of clear differentiation between the Soviet Navy's various tasks, which does not spring simply from the obscurity of its terminology or the ambiguity of its exercises. Nearly all these tasks require a mix of forces (surface, sub-surface and air), a degree of sea control, and depend at least in part on the successful accomplishment of other tasks. A mutually supporting chain of naval tasks can easily be envisaged: for instance, an amphibious landing in Northern Norway would make it easier for the Soviet Navy to dominate the Norwegian Sea: in turn this would make it more difficult for Western carrier strike forces to attack naval and air bases in the Murmansk area: as a result, the Soviet Naval Air Force would be better able to attack Western shipping in the Atlantic: this would make it more difficult for the United States to project its military power against the Soviet Union – and so on. In short, Soviet sea power and its various missions are best seen as an integrated whole rather than broken down into artificial segments.

Admiral Gorshkov and the Soviet Navy clearly recognise in its versatility of purpose and use the very essence of sea power. To them it is a flexible and general-purpose instrument of state policy both in peace and war: it should not be thought of simply as a means of completing certain narrow and specific tasks. Instead, Gorshkov stressed its 'great potential in solving multiple operational tasks of an offensive character both in opposing the enemy's fleet and in operations against the shore'. He was quite clear about the need for a

harmonious, balanced development of the force of the ocean-going navy matching the demands of the time, capable of opposing any stratagems of foes and of confronting a potential aggressor with the need to solve himself the very problems which he is creating for our country.[159]

In the Soviet view it is best not to be too specific about the relative importance of the possibilities of naval power, since the way these turn out is so critically dependent on particular circumstances of time and place. In fact, according to one of Gorshkov's American counterparts, this was an approach the US Navy would be well advised to follow too:

> Gorshkov treats as obvious the specifics of how naval presence in peacetime contributes to national purpose, why a great power requires a sea-going capability, and just why increasing development of the seabed demands more naval power. It appears to me that, in contrast, we have fallen into the trap of having to explain why we need a navy in overly specific terms. Perhaps we should study Gorshkov's example. Quantitative systems analysis has carried over too far into strategic concepts. We have become too dependent upon scenarios and hypothetical campaign analyses to justify every force level: e.g. a NATO campaign of 90 days, a ground war in Asia, a so-called 'unilateral' war in the Mid East, etc. We have fallen into this trap from a lack of vision and because we have failed to articulate the purposes and historical perspectives of naval power.[160]

The conclusion to be drawn from this is that we should be reasonably agnostic about the Soviet Navy's precise order of priorities, not least because doing otherwise may obscure the essential fact that for the first time in its history the Soviet Navy now appreciates, and evidently intends to develop, maritime power as a general-purpose and multicapable instrument of state policy.

8 Present and Future Prospects

It is difficult to produce simple conclusions about the rise of the modern Soviet Navy. On the one hand monolithic or monocausal explanations do not do justice to the complexities both of the Soviet Union and of her maritime aspirations. On the other, the Soviet Navy has absorbed far too high a proportion of the country's resources simply to be dismissed as the product of an *absence* of policy. The Soviet Union has not acquired a blue-water navy in a fit of absence of mind, or simply through a process of institutional drift. Nor can the rise of the Soviet Navy be put down merely to a mindless compulsion to match the West at every point on the spectrum of force. It is therefore unwise to conclude either that Soviet leaders have a satisfactorily clear and simple set of maritime objectives, or that they have no objectives at all. In truth, it is possible to see two different kinds of motivation in their policy of maritime expansion, both of which need to be given their due prominence.

In the first place, there is a clear awareness of the need for a capacity to perform a number of specific missions, whose relative importance has been, and will doubtless continue to be, subject to constant change as we saw in the last chapter. But, secondly, there is also the general perception in the Soviet Union that great powers need great navies almost as a matter of course. Navies are seen as general-purpose instruments of state policy. The Soviet Union will inevitably need maritime power to counter the maritime power of her adversaries. Because the sea is increasingly important to the Soviet Union as a source of food and minerals and as a medium of international trade, she will need to protect and expand her maritime interests. As she becomes more global in her concerns, the importance of the sea as an element in her relations with distant countries will naturally grow. For this and many other reasons, it is easy to see why the Soviet Union should think she needs a navy, in the time-honoured phrase, 'for general purposes of greatness'.

Soviet maritime policies create a situation to which the West must respond now and in the future. In general terms the effect of these policies is quite easy to describe. Over the last thirty years the Soviet Union has developed from a minor naval power with largely coastal capabilities and has become a major sea power able to challenge the supremacy of the US Navy throughout the world. But it is no easy matter to define the East–West naval balance more exactly.

Basing such estimates on what American analysts like to call 'bean-counting' (that is on numerical comparisons of ships, aircraft and so forth) has obvious weaknesses. As a method, it counts what can be counted but misses out the rest – although the rest (morale, for example, or experience) may in fact be as important. Moreover, this method of investigation depends too heavily on purely procedural issues such as the particular period of time looked at, or the selection of ship totals rather than overall tonnages. All too often, it can obscure the real military difference between one *Nimitz* class 81,000 ton nuclear-powered carrier and two *Kievs*. It can also lead the analyst into fatuous exercises of comparison between totally dissimilar units or formations. Nevertheless, in a very crude way, bean-counting does help the analysts establish general trends. As we have seen, it shows that the Soviet surface fleet has actually declined in number over the past twenty years, though the average tonnage of the ships (and their military effectiveness) has doubled over the same period. We must expect both the downward trend in the number of new deliveries and the increase in average tonnage to level off before long. If they did not, the Soviet Navy could expect only one new ship (of some 36,000 tons) to be delivered every three or four years by the end of the century![1] Moreover, the pattern of Soviet construction has been such that the Soviet Navy will be faced with a large proportion of its surface fleet reaching retirement age by the mid-1990s.

It is the effects of a similar block absolescence problem in the US Navy which has halved its number of ships on the active list since 1962 and which has apparently helped to undermine Western naval predominance. In 1962, the US Navy had almost twice the combat tonnage of the Soviet Navy and its fleet included 875 surface ships.[2] Now, by virtue of Soviet construction and American decline the two navies are more or less equal in tonnage terms and the Soviet Navy actually now has 560 major combatants to the US

Navy's 350. However we can expect US trend lines to level out too. It is impossible to predict what will be the situation by the end of the century, but in view of present commitments to maintain a US fleet of 600 active units, and the option of a 7–800 ship navy being considered seriously by President Reagan, present indications suggest that both in numerical and in over tonnage terms, the US Navy will at least retain parity by the year 2000.

This kind of impression however must be balanced by others derived from investigation of the ability of each side's fleet to carry out the tasks assigned to it. What does each side expect its fleet to do? Which naval assets are, and will be, devoted to what tasks? This approach allows the analyst to compare the contending forces in a more realistic fashion; thus the effectiveness of Soviet SSBNs depends on an estimate of the effectiveness of Western strategic ASW. Nevertheless, there are problems with this type of analysis too, in particular the large number of variables in the equation which makes definite answers extremely difficult to arrive at. The naval balance, as measured by the putative outcome of a range of conflicts at sea, depends critically on a host of uncertain factors such as luck, the geography of the battle area, the weather, the availability of bases, the combat performance of previously untried weapon systems, the political situation and so forth. As the 1982 Falklands campaign so clearly shows, total prediction of future naval events is impossible.

It has been a constant argument in this book that the course of Soviet naval development (and the consequent naval balance of the future) will also be determined by a continuing interaction between political, economic and technological factors inside the Soviet Union set against a background of world events. Since we began this book, there have been no identifiable or significant changes in the distribution and exercise of political power in the Soviet Union. Brezhnev, despite some protracted absences from public view, still appears to be in control of the Party and state machines, as well as remaining Commander-in-Chief of the armed services.* The death of Michail Suslov, the Party's leading ideologist, has led to some shuffling of positions within the Politbureau, of which he was one of the most senior and influential members, but with as yet no discernible practical results. Marshal Ustinov remains Minister of Defence and Admiral Gorshkov still heads the Navy. It is impossible to say whether Brezhnev has made any arrangements for his succession, or

* He died in November 1982 and was immediately succeeded as Party General Secretary by Yuri Andropov.

if he has, whether they would be adhered to after he leaves the stage. If previous patterns are followed, it is likely that his departure will be attended by a period of uncertainty until behind-the-scenes bargaining in the Politbureau and the Secretariat produces a new distribution of offices, in which the man who emerges as General Secretary of the Party is most likely to be *primus inter pares*. The uncertainty is intensified by the fact that the average age of the present Politbureau is over 70 and that therefore there are bound to be many other changes before or after Brezhnev's departure. It is generally believed that in the period following the death of Stalin and the supercession of Khruschev, the support of military was courted by rival factions and played a significant part in the outcome. This is likely to recur, but in view of what has happened in Poland, where the Army has taken over the leading role of a discredited Party, Soviet leaders will be aware of the dangerous opportunities which political feuding might give to a military leadership conscious of the centrality of the armed forces to their country's security and world position. Even if there were to be an increase in the political influence of the armed services, it would not necessarily be to the advantage of the Soviet Navy. Such a development would inevitably be most heavily influenced by the land forces whose leaders might find it opportune to restrict the resources allocated to the fleet, especially if Admiral Gorshkov, or his successors, were not able to find support in important sections of the political, economic, industrial and bureaucratic institutions of the Soviet state.

Whatever leadership emerges, and the strongest possibility is that it will not differ substantially from the present regime, there is no doubt that its primary worry will be the poor performance of the Soviet economy, with its associated social, regional and racial tensions. Poor productivity, shortfalls in investment and a grossly inefficient managerial system, will be the main domestic problem of the next decade.[3] A new, relatively inexperienced, and possibly divided leadership is not going to find it easy to enforce the drastic political and administrative reforms which have been beyond the powers of Brezhnev and his contemporaries. Failure to produce more grain will mean continuing dependence on purchases from abroad as will attempts to improve industrial performance through technological and financial aid from the West. Here, of course, economic needs, foreign policy and defence requirements converge or maybe clash.

An active foreign policy in the recent past has led to the costly and long drawn-out entanglement in Afghanistan and expensive economic support of Cuba and other client states. Can the already strained economy sustain these demands, the 12–15 per cent of GNP devoted to defence and, at the same time, meet at least some of the expectations of the civil population? Can the economic co-operation of North America and Western Europe needed for agricultural and industrial improvement be counted on at a time when the West sees itself threatened by Russia's military strength and in response, led by a newly militant United States, has set in train a dramatic increase in its own armaments? This last develop-ment in turn has encouraged those in the Soviet Union who are haunted by the dangers of encirclement by the West, a hostile China and by fears of the disintegration of their European security system as exemplified in Poland and the increasing restiveness of other East European states.

There is nothing in past experience to suggest that Soviet leaders, entrapped in such a situation, will abandon their predecessors' determination to maintain nuclear parity with the United States as well as the range of conventional forces needed to maintain national prestige and security and to benefit from any opportunities which offer a chance of increasing their country's world influence. In naval terms, the decision of the United States to build up its naval capabilities will produce new challenges for Admiral Gorshkov's successors. Will they be able to develop doctrines and naval con-struction programmes sufficient at least to maintain the more favourable maritime balance of power which has been achieved in recent years? If they are to succeed, the skills in advocacy and the application of modern technology to naval forces which have figured so largely in his achievements will have to be maintained and enhanced.

There are two factors working in the Navy's favour, which are a continuation of the two elements in Soviet strategic and foreign pol-icy thinking and which have already favoured a growing perception of the importance of the sea in Soviet strategy. Faced with their economic difficulties and their long-established fear of the general superiority of the technology of the United States, it seems likely that a future Soviet leadership would be willing to accept a reduc-tion of nuclear arms if it could be made without loss of security. By the spring of 1982, President Reagan also appeared to be moving in the same direction. One of his major negotiating proposals was for a considerable reduction of nuclear warheads to mutually agreed equality, with at least half of those retained being sea-based.[4] The attraction of this proposal lies in the continuing acceptance of the relative invulnerability of submarine as opposed to land-based systems, an invulnerability which reduces either superpower's incentive for a pre-emptive strike. If this proposal were adopted it would of course strengthen the Soviet Navy's claim to be the prime element in the country's nuclear forces as it would approximately double the proportion of submarine-based missiles in Russia's armoury and thus give added strength to its claim that the effective deployment of its own SSBNs and any substantial hope of countering those of its enemies depends on the wide deployment of balanced naval forces.

The other factor which might favour the Soviet Navy's case is more speculative and is based on the apparent inability of the Soviet Union recently to play a strongly positive role in parts of the world where she has important interests. Since 1973, her influence in the Middle East has greatly declined. She has so far gained no advantage, and indeed may face new threats, from the rise of a militantly anti-Western but also strongly Islamic Iran. In the Far East, the long-term hostility of China, Japan and the United States seems likely to persist. Everywhere her influence seems to have been checked and she seems unable to initiate positive policies to redeem the loss. Perhaps the Soviet Navy may be able to establish that an increase in its capabilities for the exercise of diplomatic pressure or for participation in limited wars in concert with friendly local states is the only possible way out of such an impotence?

The future naval balance will depend on a whole range of answers to such currently uncertain questions as these, and this makes forecasting a more than usually hazardous activity. Nevertheless, some predictions are safer than others on the basis of present evidence. Unless there is some unexpected technological development which increases the relative vulnerability of large carriers and so justifies the argument of advocates of 'distributed force', the US Navy's lead in this kind of conventional sea control seems likely to remain for the foreseeable future. However the Soviet Navy's recent investment in powerful new classes of surface ship and reported intention to proceed with the construction of attack carriers combine with the arrival of the *Backfire* bomber and of new classes of submarine to produce an enhanced threat to this kind of maritime force. On the other hand it does not seem likely that the Soviet Navy will be able to match the US Navy's amphibious or ASW capacity. But its manifest strength in the means of strategic strike, its capacity to threaten areas close to the strategic perimeter of the Soviet Union and its ability to disrupt the West's merchant and military shipping will surely remain. More generally, although the Soviet level of dependence on the sea will doubtless continue to rise for the rest of the century, this seems unlikely to match that of the West, given the latter's geographic dispersion and absolute reliance on sea-borne trade. For this reason, the West will doubtless remain more vulnerable to conventional maritime attack than will the Soviet Union. In fact present evidence suggests that most naval balances will be at least as delicate as they are now and will maybe confirm the apprehensions of Admiral Hayward that the US Navy has lost its 'narrow margin of superiority, [and is] sliding into a grey area where neither side can be said to be ahead'.[5]

Certainly it seems more than likely that the development of the Soviet Navy will exacerbate the already worrying gap between the West's maritime requirements and its maritime resources brought about by the disproportionate rise in the relative cost of naval forces. In situations like this countries naturally tend to concentrate on those aspects of the apparent threat which are of immediate concern to them. As befits a superpower, the perspectives of the United States on Soviet naval expansion tend to be global and strategic, concentrating on the consequent threat on the broad oceans, in the Pacific, the Atlantic, the Indian Ocean as well as in European waters. Their stress is on the struggle for maritime dominance, on the spread of Soviet (naval) influence and on the strengthening of Soviet sea-based strategic deterrent forces; and, such is the dominance of American literature on this subject, that these arguments have all become familiar.

The large contribution made to the overall naval balance being made by Western Europe[6] (a contribution analysed in Table 4) shows how important are European views of the Soviet maritime threat. On the whole these tend to be more local and specific than those of the United States. The composition of most of the European navies suggests a particular stress on the necessity to provide forces for general and conventional maritime deterrence in peacetime, a readiness to contest Soviet wartime exploitation of Europe's inner waters (both in direct support of the Soviet Army and to effect transit to the high seas) and a determination to provide large numbers of escorts for the protection of NATO's Atlantic and European sea communications.

Europeans are particularly apprehensive about the possibility of the Soviet Union employing her new maritime potentialities in less-

TABLE 4   *The naval balance, 1981*

	Warsaw Pact	NATO	Of which NATO–Europe (including France)
Carriers	4	18	5
Cruisers	28	40	3
Destroyers	61	159	73
Frigates	30	145	77
Corvettes	86	37	37
Submarines (excl. SSBN)	199	212	139
Amphibious warfare ships	120	97	36

Source: Lt-Col. D. M. O. Miller, (1981) *East v West: The Balance of Military Power* (London: Salamander) p. 119.

than-absolute acts of pressure, possibly not involving the use of nuclear weapons against the United States. As a nuclear power the Soviet Union is now far more confident than she used to be. The United States no longer has 'escalation dominance'. Laurence Martin has made the important point that the naval forces of the Soviet Union would now have to be treated with considerable respect, even if they were weak, simply by virtue of her general military power.[7] But as we have seen, the Soviet Navy is not weak and Europe will have to adjust to this more threatening situation. The potency of this kind of threat must also be increased by the apparent intention of the Soviet Union to construct forces that will give her the capacity to fight an independent non-nuclear war in Europe. James McConnell has argued that such is her intention in the current Five Year Plan (1980–5). Past strategists such as N. M. Nikolskiy whose hitherto disregarded view that nuclear war had negated itself and that there should be more emphasis on conventional forces have been significantly rehabilitated. There are indications that Marshal Ogarkov (long supposed to be preparing a major work on Soviet strategy to replace Sokolovskiy's) has been sketching out the parameters of a conventional war in Europe lasting in excess of three months. The large-scale Soviet exercise *Zapad–81* in the Baltic in September of that year was entirely non-nuclear from start to finish, à quite unprecedented event.[8]

Such a conventional capacity could threaten the fragmentation of the Western alliance. Most gravely, it could decouple the United States from Europe by severing, or threatening to sever,

NATO's Atlantic communications. In the same way, maritime attack might isolate Britain from the rest of Europe. There are similar anxieties about the possibility of such salami-slicing tactics in the Mediterranean and, more particularly, around NATO's Northern Region. If NATO's maritime forces are obliged to regard the Greenland–Iceland–United Kingdom Gap as its front line, then Norway, and especially northern Norway, could well begin to think of itself as ultimately indefensible. A Soviet bid to open the straits around the north of Denmark might have the same consequence. Certainly the unfortunate Captain Pyotr Gushin's misadventure with *Whiskey* submarine no. 137 in the restricted military zone around the Swedish naval base at Karlskrona in November 1981 aroused shivers of apprehension throughout Scandinavia, especially when it was reported that the submarine carried nuclear-tipped torpedoes. The grounding of this submarine combined with sinister goings-on around the Danish island of Bornholm reported in the Copenhagen press and the persistent submarine violations of Norwegian waters (there were apparently no less than fifteen such incidents in 1981 alone) all alarm the Scandinavians and increase their sense of threat.[9] The response might be to encourage those who counsel caution and prudence, who point out the unwisdom of entering into a naval arms race with the Soviet Union, and who would seek more co-operative relationships with their powerful neighbour. Equally it might strengthen the hands of those who argue that lambs who lie down with lions tend to get eaten and who advocate more naval expenditure in defiance of countervailing economic pressures. The same is true on a wider scale for the Alliance as a whole. During the Falklands campaign, Admiral Hayward reportedly argued that recent rundowns in the Royal Navy and other European navies should be reversed since their forces were already 'too small and too inadequate' for patrolling the Mediterranean and the waters off north-west Europe.[10] But whichever way this and other arguments about the appropriate Western response eventually go, the urgency of the discussion is a considerable testament to the rise in importance of the Soviet Navy since 1949 and its likely impact on the remainder of the twentieth century.

Notes and References

We have used a short form of reference in which the author's surname is followed by the year of publication in brackets and the page number(s). Full details of the books and articles cited can be found in the bibliography.

CHAPTER 1: PROBLEMS OF INTERPRETATION

1. M. MccGwire, 'The Turning Points in Soviet Naval Policy' in MccGwire (1973a) p. 176.
2. C. R. Thorpe, 'Mission Priorities of the Soviet Navy' in Murphy (1978) pp. 159–61.
3. See, for instance, G. Till, 'Perceptions of Naval Power Between the Wars' in Towle (1982) pp. 172–93.
4. Col. P. Sidorov in the *Soviet Military Review*, no. 9, 1972, quoted by G. Jukes in MccGwire *et al.* (1975) p. 481.
5. General Staff Academy, *Dictionary of Basic Military Terms* (Moscow: Voenizdat, 1965) quoted by M. P. Gallagher in MccGwire *et al.* (1975) pp. 56–7.
6. See the debate between McConnell and MccGwire in MccGwire and McDonnell (1977) pp. 54–7, 565–620.
7. McDonnell (1977) p. 568.
8. Gorshkov (1979) pp. 120, 122.
9. N. Friedman, *US vs Soviet Style in Fleet Design* in Murphy (1978) p. 209.
10. Woodward (1965) pp. 20ff.
11. Ibid., pp. 72–4.
12. Gorshkov (1979) pp. 68–9.
13. G. Barrat, *Russia in Pacific Waters 1715–1825* (Vancouver and London: University of British Columbia Press, 1981).
14. Adm. Sir Herbert Richmond, *Sea Power in the Modern World* (London: Bell, 1934) pp. 17ff.
15. Herrick (1968) p. 143.
16. M. MccGwire, *Soviet Naval Programmes* in Murphy (1978) p. 100.
17. M. MccGwire, *The Soviet Navy in the Seventies* in MccGwire and McDonnell (1977) p. 652.

18. McConnell (1978) p. 40.
19. See letter by Captain K. W. Estes (USMC) in *Proceedings of the USNI*, November 1979, pp. 23–4.
20. See, for instance, the argument in MccGwire (1973a) pp. 3–5.
21. MccGwire (1980a) pp. 178–9.
22. Adm. Thomas B. Hayward, US Navy, *Summary of Statement concerning the FY 80 Military Posture and FY 80 Budget of the US Navy* of 2 February 1979.

CHAPTER 2: THE FRAMEWORK

1. Pethybridge (1966) is a good introduction to Stalinism and Khruschev's reforms as seen at the time, and has a useful bibliography. See also N. S. Khruschev, 'Speech to the Twentieth Party Congress of the CPSU', published by the *Manchester Guardian* in 1956.
2. Mackintosh (1962) is still the best introduction.
3. Baylis and Segal (1981) is a collection of essays with full reference to the specialised literature, and covers recent developments.
4. R. Lowenthal, 'The Soviet Union in the Post-Revolutionary Era: an Overview' in Dallin and Larson (1968) p. 1.
5. Carew Hunt (1957) and Schapiro (1970) provide an excellent background.
6. Ranft (1972).
7. V. Aspaturian, 'Foreign Policy Perspectives in the Sixties' in Dallin and Larson (1968) pp. 132–3.
8. Lowenthal, op. cit. in Dallin and Larson (1968) pp. 3–6. Also D. R. Kelley, 'The Communist Party' in Kelley (1980) p. 29.
9. W. Leonhard, 'Politics and Ideology in the Post-Khruschev Era' in Dallin and Larson (1968) pp. 54–6.
10. D. R. Kelley, 'Developments in Ideology' in Kelley (1980) pp. 185–7; based on Brezhnev's speech to the Supreme Soviet as reported in *Pravda*, 5 October 1977.
11. Kelley, ibid., pp. 194–5.
12. R. Sharlet, 'Constitutional Implementation and the Juridicization of the Soviet System' in Kelley (1980) pp. 200–7. For Brezhnev's appointments and the text of the Constitution see *Keesing's Contemporary Archives* (1977) vol. XXIII, pp. 28483–4, 28701–9.
13. *The Current Digest of the Soviet Press*, vol. XXXIII, no. 8 of 25 March 1981 and no. 9 of 1 April 1981 (Colombia, Ohio: The American Association for the Advancement of Slavic Studies).
14. *Keesing's*, op. cit., p. 28703.
15. Colton (1979) p. 3.
16. Mackintosh (1967) gives the background.
17. This and what immediately follows is based on two most valuable recent studies: Colton (1979) and Deane (1977).
18. Deane (1977) pp. 69–93.
19. Ibid., pp. 281–3.
20. Ibid., pp. 76–7, 95–127, 139, 213, 229, 233.

21. Ibid., pp. 217–18.
22. Colton (1979) p. 118.
23. Ibid., pp. 48–9.
24. Ibid., pp. 27, 245.
25. Deane (1977) pp. 268–73; J. Erickson, 'Recruitment Patterns for the Leadership' in Bertram (1980) p. 78.
26. C. Douglas-Home, 'The Militarisation of Soviet Society', *The Times*, 7 November 1978; M. Mackintosh, 'The Soviet Military's Influence on Foreign Policy' in *Problems of Communism*, no. 22, September/October 1973.
27. *Keesing's*, op. cit. (1977) p. 28703.
28. Nove (1977), Hutchings (1971) and (1976) give the background.
29. G. Sokoloff, 'Sources of Soviet Power: Economy, Population, Resources' in Bertram (1980) pp. 71–7.
30. R. Davy, 'Russia in the Eighties: What the West Can Expect', *The Times*, 9 October 1978; 'Russia in the 1980s: the Giant Grows Sluggish'. *The Economist*, 29 December 1979; Sokoloff, op. cit. in Bertram (1980) pp. 32–61.
31. The following analysis is based on *The Current Digest of the Soviet Press*, vol. XXXIII, no. 8, 25 March 1981, pp. 3–21.
32. Ibid., pp. 3–6.
33. Ibid., pp. 14–21.
34. Ibid.
35. G. R. Feiwel, 'Economic Performance and Reforms in the Soviet Union' in Kelley (1980) pp. 70–103. This should be consulted for all problems of the Soviet economy in the 1970s and 1980s.
36. *The Military Balance 1981–2* (London: IISS, Autumn 1981) contains full details of the Soviet Union's armed forces and defence expenditure.
37. Nove (1977) pp. 239–40, 350–1; P. Hanson, 'Estimating Soviet Defence Expenditure' in *Soviet Studies*, vol. XXX, no. 3, July 1978, pp. 143–50.
38. Krylov (1979) pp. 61–3. This comprehensive survey is based on Russian sources.
39. D. Holloway, 'Foreign and Defence Policy' in Brown and Kaser (1975) pp. 64–5. M. Kaser's 'The Economy: a General Assessment' and 'The Economy in 1977' in this book are particularly useful.
40. R. Hutchings, 'The Economic Burden of the Soviet Navy' in MccGwire (1973a) pp. 210–27.
41. M. MccGwire, 'The Economic Costs of Forward Deployment', ibid., pp. 137–44.
42. J. McDonnell, 'The Soviet Defence Industry as a Pressure Group' in MccGwire (1975) pp. 87–122. Also D. Holloway, 'Soviet Military Research and Development: Managing the Research Production Cycle' in Thomas and Kruse-Vaucienne (1977) pp. 189–229.
43. Kelley (1980) p. 189, Hutchings (1976) p. 41.
44. Holloway, *Soviet Military Research and Development*, op. cit., p. 210; Krylov (1979) p. 62.

CHAPTER 3: THE FOREIGN POLICY BACKGROUND

1. For authoritative treatment of the development of Soviet Foreign Policy see Mackintosh (1962), G. Stern, 'Soviet Foreign Policy in Theory
   and Practice' in Northedge (1974), and Edmunds (1975).
2. R. E. Kanet and M. Rajan, 'Soviet Policy Towards the Third World' in
   Kelley (1980) pp. 235–66.
3. Edmunds (1975) pp. 12–14.
4. What follows is based largely on Ranft (1972).
5. *Keesing's Contemporary Archives*, 1977, vol. XXIII, p. 28703.
6. L. Labedz, 'Ideology and Soviet Foreign Policy' in Bertram (1980) pp.
   22–30.
7. R. Legvold, 'The Concept of Power and Security in Soviet History' in
   Bertram (1980) pp. 5–12.
8. M. Mackintosh, 'The USSR and its New Super-power Status' in Atlantic Treaty Assoc. (1975) develops this theme excellently.
9. V. V. Aspaturian, 'Detente and Strategic Balance' in MccGwire and
   McDonnell (1977) pp. 1–30; R. Lowenthal, 'The Soviet Union in the
   Post-Revolutionary Era: an Overview' in Dallin and Larson (1968) pp.
   13–22; W. Zimmerman, 'Soviet Perceptions of the United States' in
   ibid., pp. 163–79; A. Dallin, 'The United States in Soviet Perspective'
   in Bertram (1980) pp. 31–9.
10. G. S. Dragnich, 'The Soviet Union's Quest for Access to Naval
    Facilities in Egypt Prior to the June War of 1967'; A. Z. Rubinstein,
    'The Soviet–Egyptian Influence Relationship since the 1967 War'; and
    R. O. Freedman, 'The Soviet Union and Sadat's Egypt', all in
    MccGwire *et al.* (1975). More detailed accounts of the naval negotia-
    tions will be found in M. M. El-Hussini, 'Soviet–Egyptian Relations
    1945–70, with Special Reference to Naval Matters', a University of
    London unpublished PhD thesis for 1981. H. S. P. Shoup's forthcoming
    thesis will take the story up to 1975.
11. For a full treatment of this see Theberge (1972).
12. The most perceptive although not always congruent Western discus-
    sions on this are Booth (1974) and (1977), Cable (1981), and Dis-
    mukes and McConnell (1979).
13. See Gorshkov (1974) and (1979).
14. See Dismukes and McConnell (1979), M. MccGwire, 'Naval Power and
    Soviet Oceans Development' and J. McConnell, 'Military–Political
    Tasks of the Soviet Navy' both in US Government (1976) for the best
    insight into these controversies.
15. For instance, Bagley (1977).
16. Gorshkov (1974) pp. 114–20 and (1979) pp. 244–53.
17. Gorshkov (1974) pp. 3–5. What follows is based on chapters 1–3 of
    this and chapters 1–2 of Gorshkov (1979).
18. Ibid., pp. 12–14.
19. Ibid., p. xi.
20. Gorshkov (1974) pp. 113–20; Gorshkov (1979) pp. 2–6, 245–51.
21. Gorshkov (1974) pp. 119–20; Gorshkov (1979) pp. 252–3.

22. For an authoritative analysis see Butler (1971). B. Buzan, 'Naval Power, the Law of the Sea and the Indian Ocean' in *Marine Policy*, July 1981, pp. 194ff., gives an excellent up-to-date summary of the Soviet Union's general position.
23. D. P. O'Connell, 'Transit Rights and Maritime Strategy', *Journal of the RUSI*, June 1978, pp. 11ff.
24. W. E. Butler, 'The Legal Dimension of Soviet Maritime Policy' in MccGwire (1973a) pp. 109–22. Also Janis (1976) chapter 2.
25. O'Connell, op. cit., p. 12.
26. Janis (1976) p. 27.
27. Butler (1971) pp. 52–65, 104–15, 116–33.
28. Gorshkov (1979) pp. 46–58.
29. Examples of Soviet attempts to turn international maritime law to its advantage are given in S. Roberts, 'The Turkish Straits and Soviet Naval Operations' in *Navy International*, October 1981, pp. 581–5; and E. Young and V. Sebek, 'Red Seas and Blue Seas: Soviet Uses of Ocean Law' in *Survival*, November/December 1978, pp. 255–62.
30. See A. M. Kelly and C. Petersen, *Recent Changes in Soviet Naval Policy: Prospects for Arms Limitations in the Mediterranean and Indian Ocean* (Arlington, Virginia: Center for Naval Analyses, Professional Paper No. 150, 1976). Also B. Buzan, 'Naval Power, the Law of the Sea and the Indian Ocean', op. cit.
31. Kelly and Petersen, op. cit., pp. 4–11.
32. Ibid., pp. 11, 13; Buzan, op. cit., pp. 196–200.
33. F. Griffith. 'The Tactical Uses of Arms Control' in MccGwire *et al.* (1975) pp. 637–60 speculates interestingly about this.

CHAPTER 4: THE STRATEGIC BACKGROUND

1. Accounts of the development of Soviet strategy will be found in Scott and Scott (1979) and Baylis and Segal (1981).
2. The role of the armed forces in Russia's history is authoritatively treated in G. H. N. Seton Watson (1977) 'Russia: Army and Autocracy' in M. E. Howard (ed.) *Soldiers and Government* (London: Eyre & Spottiswoode); Erickson (1962); and Mackintosh (1967).
3. Scott and Scott (1979) chapter 4.
4. Sokolovskiy (1968). The introduction gives the background to the book's publication.
5. Ibid., pp. 11–13.
6. Ibid., pp. 60, 81–109.
7. Ibid., pp. 134–6.
8. Ibid., pp. 146, 160–2.
9. Ibid., pp. 182–200.
10. Ibid., p. 203.
11. Ibid., pp. 254–5.
12. Ibid., pp. 280–7.
13. Ibid., pp. 299–300.
14. Ibid., pp. 300–3.

15. Grechko (1974).
16. Ibid., editorial introduction.
17. Ibid., p. 24.
18. Ibid., chapter 2.
19. Ibid., p. 82.
20. Ibid., pp. 151–3.
21. Ibid., pp. 154–6.
22. Ibid., p. 284.
23. Gorshkov (1974). See biographical essay in this by J. G. Hibbits, 'Gorshkov: Architect of the Soviet Navy', pp. 142–6.
24. Gorshkov (1974) pp. 1–8.
25. Ibid., pp. 11–21.
26. Ibid., pp. 66–73.
27. Ibid., pp. 89–96.
28. Ibid., pp. 123–34, 135.
29. Gorshkov (1979).
30. MccGwire (1980c) pp. 3–6.
31. Gorshkov (1979) pp. ix–xii.
32. Ibid., pp. 9–16.
33. Young and Sebek (1978) pp. 256–7.
34. Gorshkov (1979) pp. 156–8.
35. Ibid., pp. 178–84.
36. MccGwire (1980c) pp. 3–6.
37. Gorshkov (1979) p. 213.
38. Ibid., pp. 213–22.
39. Ibid., pp. 229–34.
40. Ibid., pp. 274–7.
41. Ibid., pp. 234–45.
42. Ibid., pp. 278–82.
43. MccGwire (1980c) pp. 3–6.
44. What follows is derived from McConnell (1980), a work based on a most probing analysis of the relevant Soviet strategic literature.
45. Ibid., pp. 24–34.
46. Ibid., pp. 42–67.
47. Ibid., pp. 67–88.
48. Ibid, p. 40, quoting an article on 'The Armed Forces and Military Art of the Main Capitalist States after World War II' in *Voennaya istoriya*, Moscow 1971.

CHAPTER 5: THE DEVELOPMENT OF THE SOVIET NAVY

1. Mitchell (1974) p. 404.
2. Herrick (1968) pp. 3–6. These two books contain full bibliographies and references to sources, and provide a basis for the study of the history of the Soviet Navy.
3. Herrick (1968) p. 10.
4. Ibid., pp. 19–24.
5. Mitchell (1974) pp. 371–2. 373–4.

6. Herrick (1968) pp. 24–36.
7. Mitchell (1978) p. 436.
8. Herrick (1968) pp. 47, 49.
9. Mitchell (1974) pp. 384–404.
10. Ibid., pp. 404–20.
11. Ibid., pp. 426–7 gives full details of the supplies sent taken from B. B. Schofield, *The Russian Convoys*. (London: Batsford, 1964) pp. 212–14.
12. Mitchell (1974) pp. 425, 434.
13. Ibid., pp. 434–52.
14. Ibid., pp. 453–63.
15. Herrick (1968) pp. 59–66.
16. Ibid., pp. 66–7.
17. Ibid., pp. 67–73.
18. Ibid., p. 74, n. 2.
19. Ibid., p. 74.
20. See M. MccGwire, 'The Evolution of Soviet Naval Policy 1960–74' in MccGwire and McDonnell (1975). Also MccGwire (1976b) pp. 80–6 on which the restatement is based.

CHAPTER 6: THE SOVIET NAVY: AN INVENTORY

1. Baker (1980).
2. W. Hadeler, 'The Ships of the Soviet Navy' in Saunders (1958) p. 156.
3. 'Soviet Expansion' in *Navy International*, January 1973, p. 11.
4. 'Fast Patrol Boats: Political Instruments of the USSR' in *Defence Electronics*, September 1978, p. 74.
5. *Jane's Fighting Ships (JFS)* for 1981–2 in fact lists a total of 87 but includes vessels placed in reserve.
6. The dates are those of completion for first-in-class according to *JFS*, 1981–2.
7. Vice-Adm. Sumner Shapiro, US Navy, quoted in 'US Navy Intelligence Looks at the Soviet Fleet' in *Maritime Defence*, April 1981, pp. 109–10.
8. *JFS* 1981–2 for instance counts these ships as cruisers. For the classification shift argument see MccGwire (1980c).
9. M. MccGwire, 'Soviet Naval Programmes' in Murphy (1978) p. 90.
10. Khruschev quoted in MccGwire (1973a) p. 282.
11. J. G. Hibbits, 'Admiral Gorshkov's Writings: Twenty Years of Naval Thought' in Murphy (1978) p. 18.
12. This is one of the main arguments in Herrick (1968).
13. Thus the criticisms of Rep. Claring Cannon in 1959, quoted in Polmar (1974) p. 146.
14. A. Eremenko, 'Strategic and Political Significance of Military Bases', November 1960, quoted in Herrick (1968) p. 121.
15. Quoted in Martin (1970) p. 49.
16. Kennedy (1979) pp. 50–2.
17. Quoted by Hibbits in Murphy (1978) p. 19.

18. I. Korotkin *et al.*, *Avianostsy*, 1964 and article by Rear-Adm. V. Lisiutin in *Morskoi Sbornik*, March 1965, analysed by O. Smolansky, 'Soviet Policy towards Aircraft Carriers' in MccGwire and McDonnell (1977).

19. Adm. of the Fleet V. Kasatonov (first deputy commander-in-chief of the Soviet Navy) quoted by Polmar (1974) p. 178; Vice-Adm. K. A. Stalbo, 'Aircraft Carriers in the Post War World' in *Morskoi Sbornik*, June 1978, analysed in Daniel (1979a) pp. 6–7.

20. For the strong position of the Tsarist Navy in maritime aviation, see Martin (1970) and Layman and Drashpil (1971).

21. Gorshkov, quoted in Watson (1978) p. 96.

22. Gorshkov (1979) pp. 167–9. This last point in particular is distinctly un-American. Although Gorshkov purported to describe US motivations, he was plainly dealing with Soviet ones.

23. MccGwire (1973a) pp. 201–4.

24. MccGwire (1968) p. 149.

25. As, for instance, in Robert McNamara (the US Secretary of Defense) 16 June 1962, in his celebrated speech at Ann Arbor, Michigan.

26. K. J. Moore *et al.*, 'Developments in Submarine Systems' in MccGwire and McDonnell (1977) pp. 159–60; Clawson (1980).

27. W. Schilling, 'US Strategic Nuclear Concepts in the 1970s' in O'Neill (1981) pp. 35–6.

28. K. J. Moore *et al.*, op. cit., pp. 151–2.

29. 'A Special Soviet Submarine' in *Newsweek*, 9 February 1981.

30. It should be noted however that Soviet satellites are generally reckoned to be inferior in performance and certainly have a shorter life than those of the United States.

31. Quoted in O'Neil (1977) p. 26.

32. Gorshkov (1979) pp. 201–2.

33. Ibid.

34. Quoted in Cliffe (1971).

35. Gorshkov (1979) pp. 197–8.

36. Daniel (1978a).

37. See R. B. Remnek, 'The Politics of Soviet Access to Naval Support Facilities in the Mediterranean' in Dismukes and McConnell (1979) pp. 357–92; Weinland (1978); and Watson (1978) pp. 403ff.

38. Ruge (1979) pp. 193–5.

39. J. French, 'The Soviet Navy: Achievements and Problems' in *Navy International*, April 1972.

40. Gorshkov (1979) pp. 185, 197, 209–10.

41. Quoted in Manthorpe (1976) pp. 208–9.

42. Manthorpe (1978) p. 132.

43. 'Pacifism in Red Army' in *The Guardian*, 21 May 1982; Gorshkov, quoted in Manthorpe (1976) p. 208.

44. *Pravda*, 25 July 1976.

45. J. P. Riva, 'Soviet Offshore Oil and Gas' in US Government (1976) p. 485.

46. See M. D. Davidchik and R. B. Mahoney, 'Soviet Civil Fleets and the Third World' in Dismukes and McConnell (1979). Also figures

presented by K. A. Moore of the General Council of British Shipping at a Soviet Navy Seminar held at King's College, London, 22 October 1980.
47. Ibid.
48. Rees (1977) p. 47.
49. See Athay (1971) and his 'Perspectives on Soviet Merchant Shipping Policy' in MccGwire (1973a).
50. C. C. Petersen, 'Trends in Soviet Naval Operations' in Dismukes and McConnell (1979) p. 61.
51. Blackman (1981).
52. Dunn (1980).
53. MccGwire (1973a) p. 142.
54. MccGwire (1976a).
55. The source for this is the US Joint Chiefs of Staff, *Soviet Shipbuilding Deliveries 1961–75* of 20 May 1976.
56. These figures are loosely based on *JFS* for the years in question.
57. MccGwire (1976a).
58. Jordan (1977).
59. Kehoe (1975) and Breemer (1981).
60. Gabaglio (1977).

CHAPTER 7: MISSIONS OF THE SOVIET NAVY

1. Till (1982) pp. 128–39, 188–92.
2. Quoted in Gorshkov (1979) p. 230.
3. Quoted in Martin (1970) p. 47.
4. Gorshkov (1967) quoted in Herrick (1968) pp. 34–5.
5. Ruge (1979) p. 51.
6. Gorshkov (1967) quoted in Herrick (1968) p. 35; also Gorshkov (1979) pp. 272, 274.
7. Quoted in Herrick (1968) p. 90.
8. For example, ibid., pp. 144, 153.
9. Till (1982) pp. 191–2.
10. Gorshkov (1979) p. 229.
11. Quoted and discussed in McConnell (1977) p. 600.
12. A phrase of Admiral Raoul Castex. See Till (1982) pp. 128–32.
13. Gorshkov (1979) pp. 242, 243.
14. Ibid., p. 232.
15. Ibid., p. 234.
16. Ibid., pp. 122, 217.
17. Watson (1979) pp. 144–5.
18. Figures based on Polmar (1979) p. 14.
19. S. G. Gorshkov in *Red Star*, 18 April 1970.
20. Quoted in 'The Soviet Navy in 1975' in *Proceedings of the USNI, Naval Review 1976*, pp. 206–7.
21. S. G. Gorshkov in a footnote to a 1967 article in *Morskoi Sbornik*.
22. Gorshkov (1979) p. 196.

23. Ibid., pp. 229ff.
24. Ibid., p. 215.
25. Ibid., p. 256.
26. Ibid., p. 224.
27. Ibid., p. 210.
28. Quoted in Hibbits (1978) pp. 14–15.
29. Petersen (1979) pp. 50–1.
30. Gorshkov (1979) p. 226.
31. Ibid., p. 122.
32. Ibid., p. 128.
33. Sokolovskiy (1968).
34. Quoted in Herrick (1968) pp. 104–5.
35. Gorshkov (1979) p. 135.
36. MccGwire (1968) pp. 145–6.
37. Sokolovskiy (1968) p. 300.
38. Daniel (1978a) p. 225.
39. Ibid.
40. Dismukes and McConnell (1979) pp. 21, 49–50.
41. Daniel (1979b).
42. Weinland (1979) p. 84.
43. Dragnich, 'The Soviet Union's Quest for Access to Naval Facilities in Egypt Prior to the June War of 1967', in MccGwire and McConnell (1975) p. 251.
44. McConnell (1978) p. 48.
45. Teplinsky (1973) p. 79.
46. N. Friedmann, 'US vs Soviet Style in Fleet Design' in Murphy (1978) p. 206.
47. MccGwire (1973a) pp. 350ff.
48. Quoted in Zumwalt (1976) p. 436.
49. Dismukes and McConnell (1979) p. 22.
50. Sokolovskiy, quoted in Herrick (1968) p. 93. See also ibid., p. 96 and MccGwire and McDonnell (1977) p. 625.
51. Gorshkov (1979) p. 279.
52. Ibid., p. 221.
53. Bell (1970).
54. O. M. Smolansky, 'Soviet Entry into the Indian Ocean: an Analysis' in MccGwire (1973a) p. 414.
55. Gorshkov in *Morskoi Sbornik*, 1974, quoted by Moore in MccGwire and McDonnell (1977) p. 196.
56. V. A. Kasatanov, October 1961, quoted by Ullman in MccGwire *et al.* (1975) p. 587.
57. Quoted in Ruhe (1980).
58. Petersen (1979) p. 51.
59. K. J. Moore, 'Anti-Submarine Warfare' in MccGwire and McDonnell (1977) p. 196.
60. V. P. Zhukov in an article in *Morskoi Sbornik*, quoted in Kennedy (1979b).
61. MccGwire *et al.* (1975) p. 508.
62. MccGwire (1974).

63. See MccGwire and McDonnell (1977) pp. 653ff. and MccGwire (1976b) pp. 86ff.
64. Ibid., p. 145 and MccGwire (1978) p. 41.
65. Dismukes and McConnell (1979) p. 36.
66. McConnell (1978) p. 47.
67. See Tsipis (1974) and Nathan and Oliver (1979) p. 102.
68. See, for instance, the arguments developed by Polmar (1976) pp. 110–29.
69. Senate Foreign Relations Committee Report no. 96–14, Washington DC, 1979, on the SALT II Treaty.
70. Daniel (1978a) p. 226.
71. McConnell (1978) p. 49.
72. *Izvestiya*, 31 July 1966, quoted in McConnell (1977) pp. 570–1.
73. P. Nitze in George (1978) p. 91.
74. Sokolovskiy, quoted in Herrick (1968) p. 94.
75. Gorshkov (1979) pp. 219ff. and McConnell (1977) pp. 583–4.
76. For this see articles by P. Vigor, G. Jukes and M. MccGwire in MccGwire *et al.* (1975) pp. 471, 484, 489 respectively.
77. McConnell (1977) pp. 577–80.
78. Ibid., pp. 590–2.
79. Quoted in ibid., p. 578.
80. Department of Defense Posture Statement for FY, 1979, p. 28.
81. See the commentary of Cmdr C. C. Holcomb, US Navy (then Commanding Officer of the SSBN USS *Lafayette*) in the *Proceedings of the USNI*, July 1978, p. 21.
82. George (1978) p. 91.
83. Capt. First Rank Vyunenko, 'Some Trends in the Development of Naval Tactics' in *Morskoi Sbornik*, no. 10, 1975, quoted in Kennedy (1979a).
84. Gorshkov in *Problemy Filosofi*, quoted by Hibbits in Murphy (1978) p. 10.
85. Gorshkov (1979) p. 197.
86. McConnell (1978) pp. 60–1.
87. Gorshkov (1979) p. 197.
88. Ibid., p. 263.
89. A remark made in 1961 and quoted in McGruther (1978) p. 59.
90. McConnell (1980) pp. 67–88.
91. Ibid.
92. The dates of these two are 28 April 1970 and 30 July 1972 respectively. They are quoted in Clawson (1980).
93. McGruther (1978) p. 63.
94. Gorshkov (1979) p. 140.
95. Sokolovskiy (1968) pp. 302–3.
96. Gorshkov describes this view in a 1967 article quoted by Pritchard (1972).
97. Rear-Adm. K. A. Stalbo in *Morskoi Sbornik,* March 1970.
98. Gorshkov (1979) pp. 214, 217.
99. Ibid., p. 148.
100. Ibid., pp. 144–5. See also Ruge (1979) which describes these and other operations from the German point of view.

101. Ibid., p. 77.
102. Gorshkov (1974) p. 94.
103. Capt. First Rank Vyunenko, 'Modern Amphibious Landings' in *Morskoi Sbornik*, 1963, an article discussed in Pritchard (1972).
104. Ibid.
105. Quoted in *Naval Forces*, no. 1, 1981 in 'Soviet Activities in the Baltic', p. 96.
106. See *Navy International*, August 1981, p. 634.
107. Gorshkov (1979) p. 122.
108. Ibid., pp. 242–3.
109. Ibid., p. 122.
110. Ibid., pp. 234ff.
111. For a review of such views see Herrick (1968) p. 85.
112. Uri Ra'anan in US Government (1976) p. 299; Adm. W. Crowe, US Navy, *Western Strategy and Naval Missions Approaching the Twenty-First Century* in George (1978) pp. 19–20.
113. Herrick (1968) pp. 99, 131; MccGwire (1973a) p. 511 and (1980a) p. 170, etc.
114. McConnell (1978) pp. 43ff. and in (1977) p. 581.
115. Herrick (1968) p. 131.
116. Quoted by McConnell (1977) p. 581.
117. Sokolovskiy (1968) p. 302.
118. Whelan (1979).
119. Gorshkov (1979) p. 143.
120. A possibility stressed by MccGwire in MccGwire (1973a) p. 353.
121. Gorshkov (1979) p. 118.
122. Quoted in Polmar (1979) p. 10.
123. Gorshkov (1974) p. 101.
124. MccGwire (1980a) p. 170.
125. Both arguments are to be found in Daniel (1978a) pp. 227–9.
126. For instance, Gorshkov (1979) p. 243.
127. 'Britain Claims 7 year lead over USSR in Subs Race' in *The Guardian*, 31 December 1980.
128. See Funkhouse (1973) and Stone (1979).
129. McConnell (1978) p. 49.
130. Quoted in Kennedy (1979b).
131. R. W. Herrick, 'The USSR's Blue Belt of Defense Concept' in Murphy (1978) pp. 184–5. See also ibid., p. 199.
132. O'Neil (1977) p. 26.
133. See, for instance, Ruge (1979) p. 133.
134. Gorshkov (1979) p. 120–1.
135. Ibid., p. 128.
136. An argument advanced by M. MccGwire in George (1978) p. 202.
137. See Daniel (1980) pp. 9ff.
138. Gorshkov (1979) p. 244.
139. A. N. Shulsky, *Coercive Diplomacy* in Dismukes and McConnell (1979) pp. 134–7.
140. Watson (1979) p. 318.
141. Gorshkov quoted and discussed in J. M. McConnell, 'The Soviet Navy in the Indian Ocean' in MccGwire (1973a) pp. 392–3.

142. Ibid.
143. Quoted in Dismukes and McConnell (1979) p. 12.
144. Gromyko (1969) pp. 4–5.
145. See Gorshkov (1979) pp. 237ff., 247–8. Also Till (1982) pp. 209–13.
146. Gorshkov (1979) p. 251.
147. Ibid., p. 248.
148. Smirnov (1969) p. 66.
149. Dismukes and McConnell (1979) pp. 23–7.
150. Till (1982) pp. 230, 235.
151. C. C. Petersen and W. J. Durch, 'Angolan Crisis Deployments' in Dismukes and McConnell (1979) p. 151.
152. B. W. Watson, 'Maritime Problems in the Mediterranean Sea . . .' in George (1978) p. 101.
153. Telem (1975).
154. Kidd (1972).
155. Quoted in Zumwalt (1976) p. 447.
156. Watson (1979) pp. 334–5.
157. MccGwire (1976d)
158. Dismukes and McConnell (1979) p. 295.
159. Gorshkov (1979) pp. 154–5.
160. Adm. S. Turner, US Navy. Comments on Gorshkov's 11th Article of 18 March 1974 in Gorshkov (1974) p. 136.

CHAPTER 8: PRESENT AND FUTURE PROSPECTS

1. This is an extrapolation from the figures presented in Abellera and Clark (1981).
2. Ibid., pp. 36ff.
3. *Strategic Survey 1981–2* (London: IISS) pp. 46–9.
4. Leading article, *The Times*, 11 May 1982.
5. Quoted in Zumwalt (1981) p. 140.
6. Miller *et al*. (1981) p. 119.
7. L. Martin, 'Future Wartime Missions' in Veldman and Olivier (1980) p. 58.
8. This argument has been advanced by J. M. McConnell. We are grateful to the author for his help in explaining these points to us in various discussions at Kings College London and communications through 1981. For Ogarkov's views see *Kommunist*, July 1981.
9. See 'Nordic Shivers at Soviet Threat', *Weekly Guardian*, 14 November 1981 and 'The Fears that Whiskey Brought to the Surface', *The Guardian*, 7 November 1981.
10. Quoted in 'Speed Group Fights to Reverse Cuts', *The Guardian*, 22 May 1982.

Bibliography

Abellera, James W. and Rolf, Clark (1981) *Forces of Habit: Budgeting for Tomorrow's World* (Washington: American Enterprise Institute).

Adelphi Paper (1976) *Power at Sea*, nos. 122–4 (London: International Institute for Strategic Studies).

Athay, R. (1971) *The Economics of Soviet Merchant Shipping Policy* (University of North Carolina Press).

Atlantic Treaty Association (1975) *Soviet Foreign Policy: its Many Facets and its Real Objectives* (Paris).

Baker, Arthur D. (1980) 'Soviet Ship Types', *Proceedings of the United States Naval Institute* (USNI), November and December.

Bagley, W. (1977) *Sea Power and Western Security: The Next Decade*, Adelphi Paper No. 139 (London: International Institute for Strategic Studies).

Baylis, J. and Segal, G. (eds) (1981) *Soviet Strategy* (London: Croom Helm).

Bell, C. (1970) 'Strategic Problems of the Atlantic', *Survival*, March.

Bertram, C. and Holst, J. J. (eds) (1977) *New Strategic Factors in the North Atlantic* (Oslo: Universiteitsforlagt).

Bertram, Christoph (1980) *Prospects of Soviet Power in the 1980s* (London: Macmillan).

Blackman, Ray (1981) 'Logistics Ships', *Naval Forces*, no. 1.

Booth, K. (1974) *The Military Instrument in Soviet Foreign Policy* (London: Royal United Services Institute for Defence Studies).

Booth, K. (1977) *Navies and Foreign Policy* (London: Croom Helm).

Booth, K. (1978) 'The Military Implications of the Changing Law of the Sea', a paper prepared for the 12th annual conference of the Law of the Sea Institute, The Hague, Holland.

Breemer, J. (1981) 'The Soviet High Seas Fleet of the 1990s', *Naval War College Review*, March and April.

Brown, A. and Kaser, M. (1975) *The Soviet Union since the Fall of Khruschev* (London: Macmillan).

Burt, Richard (1975) 'Soviet Sea-Based Forces and SALT', *Survival*, January/February.

Butler, W. G. (1971) *The Soviet Union and the Law of the Sea* (Baltimore: Johns Hopkins Press).

Cable, Sir James (1981) *Gunboat Diplomacy, 1919–1979* (London: Macmillan).

Carew Hunt, R. N. (1957) *The Theory and Practice of Communism* (London: Geoffrey Bles).

Clawson, Lt-Cdr Carl H. (1980) 'The Wartime Role of Soviet SSBNs – Round Two', *Proceedings of the USNI*, March.

Cliffe, Lt-Col. Donald K. (USMC) (1971) 'Soviet Naval Infantry: a New Capability', *Naval War College Review*, June.

Chief of Naval Operations (1974) *Understanding Soviet Naval Developments* (Washington).

Cohen, Paul (1971) 'The Erosion of Surface Naval Power', *Foreign Affairs*, January.

Colton, T. J. (1979) *Commissars, Commanders and Civilian Authority: The Structure of Soviet Military Politics* (Cambridge, Mass. and London: Harvard University Press).

Crowe, Vice-Adm. W. (1978) 'Western Strategy and Missions Approaching the Twenty-First Century', in J. L. George (ed.) *Problems of Sea Power as We Approach the Twenty-First Century* (Washington: American Enterprise Institute).

Dallin, A. and Larson, T. B. (eds) (1968) *Soviet Politics since Khruschev* (Englewood Cliffs, N.J.: Prentice-Hall).

Daniel, D. C. (1978a) 'Trends and Patterns in Major Soviet Naval Exercises' in P. J. Murphy (ed.) *Naval Power in Soviet Policy* (USAF).

Daniel, D. C. (1978b) 'The Soviet Navy in the Pacific: an Overview of Capabilities, Limitations and Utilisation', paper presented at the International Symposium on the Sea, Tokyo, October.

Daniel, D. C. (1979a) 'The Soviet Navy in the Pacific', *Asia Pacific Community*, Spring.

Daniel, D. C. (1979b) 'Navy' in David Jones (ed.) *Soviet Armed Forces Review Annual*, vol. 3 (Gulf Breeze: Academic International).

Daniel, D. C. (1980) 'Sino-Soviet Relations in Naval Perspective', paper prepared for the 1980 Garmisch Symposium on Sino-Soviet Relations: Implications for the West in the 1980s, 14–17 May, Garmisch, West Germany.

Deane, Michael J. (1977) *The Political Control of the Soviet Armed Forces* (London: Macdonald & Janes).

Dismukes, Bradford and McConnell, James M. (eds) (1979) *Soviet Naval Diplomacy* (New York: Pergamon Press).

Dunn, Keith A. (1980) *Power Projection or Influence: Soviet Capabilities for the 1980s* (Strategic Studies Institute, US Army War College, November).

Eller, E. M. Rear-Adm. USN (1955) 'Soviet Bid For Sea', *Proceedings of the USNI*, June.

Edmunds, R. (1975) *Soviet Foreign Policy 1962–1973* (London: Oxford University Press).

Emery, David F. (1978) 'The Soviet Naval Threat to NATO Europe', *Strategic Review* (Fall).

Erickson, J. (1962) *The Soviet High Command: A Military Political History, 1918–1941* (London: Macmillan).

French, John (1972) 'The Soviet Navy: Achievements and Problems', *Navy International*, April.

Fry, Renita (1979) 'The Doctrinal Legitimacy of Gorshkov's Writings: Measuring the Measures', *Naval War College Review*, February.

Funkhouse, J. T. (1973) 'Soviet Carrier Strategy', *Proceedings of the USNI*, December.

Gabaglio, V. (1977) 'Eastern Navies', *Aviation and Maritime International*, July.

Gasteyger, C. (1970) 'World Politics on the Seven Seas', *Survival*, March.

George, James L. (1978) (ed.) *Problems of Sea Power as We Approach the Twenty-First Century* (Washington: American Enterprise Institute).

Gorshkov, S. G. (1967) 'The Development of Soviet Naval Art', *Morskoi Sbornik*, February.

Gorshkov, S. G. (1974) *Navies in War and Peace*; published as *Red Star Rising at Sea* (Annapolis: US Naval Institute Press).

Gorshkov, S. G. (1979) *The Seapower of the State* (London: Pergamon).

Grechko, Marshal A. A. (1974) *The Armed Forces of the Soviet State: A Soviet View* (translated and published under the auspices of the USAF) (Washington: US Government Printing House, 1977, 1st Soviet edn, spring 1974).

Gromyko, A. A. (1969) *The International Situation and Soviet Foreign Policy* (Moscow: Novosti).

Hanson, P. (1970) 'The Soviet Merchant Marine', *Survival*, May.

Herrick, R. W. (1968) *Soviet Naval Strategy: Fifty Years of Theory and Practice* (Annapolis; US Naval Institute Press).

Hibbits, John G. (1978) *Admiral Gorshkov's Writings* in Murphy (1978) op. cit.

Howe, J. T. (1971) *Multicrises: Seapower and Global Politics in the Missile Age* (Cambridge, Mass.: MIT Press).

Hudson, G. E. (1976) 'Soviet Naval Doctrine and Soviet Politics', *World Politics*, October.

Hutchings, R. (1971) *Soviet Economic Development* (Oxford: Blackwell).

Hutchings, R. (1976) *Soviet Science, Technology, Design* (London: Oxford University Press for Royal Institute of International Affairs).

Jacobsen, C. G. (1980) 'Strategic Considerations Underlying the Development of Soviet Naval Power', *Canadian Defense Quarterly*, Spring.

Janis, Mark W. (1976) *Sea Power and the Law of the Sea* (Lexington, Mass.: Lexington Books).

Jones, David (ed.) *Soviet Armed Forces Review Annual*, vol. III (Gulf Breeze: Academic International).

Jordan, J. (1977) 'The Russians in Retrospect', *Navy International*, August.

Jungius, Adm. Sir James (1979) 'The Balance of Power at Sea', *NATO Review*, December.

Kassing, David (1976) *Changes in Soviet Naval Forces* (Alexandria, Virginia: Center for Defense Analyses, Paper No. 183).

Kehoe, Capt. J. W. (1975) 'Warship Design: Ours and Theirs', *Proceedings of the USNI*, August.

Kelley, D. R. (1980) *Soviet Politics in the Brezhnev Era* (New York: Praeger).

Kennedy, Lt-Cdr Floyd D. (1979a) 'Soviet Doctrine on the Role of the Aircraft Carrier', *Naval War College Review*, February.

Kennedy, Lt-Cdr Floyd D. (1979b) 'Attacking the Weakest Link: the Anti-support Role of Soviet Naval Forces', *Naval War College Review*, September.

Kidd, Adm. Isaac C. (1972) 'View from the Bridge of the Sixth Fleet Flagship', *Proceedings of the USNI*, February.

Kime, Steve F. (1968) 'A Soviet Navy for the Nuclear Age', *Parameters* (Journal of the US Army War College) vol. X, no. 1.

Krepon, M. (1977) 'A Navy to Match National Purposes', *Foreign Affairs*, January.

Krylov, C. A. (1979) *The Soviet Economy: How it Really Works* (Lexington, Mass.: Lexington Books).

Langdon, Frank (1977) 'Japan–Soviet 200 Mile Zone Confrontation', *Pacific Community*, October.

Layman, R. D. and Drashpil, B. V. (1971) 'Early Russian Shipboard Aviation', *Proceedings of the USNI*, April.

Linebaugh, Ruth M. (1976) 'Ocean Mining in the Soviet Union', *Marine Technology Society Journal,* vol. 14, no. 1, July.

Mackintosh, J. M. (1962) *Strategy and Tactics of Soviet Foreign Policy* (London: Oxford University Press).

Mackintosh, J. M. (1967) *Juggernaut: A History of the Soviet Armed Forces* (London: Secker & Warburg).

Manthorpe, Capt. William H. J. (1976) 'The Soviet Navy in 1975', *Proceedings of USNI, Naval Review 1976.*

Manthorpe, Capt. W. H. J. (1978) 'The Influence of Being Russian on the Officers and Men of the Soviet Navy', *Proceedings of USNI, Naval Review 1978.*

Mariner (1979) 'Admiral Gorshkov, Naval Genius or Political Opportunist', *International Defence Review*, no. 5.

Martin, Cmdr T. G. (1970) 'A Soviet Carrier on the Horizon', *Proceedings of the USNI*, December.

McConnell, James M. (1976) 'The Military–Political Tasks of the Soviet Navy in War and Peace', in US Government Printing Office (1976) op. cit.

McConnell, J. M. (1977) 'The Gorshkov Articles, the New Gorshkov Book, and their relation to Policy', in MccGwire *et al*. (1977b) op. cit.

McConnell, J. M. (1978) 'Strategy and Missions of the Soviet Navy to the Year 2000', in George (1978) op. cit.

McConnell, J. M. (1980) *The Interacting Evolution of Soviet and American Military Doctrines* (Alexandria, Virginia: Center for Naval Analyses, Memorandum 80–1313).

MccGwire, M. K. (1968) 'The Background to Russian Naval Policy', *Brassey's Defence Annual.*

MccGwire, M. K. (ed.) (1973a) *Soviet Naval Developments* (New York: Praeger).

MccGwire, M. K. (1973b) 'Soviet Naval Programmes', *Survival*, September/October.

MccGwire, M. K. (1974) 'East–West Interaction at Sea', *Navy International*, December.

MccGwire, M. K. (1976a) 'Maritime Strategy and the Superpowers', in Adelphi Paper 123, *Power at Sea* (London: International Institute for Strategic Studies).

MccGwire, M. K. (1976b) 'Naval Power and Soviet Oceans Power', in US Government Printing Office (1976) op. cit.

MccGwire, M. K. (1976c) 'Western and Soviet Naval Building Programmes 1965–76', *Survival*, September/October.

MccGwire, M. K. (1976d) 'The Development of Soviet Naval Interests in the Indian Ocean', *Interstate*.

MccGwire, M. K. (1977) 'Changing Naval Operations and Military Intervention', *Naval War College Review*, Spring.

MccGwire, M. K. (1978) *Soviet Naval Doctrine*, a paper prepared for Joint CFIA–RSIA–RRC Seminar on Soviet Military Doctrine at Harvard University, Spring 1978.

MccGwire, M. K. (1980a) 'The Rationale for the Development of Soviet Seapower', *Proceedings of the USNI, Naval Review 1980*.

MccGwire, M. K. (1980b) 'Soviet Military Doctrine Contingency Planning and the Reality of World War', *Survival*, May/June.

MccGwire, M. K. (1980c) 'A New Trend in Soviet Naval Development', *Naval War College Review*, July/August.

MccGwire, M. K. (1980d) 'Soviet Seapower – a New Kind of Navy', *Marine Policy*, 4 October.

MccGwire, M. K., Booth, Ken and McDonnell, J. (eds) (1975) *Soviet Naval Policy: Objectives and Constraints* (New York, Washington, London: Praeger).

MccGwire, M. K. and McDonnell, J. (eds) (1977) *Soviet Naval Influence: Domestic and Foreign Dimensions* (New York, Washington, London: Praeger).

McGruther, Ken R. (1978) *The Evolving Soviet Navy* (Newport: Rhode Island: Naval War College Press).

Miller, Lt-Col., D. M. O. *et al.* (1981) *East v West: The Balance of Military Power* (London: Salamander).

Miller, Steven E. (1979) 'Assessing the Soviet Navy', *Naval War College Review*, September.

Mitchell, D. W. (1974) *A History of Russian and Soviet Sea Power* (London: Andre Deutsch).

Morris, E. (1977) *The Russian Navy: Myth and Reality* (London: Hamish Hamilton).

Murphy, Paul J. (ed.) (1978) *Naval Power in Soviet Policy* (published under auspices of the USAF).

Nathan, J. A. and Oliver, J. K. (1979) *The Future of US Naval Power* (Bloomington and London: Indiana University Press).

Nitze, Paul H. (1979) *Securing the Seas* (Boulder, Colorado: Westview Press).

Northedge, F. S. (1974) *The Foreign Policy of the Powers*, 3rd edn (London: Faber & Faber).

Nove, Alec (1977) *The Soviet Economic System* (London: Allen & Unwin).

O'Neil, William D. (1977) 'Backfire: Long Shadow on the Sea Lanes', *Proceedings of the USNI*, March.

O'Neill, Robert (ed.) (1981) *New Directions in Strategic Thinking* (London: Allen & Unwin).

Ostreng, Willy (1977) 'The Strategic Balance and the Arctic Ocean: Soviet Options', *Cooperation & Conflict*, vol. I.

Petersen, Charles C. (1979) 'Trends in Soviet Naval Operations', in Dismukes and McConnell (1979) op. cit.

Pethybridge, R. W. (1966) *History of Post War Russia* (London: Allen & Unwin).

Polmar, N. (1972) *Soviet Naval Power* (New York: National Strategy Information Center).

Polmar, N. (1974) 'The Soviet Aircraft Carrier', *Proceedings of the USNI, Naval Review 1974*.

Polmar, N. (1976) 'Thinking about Soviet ASW', *Proceedings of the USNI, Naval Review 1976*.

Polmar, N. (1978) 'The Soviet SLBM Force', *Air Force Magazine*, March.

Polmar, N. (1979) *The Modern Soviet Navy* (London: Arms & Armour Press).

Price, Capt. C. E. (1970) 'The Soviet Concept of Sea Power', *Seaford House Papers*.

Pritchard, Charles G. (1972) 'The Soviet Marines', *Proceedings of the USNI*, March.

Ra'anan, Uri (1976) 'The Soviet View of Navies in Peacetime', *War College Review*, summer.

Ranft, B. McL. (1972) 'The Aims of Soviet Policy: Ideological or National', *The Naval Review*, April.

Rees, D. (1977) *Soviet Sea Power: The Covert Support Fleet* (London: Institute for the Study of Conflict).

Rees, D. (1978) 'The Gorshkov Strategy in the Far East', *Pacific Community*, January.

Rohwer, J. (1981) 'Admiral Gorshkov and the Influence of History Upon Sea Power', *Proceedings of the USNI, Naval Review 1981*.

Ruge, Friedrich (1979) *The Soviets as Naval Opponents 1941–5* (Cambridge: Patrick Stephens).

Ruhe, William J. (1980) 'Soviet Wartime Submarine Strategy Analysed', *Defence Electronics*, August.

Sager, Karl-Heinz (1977) 'Soviet Merchant Fleet: Competition, Order or Chaos', *Defence Transportation Journal*, April.

Saunders, M. G. (1958) *The Soviet Navy* (London: Weidenfeld & Nicolson).

Schapiro, L. (1970) *The Communist Party of the Soviet Union* (2nd edn) (London: Eyre & Spottiswoode).

Scott, H. F. and Scott, W. F. (1979) *The Armed Forces of the USSR* (Boulder, Colorado: West View Press).

Sick, Lt-Cmdr Gary G. (1970) 'Russia and the West in the Mediterranean: Perspectives for the 1970s', *Naval War College Review*, June.

Smirnov, Vice-Adm. N. I. (1969) 'Soviet Navy in the Mediterranean', *Survival*, February.

Smith, Clyde (1974) 'Constraints of Naval Geography on Soviet Naval Power', *Naval War College Review*, September.

Sokolovskiy, Marshal V. D. (1968) *Soviet Military Strategy* (3rd edn: Moscow) translated and edited with an analysis and commentary by Harriet Fast Scott (London: Macdonald & Janes, 1975).

Solecki, Jan J. (1979) 'A Review of the USSR Fishing Industry', *Ocean Management*, no. 5.

Somara, Y. (1980) 'Soviet Sea Power in the Pacific', *Naval Forces*, no. II, 1980, vol. I.

Stone, Norman L. (1979) 'ASW: The Soviet View', *Military Electronics/Countermeasures*, July.

Telem, Adm. Benyamin (1975) 'Naval Lessons of the Yom Kippur War', in L. Williams (ed.) *The Military Aspects of the Israeli–Arab Conflict* (Tel Aviv: University Publishing Projects).

Teplinsky, B. (1973) 'America's Naval Programmes', reprinted in *Survival*, March/April.

Theberge J. D. (1979) *Soviet Sea Power in the Caribbean: Political and Strategic Implications* (New York, Washington, London: Pergamon Press).

Thomas, J. R. and Kruse-Vaucienne, U. (eds) (1977) *Soviet Science and Technology: Domestic and Foreign Perspectives* (George Washington University Press).

Till, Geoffrey (1982) *Maritime Strategy and the Nuclear Age* (London: Macmillan).

Towle, P. A. (ed.) (1982) *Estimating Foreign Military Power* (London: Croom Helm).

Tsipis, Kosta (1974) *Tactical and Strategic ASW* (Stockholm: SIPRI).

Turner, Adm. Stansfield (1977) 'The Naval Balance: Not Just a Numbers Game', *Foreign Affairs*, January.

US Government Printing Office (1976) *Soviet Oceans Development*.

Vego, Milan (1978) 'Soviet Naval Electronics: Getting Set for the Eighties', *Defence and Foreign Affairs Digest*, November.

Veldman, Jan H. and Olivier F. Th. (1980) *West-European Navies and the Future* (Den Helder: Royal Netherlands Naval College).

Vigor, Peter H. (1975) 'Soviet Understanding of Command of the Sea', in MccGwire and McDonnell (1975) op. cit.

Walters, R. E. (1974) *The Nuclear Trap: An Escape Route* (Harmondsworth: Penguin).

Watson, Bruce W. (1978) 'Maritime Problems in the Mediterranean Sea as We Approach the Twenty-First Century', in George, op. cit.

Watson, Bruce W. (1979) *The Mission and Operations of the Soviet Navy 1956–77* (Washington: Georgetown University, thesis for PhD).

Wegener, Edward (1975) *The Soviet Naval Offensive* (Annapolis, Maryland: Naval Institute Press).

Weinland, Robert G. (1972) 'The Changing Mission of the Soviet Navy', *Survival*, May/June.

Weinland, Robert G. (1975) 'Admiral Gorshkov's Navies in War and Peace', *Survival*, March/April.

Weinland, Robert G. (1978) 'Land Support for Naval Forces: Egypt and the Soviet Eskadra 1962–76', *Survival*, March/April.

Weinland, Robert G. (1979) *Superpower Naval Diplomacy in the October 1973 Arab–Israeli War* (with Edward Luttwak) (Washington: Sage).

Westwood, Lt-Cmdr J. T. (1978) 'Soviet Naval Strategy, 1968–78: a Re-examination', *Proceedings of the USNI, Naval Review 1978*.
Whelan, Capt. Mathew J. (1979) 'The Soviet Anti-SLOC Mission', *Proceedings of the USNI*, February.
Woodward, David (1965) *The Russians at Sea* (London: Kimber).
Young, Elizabeth (1974) 'New Laws for Old Navies: Military Implications of the Law of the Sea', *Survival*, November/December.
Young, E. and Sebek, V. (1978) 'Red Seas and Blue Seas: Soviet Uses of Ocean Law' *Survival*, November/December.
Zumwalt, Adm. Elmo (1976) *On Watch* (New York: Quadrangle).
Zumwalt, Adm. Elmo (1980) 'Gorshkov and his Navy', *Orbis*, fall.
Zumwalt, Adm. Elmo (1981) 'Naval Battles We Could Lose', *International Security Review*, summer.

Index

Aden, 39
Afghanistan, 40, 58, 82, 132, 208
Africa, in Soviet foreign policy, 47, 52, 164, 195
Alafuzov, Admiral, 104, 153
Albania, 198
Alexandria, 121, 201
Algeria, 39
Amur river, shipbuilding at, 135
Angola, 39, 192, 198
Arabian Sea, 47
Arab–Israeli wars, (1967), 195, 199, (1973) 5, 114, 157, 192, 195, 200–1
Asia, 52, 77, 78, 195, 197
Atlantic Ocean, 77, 144, 188, 211, 212–13
Australasia, 77
Azov Sea, 177

Baltic Fleet, 85, 89, 116, 124, 153, 178–80, 212
Baltic Sea, 55, 60, 78, 90, 118, 154, 191
Bangladesh war (1975), 195
Berbera, 121
Black Sea, 60, 78, 90, 118, 154, 177, 183, 200
Black Sea Fleet, 118, 120–1, 124, 191
Brezhnev, L.
    Constitution (1977) 20–2
    Doctrine, 18, 42
    on Soviet economy, 30–2
    political primacy of, 12, 17, 19–21, 31, 62, 207–8

sympathy with military, 26–7, 36, 61, 70
Bulgaria, navy, 140, 141

Cam Ranh Bay, 122
Caribbean, 195
Caspian Sea, 89, 124
China, Soviet relations with, 15, 16, 19, 43, 44, 46, 48, 58, 93, 179, 191, 197, 209, 210
Communist Party of the Soviet Union (CPSU)
    Central Committee, 13, 21, 26, 35, 62
    congresses of: 20th (1956), 13; 23rd (1966), 167; 24th (1971), 20; 25th (1976), 26, 31; 26th (1981), 21, 30, 164
    control of armed forces and strategy, 15, 17, 22–7
    leading role of, 13–14, 18–20, 21, 122
    military membership of, 26
    Politbureau, 13–15, 17, 21–2, 24–6, 29, 36, 208
    Secretariat, 13–14, 17, 26, 35, 208
Crowe, Admiral W. (USN), 181
Cuba, 39, 40, 47, 62, 73, 148, 149, 188, 192, 195, 196, 209
Cyprus, 192
Czechoslovakia, 18, 180

Denmark, 213
Diego Garcia, 57
Dombrovskiy, Admiral, 143

East Germany (GDR), 140–1
Egypt, 47, 121, 164, 192, 198, 199
   Soviet naval facilities in, 121–2,
      164
Ethiopia, 47–8, 121, 164, 192
European Economic Community
   (EEC), 45–6

Falkland Islands campaign (1982),
   207, 213
Filanov, Admiral, 181
Frunze, naval academy, 127, 142

Gervaise, Professor, 142, 154
Gorki shipbuilding complex, 135
Ghana, 193
Gorshkov, Commander-in-Chief
   Soviet Navy
   career, 71–4, 89, 92, 122, 207–8
   major publications: *Navies in War
      and Peace*, 3, 4, 48–53, 74–6,
      78, *The Sea Power of the State*,
      3, 48–50, 53, 76–80, 147
   on: aircraft carriers, 104;
      amphibious operations, 175,
      177–8; anti-SSBN
      operations, 160–1, 164,
      170–1; balanced fleet, 79, 80,
      92, 102, 149–50, 203–4;
      command of the sea, 146–7;
      decisive battle, 150–1;
      lessons of history, 4–5, 74,
      146, 153, 168–9, 172, 177,
      183–4, 190; local wars, 180,
      185, 192; maritime
      interdiction, 181, 183–4;
      merchant marine, 129; naval
      art, 79; naval aviation 116;
      naval diplomacy, 194–6;
      Russia's maritime history,
      7–8, 74–6, 87; science and
      technology, 20, 27, 36, 51,
      76, 78–9, 147, 152, 160, 167;
      surface ships, 172;
      submarines, 108; tactics, 151;
      training, 128
Great Britain, 53, 89, 93, 213
Grechko, Marshall, 20, 26, 36,
   68–71, 72, 73

Greenland–Iceland–UK Gap, 121,
   157, 166, 185, 213
Grishanov, Admiral, 124
Gromyko, A. 194
Guinea, 149, 188

Hayward, Admiral (USN), 12, 211,
   213
Herrick, R., 9, 91, 160, 181
Holloway, Admiral (USN), 116

India, 121
Indian Ocean, 46, 55, 57, 157, 188,
   191–2, 195, 201–2, 211
Iran, 47, 210
Israel, 46–7, 192, 199
Isachenkov, Rear-Admiral, 173

Japan, 45, 70, 77, 87, 89, 93, 121,
   197
Jeune Ecole, 10, 86
Jordanian crisis (1970), 200

Kampuchea, 122
Khruschev, N., 17, 44
   economic policies, 29, 36
   proclamation of a new era (1956),
      13, 38–9
   superceded (1964), 13, 19, 62,
      207
   views on military matters, 24, 26,
      35, 73, 91–2, 102, 104, 135,
      145, 176, 182
Kiev, Higher Naval Political School,
   128
Kola peninsular, 120, 188
Korea, 89, 147, 180
Korsakov, Pacific naval base, 120
Kronstadt, naval mutiny at (1921),
   85, 127
Kurile Islands, 89, 121
Kuznetsov, Admiral, 72, 87, 92

Latin America, 52, 54
Lenin, V., 20, 85
Leningrad
   in Great Patriotic War, 88–9, 177
   Frunze Naval Academy, 127
   Nakhimov Naval School, 127
   shipbuilding yards, 134, 135, 170

London Naval Conference (1935), 57, 87

Magadan, Pacific naval base, 120
Main Political Administration of Army and Navy, 24–5
Malenkov, G., 44
Malinovskiy, Marshal, 69, 72, 73
Mao Tse Tung, 41
Marxism–Leninism, 10–11, 16–22, 39, 40–4, 79
McConnell, J., xiii, 82, 165, 173, 181, 211
MccGwire, M., xiii, 9, 12, 76–7, 80, 93, 160, 163–4, 181, 201
Mediterranean, 57, 75, 77, 164, 183, 193, 213
    Soviet naval presence in, 50, 120, 195, 196, 198–9, 200–1
Middle East, in Soviet policy, 44, 46–7
Military Doctrine, 3, 4
Military Science, 3–4
Moorer, Admiral (USN), 159
Morocco, 192, 199
Mozambique, 39, 192, 197
Murmansk, 60, 153, 177, 178, 188, 203

Nakhimov Naval School, 127
NATO, 38, 45–6, 50, 77, 82, 93–4, 149, 183, 189, 211
New School, naval theories of, 85–6, 143, 153–4
Nikolayev, shipbuilding yard, 134
Nikolskiy, N., strategist, 212
Northern Fleet, 120, 124, 179
Norway and Norwegian Sea, 164, 203, 213
Nuclear weapons
    influence on strategy, 15, 78, 81
    in maritime operations, 63, 65–7, 70, 152, 176, 178–9

Oceanography, 129
Offshore defence forces, 95–8
Ogarkov, Marshal, 212
Okean-70, naval exercise, 149, 156, 176, 178
Okhotsk, Sea of, 171

Pacific Fleet, 87, 120–1, 124, 179
Pacific Ocean, 60, 77, 90, 188, 211
Persian Gulf, 47, 51, 77, 195, 197
Peter the Great, 6, 7, 116, 134, 137
Petropavlovsk, Pacific naval base, 120, 121
Petrov, Professor, 142, 154
Philippines, 54
Poland
    political crisis in, 27, 184, 209
    navy and naval shipbuilding facilities, 140–1
Polaris, 63, 93, 94, 109, 111, 139, 163
Porkalla, Finnish naval base, 92
Port Arthur, 92
Poseidon, 63, 113, 163, 169
Projection of power, 10

Romania, 46, 140, 141
Russian Imperial Navy, 6–8, 59–61, 107, 134, 139, 153, 181

Saudi Arabia, 47
Sea command/control
    Soviet changing attitudes to, 68, 86, 142–8, 171–2
Severodvinsk, HQ Northern Fleet and submarine building yard, 120, 170
Ships (Soviet Navy)
    surface ships: aircraft carriers, 102–7, 144–5, 159, *Kiev*, 105, 116, 150, 157, 162, 206, *Leningrad*, 105, *Moskva*, 73, 105, 149, 172, 198; cruisers, 100–2, *Chapaev*, 100, 137, 154, *Kara*, 101, 140, 162, *Kirov*, 101–2, 112, 140, 150, 159, 172, *Kresta I*, 101, 105, 140, 149, 156, 157, *Kresta II*, 101, 162, 200, *Kynda*, 100, 102, 139, 156, 157, 200, *Nikolayev*, 5, *Sverdlov*, 100, 137, 154, 180; destroyers, 98–100, *Kanin*, 99, 100, *Kashin*, 99, 100, 157, *Kildin*, 99, 156, *Kotlin*, 98, 99, 139,

Ships (Soviet Navy) – *continued*
      180, *Krupny*, 99–156,
      SAM-Kotlin, 99, *Skory*, 98,
      139, 180, *Sovremenny*, 100,
      150, *Tallinn*, 98, *Udaloy*, 99,
      100; frigates and minor
      combatants, 95–100, *Aist*,
      118, *Alyosha*, 96, *Grisha*, 97,
      Gus, 118, *Kola*, 95, *Komar*,
      96, 155, 199, *Koni*, 95,
      Krivak, 95–6, *Lebed*, 118,
      Mirka, 95, *Osa*, 96, 97, 155,
      199, *Petya*, 95, *Nanuchka*, 96.
      97, 155, 157, *Poti*, 140, *Riga*,
      95, *Sarancha*, 96, *Tarantul*,
      96; intelligence gathering
      ships (AGI), *Primorye*, 115;
      supply and amphibious
      warfare ships, *Alligator*, 117,
      192, *Berezina*, 133. *Boris
      Chilikin*, 132, *Ivan Rogov*,
      117, 178, 179, *Magomet
      Gadzhiev*, 198, *Polnochny*,
      117, 192, *Ropucha*, 117
   submarines: ballistic missile firing,
      107–11, 160–75, *Delta*, 110,
      113, 165, 169, 171, 174,
      Golf, 109, 173, *Hotel*, 109,
      124, *Typhoon*, 110, 113, 165,
      171, *Yankee*, 109, 111, 113,
      163, 167, 169, 171, 173, 174;
      cruise missile and torpedo
      attack, 111–14, *Alpha*, 113,
      162, 163, *Charlie*, 112, 157,
      160, *Echo I and II*, 111, 156,
      157, *Juliett*, 111, 156, 157,
      November, 113, *Oscar*, 112,
      160, *Papa*, 112, *Quebec*, 112,
      154, *Romeo*, 140, *Tango*,
      113, 163, *Victor*, 113, 163,
      Whiskey, 111, 112, 140, 154,
      156, 181, 213, *Zulu*, 108,
      109, 112, 139, 154, 182.
Ships (United States Navy)
   surface ships: aircraft carriers,
      Constellation, 157,
      Enterprise, 107, *F. D.
      Roosevelt*, 157, *Forrestal*,
      107, 157, *Independence*,

157, *Iwo Jima*, 157, *J. F.
      Kennedy*, 157, *Nimitz*, 107,
      206
   submarines: *Polaris*, 63, 93, 94,
      109, 111, 139, 153, 163,
      Poseidon, 63, 113, 163, 169,
      Trident, 164, 165
Smirnov, Vice-Admiral, 196
Sokolovskiy, Marshal, 62–8, 145,
      153, 155, 160, 167, 176, 182,
      185, 191, 212
Somalia, Soviet naval facilities in,
      39, 47, 149, 121–2, 164, 188
Soviet Navy
   aircraft carriers, 102, 137, 146,
      151, 157, 197, 210 (*see also
      under* Ships)
   amphibious capability, 116–18,
      175–80, 197, 210
   bases, 39–40, 117, 120–2, 141
   colleges, 24, 71, 72, 127, 142
   command and staff structure, 122
   cruisers and battle cruisers,
      100–2, 107, 137, 140 (*see
      also under* Ships)
   destroyers, 98, 100, 107, 137 (*see
      also under* Ships)
   defensive role of, 152–60, 161–6
   economic burden of, 34–7, 49,
      86–7
   exercises: *Okean-70*, 149, 156,
      176, 178; *Vesna-1975*, 5, 76,
      115, 125, 149, 151, 165, 182,
      184, 188, 191; *Zapad-81*, 212
   fleets and fleet areas, 118–21,
      124, 129, 154
   forward deployment, cost of,
      34–5, 148–9
   foreign policy support, 39–41,
      43–4, 46–7, 48–53,
      193–204, 210
   growth and purposes of, 9–12, 17,
      40–4, 84–94, 205–7, 213
   intelligence ships, 115
   Mediterranean Squadron, 120,
      198 (*see also under*
      Mediterranean)
   merchant marine, support from,
      132–4, 158–9

Soviet Navy – *continued*
mine warfare and vessels, 96, 141, 154
missiles used by: **surface to surface**, SS–N–1 (*Scrubber*), 99, 156, N-2 (*Styx*), 96, 99, N-3 (*Shaddock*), 101, 111, 156, N-4, 174, N-5, 174, N-6, 174, N-7 (*Siren*), 112, N-8, 110, 165, N-9, 96, N-11, 99, N-12 (*Sandbox*), 105, NX-13, 109, 163, 174, N-14, 101, N-15, 113, N-18, 110, N-19, 101, 112, NX-20, 110; **air to surface,** AS-2 (*Kipper*), 115, 116, AS-3 (*Kangaroo*), 115, AS-4 (*Kitchen*) 115, AS-5 (*Kelt*), 115, AS-6 (*Kingfish*), 115, 186
naval aircraft: **fixed wing**, BE-12 (*Mail*), 116, I1-38 (*May*), 116, 162, 188, MiG-23 (*Flogger*), 188, TU-26 (*Backfire*), 115, 116, 160, 188, 189, 210, TU-95 (*Bear D*), 115, 157, 188, TU-95 (*Bear F*), 116, TU-142, 162; **helicopters**, *Helix*, 116, *Hormone A*, 101, 105, 116, *Hormone B*, 116, TU-16 (*Badger*), 115, 156, 157, TU-22 (*Blinder*), 115, Yak-36 (*Forger*), 105, 116
naval air force, 114–16, 150–1, 162–3, 172, 180, 188–90, 203
naval infantry, 117–18, 176, 181
nuclear weapons and strategy, 49, 65–7, 70–1, 94, 166–76, 178
offshore defence force, 95–8, 155, 191
personnel, 125–8, 170
political officers, 24–5, 124, 128
protection of shipping role, 190–3
priorities of, 202–4
reconnaissance satellites, use of, 104–5, 149

roles of in Soviet strategy, 59–83, 208
sea control: initial rejection of, 68, 86, 142–4; acceptance of, 144–8, 149; methods of achieving, 147–52; in Pro-SSBN task, 171–2
sea denial, 145–6
ship design and construction, 134–40
shipyards, 107, 121, 134, 135, 170
strategic strike role, 166–75, 210
submarines, 137, 150–1, 154, 185 (*see also under* Ships)
Sovietskaya Gavan, Pacific Fleet base, 120
Soviet Union (USSR)
Armed Forces: Air Defence Force, 59, 63, 67, 70; Army, 59, 71, 84; Strategic Air Force, 70, 81; Strategic Rocket Forces, 59, 63, 65, 70, 81
arms control and disarmament, attitude to, 45–6, 56–8
defence: Council of, 26, 61; expenditure, 27–8, 32–7, 209; industries, 35–7, Ministry, 61, 91, 122
economy, problems of, 14, 15, 28–32, 208
fishing industry, 54, 129–30, 193
foreign policy, 38–58, 194, 208; China, relations with, 15, 16, 43, 46, 48, 58, 209, 210; Third World, relations with, 19, 39–44, 133, 193, 197; United States, relations with, 13, 15, 16, 33, 37, 38–9, 40–5, 48, 51, 53, 58, 81, 84, 93, 197, 209, 210
ideology, significance of, 10–11, 16, 17–22, 40–4
merchant marine, 53, 129–34, 193
political system, 13, 14, 20–2, 27–8, 42 (*see also* Communist Party)
population problems, 30, 127

Soviet Union – *continued*
strategic doctrine: development
of, 59–83, 168–9; limited
nuclear war, 173–4, 211–12;
nuclear strike by SSBN,
168–75; witholding strategy,
168–70
Stalbo, Vice-Admiral, 104–5, 117,
176, 182, 197
Stalin, J., 13, 20, 23, 26, 38–9, 42,
44, 61, 87, 88, 90–1, 92, 94,
137, 144, 145, 154, 208
Suez Canal, 46
Suslov, M., 207
Sweden, 213
Syria, 121, 192, 193

Taiwan, 78
Thailand, 78
Tito, J., 41
Trident, 164, 165
Turkey, 55, 183

United Nations Conference on the
Law of the Sea (UNCLOS),
Soviet position at, 53–6
United States (USA), 15, 16, 18, 38,
40, 43, 44–5, 51, 77, 79, 87,
89–91, 93
United States Marine Corps, 118
United States Navy (USN), 158,
192, 197, 206–7, 209–11;

afloat support in, 132–3; ASW
capability, 171, 185, 207;
foreign policy role, 194
Ushakov, Admiral, 7
Unistov, D., Soviet Defence
Minister, 26–7, 35, 61, 122, 207

Vesna-75, naval exercise, 5, 115,
125, 149, 151, 165
Vietnam, 39, 40, 46, 122, 192, 196
Vietnam war, naval operations in,
147, 180
Viktorov, Admiral, 87
Vladivostock, Pacific Naval base,
120, 121, 153
Voroishilov naval academy, 72, 142

Warsaw Pact, 46, 61; navies of,
140–1, 149, 196
Washington Naval Conference
(1921–2), 57, 87
West Germany (FGR), 87, 88, 89,
93, 137
White Sea, 55

Yepishev, General, 149, 197
Yemen, 149, 197

Zhdanov, Black Sea, shipbuilding
yards, 135
Zhukov, Marshal, 26, 91